PRAISE FOR

SPOILER ALERT: THE HERO DIES
ONE OF *KIRKUS REVIEWS'*
BEST BOOKS OF THE YEAR

"A more heartbreaking, honest, funny, and insightful book on the subject of loss can be found nowhere."
—J.J. Abrams, writer-director-producer, *Lost, Alias, Westworld, Star Trek, Star Wars: The Force Awakens*

"Sexy and sweet, charming and funny, Michael Ausiello somehow manages to turn a story of loss into a hopeful tale that shines with warmth and wit."
—Lauren Graham, star of *Gilmore Girls* and *Parenthood* and *New York Times*–bestselling author of *Someday, Someday, Maybe* and *Talking as Fast as I Can*

"Like some of Michael's favorite TV shows, his book is heartfelt, smart, funny, insightful, and packs an enormous emotional punch. I can't recommend it more."
—Greg Berlanti, writer-director-producer, *The Flash, Arrow, Everwood, Dawson's Creek, Brothers & Sisters*

"Tender, profoundly poignant, and cleverly written with equal parts wit and integrity, the book is grounded in the realities of modern relationships and the grim fate of mortality. A heartbreaking memoir infused with dark humor and composed with true love."
—*Kirkus Reviews* (starred review)

"*Spoiler Alert: The Hero Dies* is a haunting and profoundly sad story, but it's brightened by witty writing, comedic interludes and the two charismatic, endearing and appealing heroes at the book's center."
—Shelf Awareness

"What Ausiello has done is made certain that Cowan's one special life will never be forgotten. The hero died, but the spirit lives."
—*Lambda Literary Review*

"As hate threatens to strangle our country, take a look at what love looks like."
—*Newark Star-Ledger*

"This is, without question, the best book I have ever read."
—*The Huffington Post*

SPOILER ALERT:
THE HERO DIES

A Memoir of Love, Loss,
and Other Four-Letter Words

Michael Ausiello

ATRIA PAPERBACK

NEW YORK   LONDON   TORONTO   SYDNEY   NEW DELHI

ATRIA
PAPERBACK

An Imprint of Simon & Schuster, Inc.
1230 Avenue of the Americas
New York, NY 10020

Certain names and identifying characteristics have been changed, including the names of all of Kit's doctors.

First Atria paperback edition September 2018

ATRIA PAPERBACK and colophon are trademarks of Simon & Schuster, Inc.

For information about special discounts for bulk purchases, please contact Simon & Schuster Special Sales at 1-866-506-1949 or business@simonandschuster.com.

The Simon & Schuster Speakers Bureau can bring authors to your live event. For more information or to book an event contact the Simon & Schuster Speakers Bureau at 1-866-248-3049 or visit our website at www.simonspeakers.com.

Interior design by Laura Levatino

Manufactured in the United States of America

10 9 8 7 6 5 4 3 2

Library of Congress Cataloging-in-Publication Data

Names: Ausiello, Michael, author.
Title: Spoiler alert : the hero dies : a memoir of love, loss, and other
    four-letter words / by Michael Ausiello.
Description: First Hardcover Edition. | New York, NY : Atria Books, [2017] |
    Description based on print version record and CIP data provided by
    publisher; resource not viewed.
Identifiers: LCCN 2017012865 (print) | LCCN 2017039461 (ebook) |
    ISBN 9781501134982 (ebook) | ISBN 9781501134968 (hardcover)
Subjects: LCSH: Same-sex marriage--United States. | Gays--Family
    relationships--United States. | Love. | Bereavement--United States.
Classification: LCC HQ1034.U5 (ebook) | LCC HQ1034.U5 A87 2017 (print) | DDC
    306.84/80973--dc23
LC record available at https://lccn.loc.gov/2017012865

ISBN 978-1-5011-3496-8
ISBN 978-1-5011-3497-5 (pbk)
ISBN 978-1-5011-3498-2 (ebook)

To Kit—olive juice, always and forever . . .

Previously on . . .

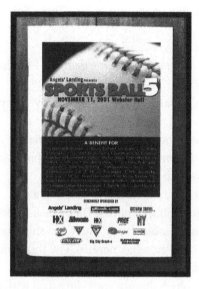

Our relationship was over before it began.

Less than fifteen minutes into our first date, I discovered that the tall drink of water sitting across from me by the name of Kit Cowan watched zero television, although he admitted to rewatching (over and over again) old episodes of *AbFab* on his VCR. This explained the glazed-over look in his eyes when I mentioned that my favorite current series was *Felicity*, starring my soul mate/kindred spirit Keri Russell.

"Oh, wait—is she the one whose haircut almost got the show canceled?" he exclaimed, way too proudly, as if bragging, *See, I know stuff!*

"Yes," I sighed, with an exaggerated eye-roll that properly conveyed my half-serious contempt that he had just reduced Queen Keri to a Trivial Pursuit question.

"I'm actually going to be on *Felicity*," I boasted. "I'm going to make a cameo in the episode where she graduates, as part of a story I'm writing for *TV Guide*. I'm flying out to L.A. in January to shoot it."

"So you're a bit of a celebrity?" he asked, rhetorically.

"Hardly a celebrity," I clarified, before deadpanning, "But, generally speaking, I am a pretty big deal. You should be aware of that."

Kit let out a fairly noisy cackle, as the waitress at Corallo Trattoria, a well-reviewed Italian restaurant in New York's SoHo district, dropped off the wine list.

"Should we order a bottle?" Kit inquired.

"Actually, I'm not much of a wine drinker," I replied.

"Ever?" he asked.

"Pretty much," I said. "I don't particularly enjoy the taste. Same goes for beer."

I could see him processing this new information as he unfurled his napkin and rested it on his lap with a poised precision that suggested to me he had grown up around money.

"We could do cocktails instead . . ." he replied.

"I think I'm just going to have a Diet Coke," I declared with an opposing mix of embarrassment and "Sorry, but this is how I roll" swagger.

"Diet Coke?" he responded, bemused by this sudden twist.

"Yeah, I'm not a big alcohol drinker."

"You're not an alcoholic, are you?" he asked with a raised eyebrow.

"Nope, I've just never been a big drinker," I asserted, without divulging that what I really disliked about alcohol was the empty calories and the loss of control. "I do, however, love the taste of Diet Coke," I added, "especially when it comes from a fountain versus a bottle or a can."

"Oh, so you're a Diet Coke *connoisseur*?" he said, mockingly.

"If you must slap a label on me, sure," I shot back. "But it's actually more of a diet *cola* connoisseur since I'm also open to a nice Diet Pepsi."

"Oh, this is good to know," he said, adopting a faux-serious tone, before pulling out of his pocket a small notepad which was affixed to an even smaller pencil. He flipped through to what I assumed was a clean page and proceeded to dictate a message to himself. "He is a connoisseur of Diet Coke . . . *and* Diet Pepsi," he said slowly and with an air of satirical judgment. He then closed the book, tucked it back into his pocket, and half-smiled at me as he took a swig of water.

Holy. Fucking. Shit. He was keeping a running list of my eccentricities? Or was it a red-flag tally? In either case, it was a little unsettling but mostly goddamn hilarious. He was hot and could flawlessly land a comedic bit without breaking a sweat? Things were looking up.

"You should probably keep that pad out," I informed him, cryptically and sassily. "That list is going to get a lot longer tonight." I then punctuated my retort with my own carefully timed sip of water, as if to say, *Game. On. Playa.*

That saucy interplay set the tone for what ended up being an enormously entertaining, enlightening, flirtatious, and fun dinner, during which I learned that he had not, as I'd assumed, been born with a silver spoon in his mouth. As Kit (whose birth name is Christopher) explained, he had grown up the only child of a toolmaker dad and a quilt-making mom in a small Podunk town in Pennsylvania called Millersburg—"not to be confused with Millersville," he clarified—whose biggest claim to fame was that it "didn't have a single traffic light" within its one-square-mile border. "Everyone knew everyone's business," he sighed. "Not an ideal environment to grow up secretly gay."

After high school, he had attended the local Harrisburg Area Community College, where he majored in photography, before completing his four-year education at RIT (Rochester Institute of Technology), graduating with a bachelor of fine arts degree in Photographic Arts and Sciences. He had then continued his education at the University of Miami, where, with the help of a full scholarship, he had earned his master's in Art and Art History. I decided not to ruin a perfectly fine evening by telling him that what I knew about photography and art could have fit on the head of a pin.

Kit had lived and worked in Miami after graduation, before deciding to make the move to New York with nothing but himself and a huge U-Haul filled with select vintage furniture and photography equipment. A friend of a friend had connected him with a woman whose behaviorally challenged son Kirby was looking for a roommate to share a spacious, rent-controlled three-bedroom apartment on the Upper West Side. In exchange for dealing with her son's myriad idiosyncrasies, Kit only had to pay an unheard-of $400 a month for his very own bedroom and bathroom, and use of the unit's common areas if he should so please. "It was a sweet deal," he noted, although not one without its drawbacks. Kit warned me that in addition to being untidy,

Kirby didn't deal well with people who were different from him, which was why he never explicitly looped him in on his sexual orientation. Despite Kit's discretion, I got the sense that the relationship was not a healthy one.

Kit was also not out to his parents—which was odd and slightly concerning given that he was twenty-eight years old and it was 2001.

Almost immediately after arriving in New York a year ago, he had landed a job as assistant creative director for the fast-casual restaurant chain Così, where he oversaw the design and implementation of all of the franchise's visuals, from menu boards to napkins to store signage.

"I love my job," he shared, "but the atmosphere can be a little intense. I'm constantly reminding my coworkers, 'At the end of the day, we're just selling sandwiches, people.'"

He also confessed to being a major computer nerd and an acolyte of Steve Jobs.

"Oh, wait—is he the guy with the apples?!" I sassed, before sarcastically explaining to him that "We in the business refer to that as a callback."

Cut to Kit's similarly exaggerated, extremely playful eye-roll.

Oh, yes, ladies and gents, I was on fire.

I presented Kit with the CliffsNotes rundown of my life story, offering snapshots of my small-town New Jersey upbringing (although apparently not nearly as small as his), my escape to the West Coast to attend college at USC, my obsession with—and subsequent career in—television, which led to my gig at *TV Guide*. I also divulged to him that I had lost both of my parents by the age of twenty-two—"my mom to cancer, my dad to heart disease"—to which he expressed genuine sympathy but not (and this was important) pity.

Our boyfriend history was fairly similar. We had both had one major prior relationship of similar duration (three years) and end date (less than two years ago). Our girlfriend history, however, diverged greatly, in that I'd never had one and he, well, had. And a serious, adult one at that.

All told, what we lacked in common interests we more than made up for in snark-filled chemistry.

I wrapped up dinner wanting to know more about him. I got the distinct impression he felt the same about me.

We split the bill, proceeded outside, and faced that awkward "what do we do now" quandary. It was clear that neither of us wanted the evening to end.

"We could go back to my place and hang out," Kit suggested, sheepishly.

"I don't know . . ." I hedged.

"We don't have to have sex," he assured me. "We could just . . . hang out."

"I'm not sure I'd be able to restrain myself . . ."

And with that, Kit pulled out his notebook and pretended to write, "No. Willpower."

I stood there silently and smiled, giving *his* perfectly timed callback room to breathe. I wanted so badly to make out with him right there on the street. I resisted on account of not wanting to get gay-bashed. Yes, it was 2001. It was also, you know, 2001. But it was an exercise in extreme self-control.

It had been forty-eight hours since Kit and I first laid eyes on each other at New York's Webster Hall, the site of the Gay Sports Ball, an annual event that was a mashup of my favorite things: gay athletes and gay music, and, if I was lucky, gay tonsil hockey. My BFF and wingman Matt Eriksson was my plus one, and it would be our first social outing since the events of 9/11 exactly two months earlier.

Like most New Yorkers, I became something of a hermit in the weeks following 9/11. I would head straight home to my one-bedroom apartment in Bloomfield, New Jersey, after putting in a full day at *TV Guide*'s midtown Manhattan offices and lose myself in fresh episodes of my then-obsessions *Friends, Felicity, Gilmore Girls, 24,* and such. The idea of going to a bar to continue my elusive pursuit of a cute boyfriend amid fears of another terrorist attack, an approaching war, and anthrax-laced snail mail did not interest me. I also just wasn't in the mood for revelry of any kind. The world was falling apart, and I needed to focus my full-time attention on whether Felicity was going to choose Ben or Noel.

"If anything can snap me out of my 9/11 funk, it's a gay athlete," I joked to Matt, who, luckily, was also ready to dip his toe back into NYC nightlife.

And for what it's worth, I was an avid runner. Which technically made me an athlete, too. So I wasn't so much attending the Gay Sports Ball 2001 to stalk hot guys as I was going there to kick it with my peeps. Yep, that was my story and I was sticking to it.

Within minutes of Matt and me making our first loop through Webster Hall, I spotted someone I knew—Nate. We were both members of GAAMC (Gay Activist Alliance of Morris County), New Jersey's longest-operating LGBT organization. We had become acquainted through the twentysomething support group, but this was the first time I'd seen him out in the proverbial wild. He was with a small gaggle of friends, one of whom immediately caught my eye. This particular slice of heaven was tall, probably six-two or six-three. Slim build. Aquiline nose. Smart glasses. Sexy in a nerdy kind of way. And I could tell by the way he was chomping on his little cocktail straw that he didn't lack confidence.

Sign. Me. Up.

A quick round of introductions yielded the hottie in question's name: Kit.

I caught up with Nate, all the while making googly eyes at Kit. Lucky for me, the googly eyes were being returned (and then some). Houston, we had a spark.

And . . . we had a problem. Nate and his entourage wanted to move onto the dance floor.

Now, what happened next would be the subject of much heated debate over the course of our entire thirteen-and-a-half-year relationship. According to Kit, I immediately lunged toward him, desperately crying out, "No! Don't go!" I, however, recall taking a more subtle approach, something along the lines of "You sure you don't want to hang out here a little longer, you handsome sexy fuck?"

Regardless, Kit ended up staying behind with me, while Nate and his crew (which now included Matt) moved on to gayer pastures.

Maybe it was the residual high from my one-sided flirtation with the captain of the flag football team downstairs, but the moment Kit and I were alone, I boldly moved my lips toward his and yanked that cocktail straw right out of his mouth and into mine.

"Excuse you," he mock-reprimanded me, as I smiled sheepishly at him.

Without missing a beat, he charged at me and snatched the straw back.

"Oh, I see how it's going to be," I sassed.

We would repeat this unusual mating ritual continuously over the next nine minutes, our mouths never once touching. The pace of our straw-play gradually sped up and ended in him kissing me.

Holy shitballs. He looks like that and he's an A+ kisser?!

I immediately charged back at him and stole a second kiss. And then a third. And then a fourth. By the tenth, we decided to make ourselves more comfortable on one of the nearby sofas, on which we continued practicing an aggressive form of CPR on each other for the next hour or so. We eventually came up for air, exchanged phone numbers, shared one final kiss, and met up with our respective posses. The Cheshire grin on my face filled Matt in on my rendezvous more than words ever could have. Not to say I didn't use some words.

"That was . . . highly enjoyable," I said to him, attempting to play it cool. "I think I'm going to see him again, Matt."

Back to our first date: I ultimately caved and agreed to relocate to Kit's apartment, but I vowed to keep sex off the table for now. I needed to delay introducing Kit to my childhood alter ego—"Fat Mike"—as long as possible. I was convinced that if he were to find out too soon that hiding under my comfortably fitting clothes were pockets of loose skin and rows of faded-but-still-noticeable stretch marks—a by-product of my supersized teenage years—he would promptly run in the other direction. Best to leave Kit thinking there was a Marky Mark–caliber six-pack waiting for him underneath my disco shirt. If and when the day came that he learned the truth about my uniquely proportioned midriff, I'd already have my hooks deep enough into him that it wouldn't even matter.

We hopped in a cab uptown to his pad on 68th and Central Park West, copping various PG-13–rated feels the entire way. As we entered his fourth-floor apartment, he warned me, "My roommate is here, but we can hang out in my room." I hoped he had noise-canceling earplugs for when Kit and I banged. Oh, right. Fat Mike had already declared tonight a sex-free zone. Ugh. Fuck off, Fat Mike!

He led me through the long, narrow entryway, which was not nearly as polished and put-together as Kit. In fact, it was falling apart. The wall paint was peeling and the original wood flooring was extremely worn. And the entry didn't look like it was in mid-renovation. It looked like it was the victim of severe neglect.

I caught a fleeting glimpse of the sizable living room, which, much like the hallway, was a homely, poorly lit sight. What little furniture there was appeared old, dusty, and mismatched. In the distance I'm pretty sure I saw a banana peel on the floor, right next to . . . a dinner roll? What the fuck was this place? I'd known he was too good to be true.

There was no sign of the alleged roommate. Before I could take in the rest of the apartment, Kit opened his bedroom door and invited me in. I was worried about what might be waiting for me on the other side. Mannequins covered in the excised skin of Kit's exes? A trophy case filled with blood slides from his victims? Weapons of mass destruction?

As I stepped foot inside the room, it became immediately clear that his bedroom was—drum roll, please—everything the rest of the apartment wasn't: clean, organized, stylish, and impeccably curated. It was packed with interesting, artful touches. The headboard behind his bed wasn't a headboard at all, but two vintage wooden door frames leaning up against the wall. He had two distinct workspaces; one featured a desktop Apple computer surrounded by little curiosities like an orange ceramic octopus, a miniature green army figurine, a white plastic bowling pin, and a Rubik's Cube; the other one was mostly bare, save for a paper cutter and a three-hole puncher and some photography equipment. There was a huge, designer-looking black clock hanging in the center of the wall not far from an equally oversized designer-looking calendar, which was right next to a poster that looked like it was ripped off the wall of a 1940s kindergarten class or pediatrician's office. It was an illustration of a generic young boy's head with arrows identifying his eyes, ears, mouth, and nose.

Everything just looked smart.

What his bedroom did not have, unsurprisingly, was a decent television. There was a dusty, eleven-inch, rabbit-eared relic of the eighties resting on his bookshelf next to VHS box sets of his aforementioned obsession *AbFab*.

"I don't spend much time in the rest of the apartment," Kit shared. "As I told you, my roommate is kind of troubled."

"Hey," I whispered, as I lunged toward him and kissed him. I did not know who this bold, aggressive, confident Michael Ausiello was, but I liked him. Kit's lips were every bit as pins and needles–inducing as I remembered. We stood there in the middle of his bedroom and made out like high school students in the parking lot of a 7-Eleven. He at one point reached under my shirt to cop a feel, but, like a good goalie, my ribbed tank top blocked his shot.

"Has anyone ever told you that you're a good kisser?" I cooed, breathlessly.

"You're not so bad yourself," he replied, before continuing to devour me.

After about thirty more minutes of major mouth-to-mouth stimulation and light grabbing and groping, I asked to use his restroom, partly because I really had to pee and partly because we were getting dangerously close to transitioning from heavy petting to loud banging.

"Sure, follow me," he said, as he led me out his bedroom's other door, through a different decaying hallway, and into his private bathroom. Still no sign of the roommate. Kit flipped the light on for me all gentleman-like.

"Thanks," I said, as I closed the door behind me. The bathroom still had all of its prewar bones, giving it a classic New York bathroom vibe.

There was subway tile lining the walls, a huge ceramic tub, a tank-less toilet. It was a sea of white. And what few surfaces existed were completely bare.

As I stood and peed, I continued my visual inspection. I noticed the mirrored medicine cabinet. I wondered what was hiding inside. I also questioned why it mattered so much. Was I looking for a second toothbrush–type smoking gun? Was I trying to sabotage my own happiness? "Chill the fuck out and just enjoy yourself," I said to myself.

I finished tinkling, flushed the toilet, and . . . opened the medicine cabinet.

Much like the rest of the bathroom, its contents were sparse. There was a stick of deodorant, a tube of toothpaste, your standard-issue toothbrush—just the one, thank heavens!—a small jar of mouthwash, all of which had been (curiously) stripped of their labels. On the bottom shelf, tucked into the corner, were two miniature plastic dinosaur figurines hugging each other—adorable! Oh . . . hold up a second. On closer examination, they weren't hugging at all. The Triceratops was brazenly riding the Apatosaurus from behind in what appeared to be a consensual act. Hmm . . . Slightly disturbing but not a deal-breaker.

On the top shelf rested a wooden paddle with red-and-black illustrations etched into the wood. Only after picking it up and reading the words "Peter Meter"—and noticing that it was shaped like a cock—did I realize it was a measuring stick. A penis measuring stick. The units (in ascending order) were as follows:

* Should have been a girl
* Just a water spout
* 95% imagination
* Seen better days, but not much
* Just a teaser
* Woman's home companion
* A secretary's delight
* For large girls and small cattle
* Home Wrecker size
* For Barroom Betting only
* WOW!

The paddle, combined with the fornicating prehistoric reptiles, suggested three things to me about the man waiting for me in the other room: He liked himself a vintage novelty item; he had a cheeky relationship to—and an unapologetic attitude toward—sex; and he was a size queen.

That last one worried me. What if my "woman's home companion"–sized endowment wasn't big enough for him? What if he was aiming for someone in the "secretary's delight" range?

We weren't having sex tonight anyway, so I could set those fears aside for another day.

We ended up sucking face for another fifteen minutes before I cabbed it to Port Authority to catch a bus back to Bloomfield. On the way home, as I replayed the night's big moments in my head, I was forced to confront a simple truth: This thing with Kit felt . . . special. Although I'd only had one prior long-term relationship, I'd been on enough dates by the age of twenty-nine to know that one of these things was not like the other. Yes, there was the obvious physical attraction, but it was more than that. There was an in-sync-ness. A connection. A shorthand. It was like we got each other, without fully knowing at this point exactly what it was we were getting.

The best part? "Fat Mike" wasn't shitting on my post-date high. And, for that matter, neither was "Gay Shame Mike." Or "Survivor's Guilt" Mike. All the Mikes that for the past fifteen years had conspired to convince me that because my parents had died, or because I wasn't straight, or because I was once 250 pounds, I didn't deserve to be happy. Or to be loved. They kept their collective mouths shut the entire way home and allowed me to just *be*. I had never enjoyed a bus ride to New Jersey more.

1.

It was the occasion of my forty-second birthday—and a few months into my thirteenth year with Kit—and I wanted to do something special for myself. So I planned a double-date weekend getaway to the decaying seaside wonderland that is Atlantic City with our best gay friends Nick and Brandon joining Kit and me.

I rented a car, booked two rooms at the super-swank new (and now shuttered) Revel Casino Hotel, and made high-end dinner reservations at American Cut steak house. I confirmed that they had a decent seafood selection, because although I publicly labeled myself a vegetarian I was *technically* a pescatarian, which basically made me a big ol' hypocrite.

I was super-excited about my birthday weekend extravaganza, mostly because the itinerary featured some of my favorite activities: gambling, food, four-star accommodations, and . . . Kit. Add to that the fact that we were renting a car and not using public transportation—thus giving us the freedom to tack on a few of our signature NJ stops, namely Kit's beloved Target in Clark and IKEA in Elizabeth—and you had the makings of an epic birthday adventure.

We checked into Revel on Saturday morning and . . . my God, it was immense and slick and expensive and totally out of place in Atlantic City. I was sad to hear it was on its deathbed. In fact, Revel had only a few months to find a buyer before being forced to close its doors for good. The idea that this gargantuan $2 billion complex, barely a year old, could end up just another abandoned Atlantic City attraction was shocking and sad and . . . oh, my fucking God, the view from our oceanfront suite on the twenty-eighth floor was *spectacular*.

Kit and I entered the room, made a beeline to the window, and just stood there for five minutes, staring out at the Atlantic. So serene. So peaceful. So *not* New York. Honestly, we could have been happy just camping out in Room 2806 for the entire weekend and ordering room service and taking naps and thinking about having sex.

Kit immediately unpacked his toiletries, claimed his side of the bed (the right-hand one), and then we made our way down to the casino to enjoy some slot fun before meeting up with Nick and Brandon for dinner. I darted over to the 25-cent Double Diamond corridor, and the more fiscally conservative Kit parked himself in front of the penny slots. Frugal Kit was one of my favorite Kits, and this was especially true when he was in Atlantic City, where lowered stakes sometimes yielded greater joy. I found the juxtaposition of this über-stylish, successful design snob setting up shop in the penny-slot carousel alongside thrifty senior citizens so wrong yet *so* right. He fit right in. Sights like that made me look forward to our lives as an elderly couple, living out our twilight years in some classic, renovated brownstone on the main drag in quaint upstate Hudson, New York, the ground floor serving as our gift shop—featuring a mix of Kit's Pretty Bitter stationery line, impeccably curated novelty items from local designers, and maybe if Kit let me, a small area of Smurf collectibles—and the upper levels functioning as our home.

Thirty minutes into our slot play, Kit paid me a visit in the Double Diamond district to tell me he was heading to the room to take a nap and maybe have a bowel movement. (When you've been together for more than a decade, there's no shame in that level of specificity.) He kissed me goodbye and I turned my attention back to winning some cold hard cash.

As my reserves started to dwindle, I decided it was time to reach out to the Universe for a little help.

"Come on, Universe . . ." I began. "I've had a rough life. There was the gay bullying in high school. All my obesity trauma. My mom's death at sixteen. My dad's death at twenty-two. My whole tragic life has been building to this magic moment . . . it's time something swung my way. And that *something* is three double diamonds in a row."

Minutes later, the fucking Universe responded with . . . *three. double. diamonds. bitches. step. off.*

Bells were ringing. The simulated-yet-still-intoxicating sound of coins crashing into the payout tray filled the air. Confetti started falling from the ceiling. Flashbulbs were going off. Crowds began forming. There might've been a balloon drop. In the distance, I could see a local news crew approaching.

And then I glanced at the award counter. It was climbing. $100, $200, $300, $400, $500—please don't ever stop!—$600, $700 . . . and that's where it stopped. I had won $700. Holy shit. *Thank you, Universe, for the birthday gift.* I took a deep breath and then I proceeded to do something completely out of character for a slot addict: I cashed out.

And the best was still to come—sharing the news with Kit.

With seven crisp $100 bills in my pocket, I marched up to the twenty-eighth floor dreaming of all the possible fun ways I could break the news to him. I entered our room and first thing I noticed was *that view.* The second thing I saw was Kit sound asleep in the bed. And, in that moment, I felt a wave of happiness and gratitude wash over me. Like I had hit the figurative jackpot in addition to the literal one.

I proceeded over to the bed and slowly, gingerly placed one $100 bill after another down on the nightstand next to Kit until all $700 were laid out like the climax to a magic trick. I then took a seat in front of the floor-to-ceiling window overlooking the ocean and waited for him to wake up.

After fifteen minutes I said, "To hell with this waiting shit," and began the slow and steady process of waking him up. First I kissed him gently on the cheek. That triggered some light facial twitches but not much else, so I kissed him more forcibly, this time on the forehead. There: two open eyelids.

"What time is it?" he asked drowsily.

"It's 5 p.m. We have to get ready for dinner soon. We have 6 p.m. reservations."

"How did you make out?" he asked, not yet noticing the huge cache of cash a mere ten inches from him.

"I did OK," I downplayed.

He sat up, looked over at the nightstand, and saw the cash spread out like a royal flush. Without missing a beat, he quipped, "We're rich, bitch!"

He picked up the bills—one at a time—and proceeded to count them as I sat next to him on the bed and excitedly replayed the entire experience.

With our 6 p.m. dinner reservation fast approaching, we showered and threw on some fancy duds. Kit spent a little extra time in the bathroom due to some ongoing bowel discomfort. In the end, we still arrived at the restaurant a few minutes before six. I did not like to be late for anything, especially my own birthday dinner. Nick and Brandon weren't nearly as time-conscious. It was nearing 6:05 and they were still nowhere in sight. Their tardiness was made all the more irritating considering that their commute consisted of a ten-second elevator ride.

Perhaps they were busy commiserating about the big scoop Kit and I had dropped on them during the car ride to Atlantic City. Roughly thirty minutes into our two-hour trek, I—with Kit seated beside me—looped our best gay-couple friends in on our little secret: For the past six months—ever since we had cashed out on our gut-renovated-by-Kit, two-bedroom, two-bath apartment in Hell's Kitchen—we'd been maintaining separate residences in different parts of the city.

Kit and I were relieved to be sharing the news with someone other than our cat, Mister Scooch. And Nick and Brandon—who were navigating through their own long-term relationship woes—felt like a safe, nonjudgmental audience. Plus, we were spending the entire weekend with them, so it was better to come clean now rather than risk one of us letting it slip at the blackjack table (that's the one with the big wheel and tiny ball, right?).

"We are *not* broken up," I stressed to our backseat riders as I barreled down the southbound express lane of the Garden State Parkway in our rented-for-the-weekend sedan. "We just decided to give ourselves a little breathing room. We're trying it for a year. Also, we're keeping it on the DL, so don't tell anyone, please."

"I already tweeted about it," cracked Nick, not missing a beat. Despite his best diffusing-with-humor efforts, I could tell by the way he was shuffling in his seat that he was surprised. And maybe a little worried for us. Brandon was a little harder to read.

"How's it working out for you?" Nick asked, his concern giving way to genuine curiosity.

I briefly took my eyes off the road to look at Kit. We both smiled at each other.

"It's going . . . well," Kit informed them, a tinge of pride—and relief—in his voice, as I nodded in agreement.

It was a far cry from where we had been last June when Kit came home from work one night and informed me, two months ahead of our closing, that he had signed a one-year lease on a modest $1,300/month one-bedroom apartment across the river in Williamsburg, Brooklyn. For *himself.* I was livid.

"You signed the lease?" I fumed. "Without the two of us having a conversation first?"

"We've been talking about this idea for *weeks*," Kit fired back, loudly and defensively, as if utterly gobsmacked by my incensed reaction. "Don't act like this is coming out of nowhere."

"Yes, we've been *talking about it*," I countered. "But we never *agreed* to it. Thanks for including me in your big decision."

Back in May when we were getting ready to put our apartment on the market, Kit first raised the idea of us staying consciously coupled while securing separate crash pads, arguing that it might help remedy our considerable, seemingly insurmountable codependency issues. The idea seemed nuts to me. Couples who have been together for more than a decade don't just move into separate apartments. And if they do, it must mean that something is terribly wrong with the relationship. What would we tell people? How would it look? Who would get custody of Mister Scooch?

It also felt like the textbook first step in a soft breakup. Like it was easier to call it quits if we convinced ourselves that we weren't actually calling it quits. We were just, you know, moving into separate homes. No big whoop.

But I agreed with Kit on one thing: Something had to change. Our relationship was in serious trouble. For starters, our sex life was riding on fumes. It had been for years. But now that we both had crossed into the gay dinosaur decade that was our forties and could see sexual extinction on the horizon, we began to seriously ask ourselves, "Is *this* it? Should we maybe find out what else—or *who* else—is out there for us before we enter the decade whose name shall not be uttered?"

In a nutshell: We were starting to resent each other, but we loved each other too much to actually do anything about it. We were essentially trapped. And, to cope with the subsequent feelings of anger and guilt and fear, he got high and I got drunk. I considered his drug of choice to be much more of a threat to our relationship, though.

It was at the point where it seemed like Kit was almost never *not* high. Our spare bedroom/office and bathroom had started to look like the pot version of Walter White's meth lab RV, with vaporizers and rolling paper and bongs and bud grinders and bud crumbs scattered throughout. And the smell of cannabis permeated our entire two-bedroom apartment. I couldn't escape it.

Every couple of weeks I would reach a breaking point and put my foot down and issue an ultimatum that mostly involved me demanding that he curtail his usage from every freakin' night to, say, every other night or just weekends or just Tuesdays or not before dinner or not after dinner or not in the morning. He would capitulate at first, before slowly reverting back to his old ways.

I felt like his parole officer, with daily check-ins to make sure he was following the rules. I would get sick of policing him and, Lord knows, he *hated* being policed. He regularly asked me to join him in stoner-land, but I always refused. Partly on principle. Partly because I didn't want to get hooked myself. And partly because I had my wine.

As Kit was off Snoop Dogging in one half of our apartment, I was in the other half channeling my inner Sue Ellen Ewing, aka *Dallas*'s legendary alcohol-addled heroine. It was probably no coincidence that as Kit's pot intake increased, so did my wine consumption—ironic, considering I detested vino when Kit and I first met. But then, about a year into our relationship, we were enjoying a comped three-night stay at The Point, a sprawling, ultra-exclusive, all-inclusive resort in the Adirondacks that ran thousands of dollars a night and accommodated a maximum of eight hoity-toity couples thrown together by happenstance (including, on this particular weekend, Barenaked Ladies' original front man Steven Page and his then wife Carolyn, who were enjoying some "couple time" away from their three young kids, and with whom Kit and I bonded because the other six couples were pretentious assholes). It was during this stay that I was compelled to venture outside of my comfort zone during our nightly communal black-tie dinner in the main dining room. The menu called for every bite of our five-course meal to be paired with a corresponding wine and not, you know, a can of Diet Coke. So as a result of Kit's gentle prodding, not to mention my own concerns about being a Debbie Downer amid a bunch of Richie Riches, I—around Course No. 3—decided to give the chardonnay a try. And, much to my surprise, after about the second or third sip, I kinda stopped hating the taste of it. And by the time we checked out on Sunday, and bid farewell to Steven and Carolyn, I actually kinda liked the stuff.

Over the next couple of years, I began gradually rotating my Diet Coke with a glass of sauvignon blanc when dining out. And even more than the taste of it, I liked how I *felt* while drinking it. I was happier, less stressed. And I realized I didn't just have to feel that way while out at a restaurant. I could pop into the liquor store after dinner and keep the party going at our apartment—on weekends *and* weeknights. I was usually home from work first, so I'd be one glass in by the time Kit arrived around seven. While scanning Seamless for our takeout options, I'd pour Kit his first glass as I dove into my second. The nectar of the gods would continue flowing through dinner and right into *RuPaul's*

Drag Race (if it was a Monday, which is when our reality obsession originally aired). Right around the time the climactic runway portion of the
show started, and certainly before Ru declared, "Silence! Bring back my
gurls," we were moving on to Bottle No. 2. Then *Drag Race* would end
and Kit would begin his sixty- to ninety-minute "wind-down time" and
I'd stay behind to catch up on *my* TV (like *Homeland* or *Grey's Anatomy*
or *The Big Bang Theory*) while polishing off the second bottle of wine.

At around eleven-thirty, Kit—fully stoned now—would rejoin me—
fully tipsy now—in the living room to watch the one-two-three punch
of *Chelsea Lately*, *The Daily Show with Jon Stewart*, and *The Colbert Report*. If I wasn't dozing off at this point, I was shooting Kit daggers for
laughing at every joke in such an annoyingly exaggerated manner that
it rendered them impotent for me, sending me storming off to bed in
a huff.

This routine played out pretty much nightly. And I was so busy
demonizing Kit for his pot dependence that I shrugged off my wine
use as the lesser—and certainly the more *legal*—of two evils. Kit occasionally called me out on the double standard, but for the most part
he didn't judge my drinking. Part of me wished he would express some
concern or take more notice, to demonstrate to me that he cared.
Because, the fact was, over the course of our relationship I went from
hating wine to tolerating wine to liking wine to loving wine to *needing*
wine.

I needed wine to quell my raging insecurity about the extra thirty
pounds I had gained in the twelve years since Kit and I met, extra pad-
ding I feared only drew more attention to how far out of my league he
was. I needed wine to dull the shame I felt over Kit and me not having had what he referred to as "big boy sex"—intercourse—in more
than two years. I needed wine to ease my guilt about waking up early
each morning and quietly jerking off to porn while Kit lay asleep next
to me, because it was easier than initiating sex and getting rejected
or, even worse, *having* sex and being reminded of how much our ro-
mantic spark had dimmed. I needed wine to drown out my suspicions
that, despite his unequivocal denials every time I point-blank asked
him, he had fallen off the infidelity wagon again, this time with a guy
named Todd, an up-and-coming interior designer he'd met through

his current gig as head photographer at Manhattan's foremost vintage midcentury furniture shop, Wyeth, and who spoke the same design language as Kit, *and*, as bad luck would have it, was the spitting image of his ultimate celebrity crush, Olympic diver Tom Daley. I needed wine to live with the part of me that felt like a pushover for not trusting my gut about Kit's infidelity because, if I did, it would mean I'd have to finally make good on my threat to leave him. I needed wine to silence the voices in my head that pointed out all the instances where I chose my job over my relationship. I needed wine to calm the part of me that worried that Kit, after eleven years, was finally coming to the realization that he could do better than me.

And for one hour every two weeks we visited our longtime couples therapist, Tony Frankenberg, and attempted to fix our broken relationship. We discussed possible solutions, one of which, now, was living apart. Other Mike-and-Kit Act 2 options included buying another apartment together, sitting the real estate market out for a year and *renting* an apartment together, and—lastly—yanking the apartment off the market and just staying put. After all, it was a *sweet* pad and we'd developed a *Friends*-like comfort with the building and many of its residents, particularly Rose, our dear sixty-year-old friend and a fellow co-op board member of Kit's, who lived one floor up from us and would regularly pop down unannounced with a bottle of wine and a fresh batch of neighborhood gossip, all delivered with the theatrics you'd expect from a woman who'd spent the past three decades working behind the scenes as a dresser on Broadway.

Despite our love of Rose, there was little chance we were going to choose the "staying put" option, since we were pretty determined to get the blazes out of Hell's Kitchen. I had initially been drawn to the once-stigmatized midtown west neighborhood for its undeniable convenience and relative affordability. But between the gentrification of nearby Ninth Avenue, triggered by a massive pilgrimage of young gays from Chelsea, and the proximity to the booming theater district, our backyard had grown into the loudest, most congested place on Earth. And we were just too old for this shit. Our tolerance level for mobbed sidewalks and idling tour buses and aggressive horn honkers and long restaurant lines had diminished significantly. Also, we were anxious to liquidate our number one asset before the housing market crashed and/or a terrorist detonated a dirty bomb in adjacent Times Square.

That was essentially where we were at when Kit decided to go rogue: We were weighing all of our options. Together. So for him to unapologetically sign the lease behind my back, before we had mutually agreed on which path to take, infuriated me. And the fact that the communication-challenged Kit struggled to articulate why he would do such a hurtful, insensitive thing—beyond saying that he felt suffocated—only confirmed my worst fears: I was losing him. And to a fucking outer borough.

So I reacted as I typically would when Kit pushed me to the emotional brink: I gave him the silent treatment. Instead of engaging in a knock-down, drag-out shouting match that Kit was *always* game for, I went in the opposite direction and shut down. It was the same dance we'd been doing for the past almost twelve years. Kit wore his emotions on his sleeve and I bottled mine up. And I did so, in large part, because I was terrified of what lay beneath. If I cracked the floodgates open even just an inch, forty-one-plus years of grief and gay bullying and fat shaming and sexual oppression could potentially come pouring out. And what would *that* look like? What would it look like to completely lose it? Combine that with Kit's default incendiary temperament and things could get ugly. Maybe even violent, as they often had with my short-fused dad.

So, instead of discussing the matter further with Kit, I froze him out until our next appointment with Tony, who attempted to put Kit's insensitive actions into words: What if his impetuous decision to slap his John Hancock on that lease wasn't a sign that he wanted to end our relationship, but, rather, his last-ditch attempt to *save* it?

Kit loved it when Tony was able to translate his complex feelings into one smartly constructed sound bite. And he seemed particularly relieved on that day, as he nodded, looked at me with a sheepish smile, and joked, "Yeah. That's the ticket."

And as frustrating as it was that Kit needed Tony's help in both diffusing the storm brewing inside him and finding the right words to articulate those feelings, I was just relieved to hear that we both still wanted the same thing: to be in a healthy, happy relationship with each other.

That session with Tony went a long way toward helping me make peace with the fact that Kit and I would soon be receiving our mail at different addresses. And, slowly, a number of silver linings came into view, like, for example, Kit would no longer be the boss of me from an interior design perspective. After ten years of willingly and (for the most part) happily letting him control every aspect of our apartment's feng shui—from the positioning of my hair gel in the medicine cabinet to the symmetry of our pillowcases when making the bed ("The opening flaps face *out*," he'd harrumph at me every time we made the bed together)—I would, for the first time since my Bloomfield, New Jersey, days, be able to see how I'd grown as an interior designer under Kit's tutelage. And Kit's current no-Smurfs-in-the-bedroom rule? Vetoed!

Suddenly, this crazy, scary idea became exciting, liberating. And now that we were at the eight-month mark, I was comfortable declaring it an unqualified success.

I was living it up in a one-bedroom apartment with an outdoor space and a washer and dryer and a fireplace, on the top floor of a circa-1800 brownstone on one of the best blocks (Jane Street) in one of the best parts of the city (West Village), which just happened to be down the street from our favorite restaurant, Benny's Burritos. Frugal Kit, meanwhile, had turned a long-neglected one-bedroom on the top floor of a two-family house in Brooklyn into the coziest, most eclectic, smartly curated safe space.

And the best part? He spent hardly any time there.

Turned out, Kit liked living the metaphorical high life, too, especially when it was within walking distance of Wyeth's SoHo headquarters. He was pretty much living in my apartment full-time. The fact that he could hit an eject button and be transported to his own personal retreat five miles away should he need a breather from me, or simply because he didn't like what was on my work-mandated TV schedule for the night, made his enjoyment of my West Village pad all the easier.

His Brooklyn home became known as our weekend pied-à-terre— a makeshift Hamptons, if you will. For all intents and purposes, though, the West Village was our home. The *apartment*, however, was mine, and Kit respected that. Sure, he served as my design sensei throughout my furniture buying and laying-out process, but he knew the buck literally and now figuratively stopped with me. He'd occasionally take certain liberties, like decorating the inside of the fireplaces with dozens of towering candles, and organizing my pantry into distinct categories like "cleaning supplies" and "toiletries" and "Target returns." And I welcomed his involvement. It meant he was feeling at home in my home.

Oh, and we were planning a big fancy vacation together—a two-week, all-inclusive African safari the coming summer. We'd done all the research and narrowed it down to two vendors. We were making our final decision by the end of the month.

With much of the uncertainty surrounding our new living arrangement in the rearview mirror, we'd started to feel comfortable sharing the news of our living situation with those close to us. Like Nick and Brandon, whose initial reaction of surprise and curiosity had now given way to . . . jealousy. They genuinely seemed envious that we had rewritten the relationship rulebook. And lived to tell the tale.

It was now 6:09 and Nick and Brandon were still MIA. As I started crafting a bitchy text to Nick, I saw the two of them hurriedly walking down the escalator toward us.

"Did you get stuck in traffic?" I sniffed.

"Yeah, the expressway was a nightmare," Nick zinged back, giving as good as he got in typical Nick fashion.

Nick and I had a crackling repartee. His vast pop culture well, combined with just an edge of acidity, made him the quintessential sparring partner. I sensed Kit felt threatened by our comedic chemistry, so I always attempted to dial it back a smidge when we were all together. Conflict Avoidance 101.

I decided to put my $700 haul toward the dinner bill, thus avoiding that awkward, nonsensical ritual where everyone else pays for a dinner *you* invited *them* to. Between the four of us, we had no trouble eating and drinking my jackpot away. It was a lovely evening, although I did notice that Kit was shifting uncomfortably in his seat through most of the meal. I assumed it was related somehow to the bowel issues he'd been experiencing. Or perhaps it was connected to the light traces of blood he had started seeing last week in his semen—a worrisome symptom that WebMD nonetheless assured us was likely nothing serious and would probably go away on its own.

After dinner, the four of us retired to the casino and did some more gambling (lightning didn't strike twice for me), and we called it a night fairly early. The next day, Sunday, Kit and I took advantage of the unseasonably warm weather and went for a stroll on the boardwalk. Even on a peak summer day, the Atlantic City boardwalk scene was pretty sad. This was *late February*. We nonetheless managed to find a few bright spots amid the blight, beginning with an arcade that had a long row of Skee-Ball machines. We both saw them at the same time, and within seconds, he was at the change machine breaking a $10 bill and I was holding two lanes for us. We were literally the only two people in the entire arcade, but I nonetheless was prepared to defend these two lanes with *my life*.

Kit divided up the quarters—a stack of twenty on my machine and a stack of twenty on his—and it was game on. Skee-Ball was the one competitive activity where Kit and I were pretty evenly matched, which was a big part of why I gravitated to it. Come to think of it, Skee-Ball was the *only* game where we were evenly matched. Kit handed me my ass at everything else, including—but not limited to—Connect Four, Phase 10, Battleship, thumb wrestling, hangman, tic-tac-toe, Yahtzee, Ms. Pac-Man, and Ping-Pong. But I could hold my own when it came to Skee-Ball. And on this fateful Sunday, hold my own I did. I was consistently breaking the 300-point benchmark with each game, while Kit was struggling to claw his way past 200 most rounds. I was on a roll.

"I hope you get a hangnail," he mock-grumbled after my third consecutive victory.

Despite his losing streak, he obviously could tell how much fun I was having and sweetly moved a few of his coins over to my pile.

In the end, we collected a huge-ass pile of tickets and excitedly marched over to the prize counter, only to discover that we barely had enough to win a dusty, partially cracked Atlantic City coffee mug. We decided to just load up on a bunch of tiny trinkets, like fish erasers and bouncy balls. Kit remained relatively passive during this redemption process until the last second, when he took a sudden interest in a big plastic case of black spider rings.

"How many points do we have left?" Kit asked the attendant.

"Sixty points," the attendant responded.

"We'll take a couple of spider rings."

And with that, we packed up our winnings and continued our trek along the boardwalk. Sad little souvenir shop? Check. Abandoned salt-water taffy boutique? Check. Pathetic, embarrassing, hopeless 99-cent store? Check—oh, fuckity-fuck-fuck.

I was hoping Kit wouldn't see the rapidly approaching sign. He was powerless to resist anything that melded forgotten treasures and steep discounts. And sure enough, much like those *Star Wars* tractor beams, the 99-cent store took hold of Kit and slowly drew him in. All I could do was watch and pray I wouldn't have to extend our hotel reservation for another night.

"Just five minutes," he promised me.

"OK," I sighed. "I'll just wait outside. Remember we have a small apartment. And we're on a tight schedule."

Kit ventured inside his price-slash wonderland, and I plopped myself down on a nearby bench overlooking the ocean, fountain Diet Coke in hand. Five minutes quickly became ten minutes. And then fifteen minutes. I was beginning to get annoyed. Every time someone who *wasn't* Kit exited the store my irritation increased. At the twenty-minute mark, just as the chilly ocean breeze began doing a number on my toes, I realized I was going to have to carry out an emergency extraction. It was unfortunate that our idyllic Atlantic City weekend had to end on such a violent note, but I was left with no other choice. Our rental was due back at the garage by 5 p.m. and we still had to squeeze in stops at Target and IKEA.

I entered the store and began to search aisle after aisle for Kit. Occasionally, a shiny bargain would jump out at me, but I resisted the temptation to stop. This was a rescue operation; I needed to stay focused. Unfortunately, Kit was nowhere to be found. I decided to send up one of our signature audio flares.

"Marco?" I whispered as I made my way through an abyss of half-price greeting cards.

Crickets.

"Marco?" I muttered as I approached the cleaning-products section. Crickets.

"*Marco*," I groaned, my voice now loud enough to evoke confused, slightly annoyed reactions from shoppers. (It was a 99-cent store, not Tiffany & Co. Simmer down, people.)

"Polo," replied a nearby voice, which I was 99 percent certain belonged to Kit.

I turned a corner, and sure enough, there was my little frugal detective, crouched down sifting through a box of what appeared to be really old party favors. I approached him and I could see the look on his face. The look of a man on a mission. The look of a man experiencing an explosion of endorphins. He stood up and proudly shoved his basket full of goodies in my face.

"This place is *incredible*," he softly shrieked. "They have stuff in here from the seventies!"

Before I could get a word in edgewise, he began to present each of his findings to me. A super-cheesy faux gold-plated miniature camera ring for his BFF and artistic soul mate Jen. Retro paper dolls, possibly to resell on eBay. A ceramic middle-finger statue—recipient TBD.

The show-and-tell exercise currently unfolding before me was not unlike the scene in *WALL-E*, when the titular robot invites Eve into his cave and excitedly introduces her to all of his prized earthly possessions. And just like that, my anger evaporated, replaced with an avalanche of warm and fuzzies. I grabbed hold of him and looked in his eyes, all serious-like.

"Hey," I said. "I love you."

I planted a kiss on his lips. And then I looked at my watch. As I was about to remind him about the tight schedule, he interrupted, "I'm wrapping up. Give me ten more minutes."

"OK, ten more minutes," I agreed. "I'll be waiting outside."

It ended up being closer to twenty more minutes—half of those minutes he spent heavily debating whether to load up on more of those middle-finger statues. "They'd make great stocking stuffers," he reasoned. (He wound up just getting the one.)

Within an hour, we met back up with Nick and Brandon, checked out of Revel, and were on the Atlantic City Expressway heading home. Before we reached the city limits, Kit was still second-guessing his decision not to snap up more of those middle-finger statues.

"That store is not going anywhere," I assured him. "We can always come back."

Despite all my timing concerns, we managed to squeeze in trips to Target and IKEA and still get the rental returned on time. And, honestly, what was I *really* worried about? Having to pay a $50 late fee? I was constantly in a rush to be somewhere other than where I was at in any given moment. And it was exhausting.

For my *actual* birthday dinner, Kit and I went to one of our favorite restaurants, Champs Diner, in Brooklyn. The menu was all vegan and the Almost Macro Bowl—complete with brown rice, sautéed kale, grilled tempeh cutlets, sauerkraut, and tahini sauce—was to effen die for. We always flirted with the idea of going off script and ordering something new—like the yummy-sounding Chik'n Parm—but we always ended up playing it safe.

"Two Almost Macro Bowls, two Arnold Palmers, and one side of vegan bacon, please," I relayed to the waitress, with an air of "You know, our usual."

As I handed the menus back to her, I noticed Kit shifting in his seat. Again.

"Are you OK?" I asked.

"Something's not right with my ass," he replied. "I feel like I've got a golf ball lodged up there."

"A . . . golf ball?" I worriedly shot back.

"Yes," he confirmed, before picking up on the fear in my eyes. "Bodge, come down off the ledge. It's probably just a big hemorrhoid."

Quick sidebar: Bodge—pronounced Boj (think "Bo Jackson," just drop the "ackson")—was one of a handful of nicknames we'd adopted for each other over the years. It arrived after our initial "Poopiedoops" and "Dooplumdoops" phase, although we never could recall its exact origin. It was as if the word had been implanted in our brains one night while we slept, and then when we woke up we were simply each other's Bodge. And there were variations. Like Bodge-lums. And Bodge-lum-doops. But mostly it was just Bodge.

Kit knew me well. My internal alert system was raised to DEFCON 1, a level not seen since a week ago when I thought I felt a lump in my testicle and raced to an urgent care facility in Chelsea to be felt up by a stranger in a lab coat, only to be told what I was feeling was just normal scrotum bits.

Now I took a deep breath, came down off the anal cancer ledge, and urged Kit to at least get it checked out. There was also the ongoing bloody semen issue, so now he had two—possibly related—reasons to see a doctor. He agreed.

Our Arnold Palmers arrived, and as I began to sip mine, I felt a second wave of panic rush over me. I wondered if there was such a thing as a golf ball–sized hemorrhoid. Could they grow that big?

The next day, Monday, Kit reached out to a colorectal specialist referred to him by his primary care physician and made an appointment for Wednesday—the same day I was scheduled to visit the Brooklyn set of *The Americans*, the FX drama series that starred my aforementioned *Felicity* crush Keri Russell.

In the twelve years since *Felicity* went off the air, I had remained fairly tight with many of the key players, particularly series co-creator J.J. Abrams (aka the guy responsible for my graduation-scene cameo), star Scott Foley (aka the guy who directed my episode and was responsible for leaving me on the cutting-room floor, a decision that has haunted him ever since, mostly because I throw it in his face whenever I see him), and, last but not least, Keri. I was very much looking forward to seeing her on Wednesday. Kit was aware of this and therefore instantly vetoed my offer to reschedule it so I could accompany him to his appointment. And I didn't fight him on it.

I probably should have, because all I could think about on that Wednesday was Kit. His appointment was at 2 p.m., and much of my time on the *Americans* set was spent looking at my watch and texting Kit to remind him to call me with a full report the second he left the doctor's office. I arrived on the Brooklyn soundstage at around 1 p.m. and spent the first ninety minutes observing a scene between Keri and TV hubby Matthew Rhys (who I knew from covering his previous TV series, the ABC drama *Brothers & Sisters*) in their characters' living room. I typically loved seeing how the TV sausage got made, but today I was disconnected from the experience. My heart was with Kit and my eyes were on my phone, waiting for some kind of communication from him. I was praying, purely for selfish reasons, that I'd hear from him before it was time for me to sit down and interview Keri and Matthew. The optimistic part of me fantasized about getting a positive report from Kit and then turning my reunion with Keri into something of a celebration.

At around two-forty-five, I got tired of waiting.

"Update, please," I texted him.

Within seconds, he wrote back, "Just got out. Hold the line."

"Call me," I replied. "I have a sec."

I found a quiet area away from where Keri and Matthew were shooting their scene and took Kit's call.

"They found something," he informed me. "But the doctor said there are a hundred things it could be other than cancer."

"They found a *growth*?" I clarified.

"Yes," he confirmed. "I'm having it biopsied on Friday. I'm going to be fine. Please don't be worried. I'm not . . . You get one more question."

"Are you in any pain?"

"The rectal exam was not fun," he said. "But I'm OK. I'm going to treat myself to some retail therapy now. I will see you tonight when you get home."

"OK, Bodge. I love you."

I hung up with him, and before I had time to process all of this new information, Lana, *The Americans*' publicist, was in my face.

"Michael, Keri and Matthew are ready for you."

Lana escorted me through the show's surprisingly spacious living room set into the dining room nook, where Keri and Matthew were waiting for me. Their faces lit up when I entered, and they both stood to embrace me. We quickly caught up, they thanked me for schlepping out to Brooklyn to visit them (after I only half-jokingly reminded them that I didn't do outer boroughs for just *anyone*), and then I pulled out my questions, placed my tape recorder on the table in front of them, and lightly, playfully grilled them about what was in store for their characters, Elizabeth and Philip, in Season 2.

Good thing I was recording their answers, because I wasn't listening to a word they were saying. All I could hear was the voice inside my head going, "It can't be happening again."

2.

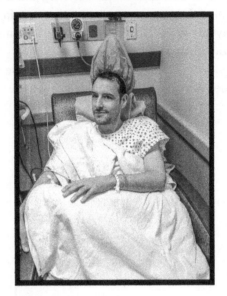

"It can't be happening again."

Nearly twenty-six years ago to the day, my mom returned home from the doctor's with my dad and informed me and my brothers, Peter and David, that a growth had been discovered inside her throat. A subsequent biopsy revealed it was cancer. She would be dead within a year.

My mom was my whole world.

She had a heart as big as Texas and a laugh that could fill a room until it was bursting with joy. And she wasn't just an animal lover; she was the kind of animal lover who would have long conversations in the kitchen with her beloved parakeet, Tweety. Then, while cooking dinner, she'd make up silly songs with random, funny lyrics.

Around seventh grade, I was pretty much fused to my mom's hip. That included shadowing her every summer at the mortgage credit check company she co-owned with my father (I was paid in Smurfs) and serving as her Sunday grocery-shopping assistant. My duties included bundle-carrying and distracting cashiers while coupons for items we hadn't purchased were deducted from our bill—remember, these were the crazy, anything-goes, pre-scanner days!

My mom also shared my love of soaps. Unfortunately, since I was a child of the Dark Ages—a time before VCRs, never mind DVRs—school proved a rather daunting obstacle to my daytime TV watching. But it was not an insurmountable obstacle. If the truancy cops had paid a little more attention to my absentee records, they'd have noticed that all of my illnesses coincided with pivotal episodes of *Days of Our Lives*. Bo and Hope's wedding? I was home with a cold. The climax of Stefano DiMera's evil prism plot? I was nursing a relentless cough. The death of Roman Brady? Nasty stomach bug.

In those instances when feigning sickness wasn't an option (or my performance was not up to snuff), I dragged out the portable tape deck, left the television on all day, and just recorded the audio. It was hardly an ideal option, but desperate times called for desperate measures.

The arrival of the VCR improved my quality of life exponentially. My mother and I developed a reliable system by which she would manually press record on the VCR every day at 1 p.m., which conveniently was right around the time she returned home from work. (You did *not* want to be in our house on the afternoons when I got home from school and a fresh episode of *Days* was not waiting for me on the VCR, the result of my mom running late at work or forgetting altogether. The tension could be cut with a knife. Thankfully, my mom's success rate was *very* high.)

My dad, however, was embarrassed by my love for "Love in the Afternoon." Whenever I got grounded, it wasn't my outdoor privileges that he revoked; it was my soaps. Daytime *and* nighttime.

"Thank God for my mother!" is a thought that crossed my mind quite often, but *especially* when my father took my soaps away. She always managed to get him to cut back on my sentence—a one-week ban often became a one- or two-day ban, and even then, Mom would record the shows for me behind his back.

My mom was also a pit bull, who defended those close to her, present company especially. I'll never forget the time at our dinner table when my older brother, Pete, snidely referred to me as a "fat girl." He often did that, but for whatever reason, this time it struck a nerve in my mom—so much so that this five-foot-seven woman stood up and slapped him across the face so hard that he was thrown off his chair and onto the floor.

Unlike my smack-happy father, my mother rarely resorted to violence when punishing us. In fact, the blow she leveled at my brother ended up hurting her more than it did him. She was not herself for days afterward. At church that Sunday, she even refrained from receiving Communion—she was *that* torn up. To this day, I'm not sure if it was the implication that I was gay or if it was the intolerance that my brother's comment foretold that so upset her. (By the way, Pete has long since accepted, embraced, and even championed his gay brother.)

Through it all, my mom was surrounded by a cloud of smoke. Oh, man, did she smoke—as much in a day as every character on *Mad Men* would in a season, combined. Morning, noon, and night, she had a cigarette in her mouth. On airplanes, in cars, at work—there was never a bad time to take a puff, as far as my mom was concerned. She would buy them by the carton, and if she ran out (or came close to it), she would send me to the corner store to pick her up a pack. (I couldn't help but feel like her drug mule.) Deep down, though, I knew that it wasn't good for her. I feared she would die of lung cancer. One night, I even ran downstairs crying after having a nightmare that she had died.

"I'm not going to die, Michael," she assured me. "Now go back to sleep."

But I nonetheless worried that the most important person in the world would be taken away from me.

And in the end, she would.

The eleven-month period between her diagnosis and death was a dark, debilitating stretch. The emotional roller coaster of fear, hope, sadness, disappointment, and ultimately, abandonment haunts me to this day. Because I spent so much time with my mother, I was given a bird's-eye view of the entire ordeal—I even accompanied her to her daily radiation treatments. And as I held her hand in the emergency room on December 27, 1988, I looked on as she opened her eyes, glanced at me, and let out a barely audible "Michael." It was the last word she would ever speak.

This couldn't be happening again.

I considered confiding in Keri and Matthew what I was going through, if only to hear them offer me a comforting, if illusionary "Everything will be OK." I ultimately decided against it. I was there for professional reasons, not to dump a lifetime's worth of cancer baggage on them. So after wrapping up the interview, I packed up my tape recorder, hugged them goodbye, and ventured back into Manhattan, anxious to see Kit and find out more about today's visit. And maybe uncover something that would reassure me that it *wasn't* happening again.

I arrived home to an empty apartment—save for our exhaustingly needy cat, Mister Scooch. If your hands weren't penetrating his purr zones (i.e., his neck, his ear flaps, and the top of his head) within fifteen seconds of walking through the door, you could be hit with a relentless "Meow" assault. There was no escape. My attempts to distract him with catnip-laced toys and fish-flavored treats proved unsuccessful, so I set down my work satchel, popped open a Diet Snapple, sat on the couch, and gave him what he needed. He was a selfish bastard, but he was *our* selfish bastard.

"Scooch" was borrowed from the made-up word Kit endearingly assigned to my residual pouch of childhood belly fat, while "Mister" was just thrown in so folks knew that he was a not-to-be-fucked-with breed of pussy. Kit and I were legally allowed to bend and twist the name as we saw fit, which led to such colorful variations as Scoocher, the Scoochinator, Scoochopolis, but everyone else had to refer to him by his full, formal moniker, Mister Scooch. Also, if you were writing him a note, it was "Mister," not "Mr." Kit was very particular about that.

Mere minutes into my QT with Scoocherino, Kit bounded through the door with shopping bags dangling from both hands. Scooch jumped off the couch and raced over to greet him. Scooch liked me well enough, but he *worshipped* Kit. It probably had something to do with the fact that when Kit sat down to pet him, he, unlike me, wasn't *also* checking his iPhone. Or scrolling through the DVR. Or reading the mail. Or drinking Snapple. He was 100 percent focused on the task at hand. His heart was in it. And this level of dedication and commitment did not go unnoticed by Scooch Potato.

The two of them hadn't always been thick as thieves.

When we first adopted Mister Scooch a decade ago from the East 38th Street branch of the Bideawee animal shelter as a belated thirty-second birthday present for me, Kit—still scarred from the time he came home from middle school and learned his beloved childhood cat had run away—kept Scooch at an emotional and physical arm's length. When I suggested that it seemed like he was taking a liking to our little rug rat, he rolled his eyes and sneered that he would "trade him in for a new flat-screen" in a heartbeat, as if Best Buy were running some kind of cats-for-TVs promotion. He would go on to level that threat directly at Mister Scooch himself whenever he misbehaved.

But anyone with a working pair of retinas could see that Scooch was slowly chipping away at Kit's armor. Among the telltale signs: the way he would proactively make a little extra room on the chaise lounge just in case the spirit moved Scooch to curl up next to him (it always did); how he'd stealthily slip a new cat toy into our Target basket when I wasn't looking; the speed with which he would whip his camera out every time Scooch hilariously forgot to dial back his manspread after licking his naughty bits; the panicked look on his face when he worried if Scooch's latest choking fit was caused by something more sinister than a harmless hairball.

Make no mistake—Scooch had become Kit's cat. And I wasn't the least bit jealous. I relished the front-row seat I had to their special bond. I loved the sweet, protective, shmoopy side it brought out in Kit. Mister Scooch illuminated all of the best parts of my guy *on a daily basis*. And because Scooch was in many ways the four-legged embodiment of our relationship—our mascot, if you will—when Kit showered *him* with love, it felt as if he were simultaneously wrapping his arms around *us*. It was my kind of threesome.

Their little bromance encountered its first major test about a year in, when Kit decided he was tired of walking into our perfectly renovated bathroom in our perfectly renovated Hell's Kitchen apartment and seeing an ugly-ass litter box assaulting his clean lines. That led him to take on the pet project of all pet projects: training Mister Scooch to pee and poop in a toilet.

He went online and purchased a Litter Kwitter, a pre–*Shark Tank* invention that transitioned your cat from a litter box to a human toilet in eight weeks or less using a series of litter-filled plastic discs that fit over the rim of the toilet. Each week the discs got smaller and smaller, until all that was left was a regular toilet seat.

Scooch proved to be a top-notch student, acing every step of his training. And in two months, Kit's dream of living in a litter-free home was realized. He was never more proud of himself. Kit would regale friends and family with the story of how he taught our cat to act like a human being in the one room where it mattered most. Strangers on the subway looked on in awe as Kit played for them movies on his phone of Mister Scooch hopping on the loo and unloading a half-dozen Raisinets into the water below. But Kit's biggest reward came every time he stepped foot in his prized bathroom and didn't see a litter box sullying his work of art.

But what the public didn't know—what Kit conveniently left out of his triumphant tales of yore—was that shortly after Mister Scooch ascended to the throne, he became a royal asshole. You see, once Scooch caught on to the fact that all of these seemingly entertaining hoops Kit had him jumping through were actually part of a larger plot to trick him into permanently rejecting the very essence of his cathood, he was—pardon the pun—pissed off. And every time he got ready to "call the office," as my maternal grandfather Thomas Bull would refer to the boy's room, he lodged a protest so loud it could wake Eartha Kitt. If I were fluent in Scoochspeak, I would say he told Kit, "This is fucking—pardon the pun—bullshit. I am a *cat*, for chrissakes. This is humiliating. It's not natural. I hope you get a hangnail."

Kit, meanwhile, tuned his son's ear-piercing, guttural meows out. He refused to acknowledge that his grand plan might be falling apart, even as I showed him all the negative reviews Mister Scooch was leaving on Litter Kwitter's Yelp page. As long as Scooch's meltdowns climaxed with the adorable sound of tiny cat turds hitting the water like pebbles in a pond, all was right in Kit's world (so much so that mere seconds after Scooch jumped off the commode, Kit would race into the bathroom, proudly inspect his treasures, and gleefully announce "poops!" or "just peeps!" before flushing the toilet).

But just as we were nearing the one-year mark, Scooch said to hell with diplomacy and declared all-out war. We came home from work one evening and were shocked to discover a big steaming pile of crusty brown cat apples in the middle of our bed. Kit shrugged it off as just one of the many random things felines sometimes do, but I knew a premeditated act when I smelled it. And, sure enough, while Kit was in the basement laundry room washing our sheets, Scooch slinked out of hiding and flashed me the scariest, most mustache-swirling smirk. And I knew D-Day had arrived. (*Psst: The "D" stands for dung.*)

Two days later, Scooch left us another surprise in our boudoir. And like a scene out of *Groundhog Day*, Kit schlepped our sheets back down to the basement to be cleaned for the second time in a week, all while refusing to let Mister Scooch see him sweat, because, as he reasoned to me, if Mister Scooch saw him sweat, the terrorists were winning.

Well, the terrorists won anyway.

It was a Sunday afternoon—just three days since the last incident and a week since the first—when Kit and I returned from brunch and saw that not only had the eagle landed, but it had once again left two tablespoons of excrement. And once again a stoic Kit rounded up our sheets and retreated to the laundry room. Only this time he returned with Scooch's old litter box, which for the past year had been collecting dust in our basement storage unit. In Kit's other hand was a bag of leftover litter.

I nervously, quietly sat on the edge of the couch as Kit entered the bathroom and plopped the litter box on the floor. I could then hear him filling it with litter. It was not unlike the sound of someone's pride taking a serious hit.

Kit then walked into the living room, sat on the couch next to me, and humbly concluded, "He wins."

Seconds later, Scooch sashayed out of the bedroom with a little extra spring in his step, made a beeline for the bathroom, and took the world's biggest, smelliest shit in his old litter box. And just to pour a little extra salt in Kit's wounds, he kicked a pawful of litter onto the impeccably tiled floor before exiting the bathroom, en route to the kitchen to grab a post-victory snack, flashing Kit the smuggest look as he sauntered by.

Kit did not speak to or pet Mister Scooch for the next week.

The two of them had long since moved past Toiletgate, a fact evident now as Kit placed his bundles on the table and immediately gave Scooch some lovin'. I waited my turn before walking over and giving Kit the tightest of hugs.

"Someone's going down the rabbit hole," he cracked as I held on to him for dear life.

"A little bit," I confessed. "I have questions."

"I figured you would." He nodded. "Which is why I took notes."

He pulled out a scrunched-up piece of paper containing all sorts of scribble and attempted to make out his own writing.

"It could be a fissure or a cyst or a hemorrhoid or an abscess . . ." he rattled off. "He did not seem worried, Bodge. Now look at all the stuff I got at Uniqlo. I got some things for you, too."

I found it somewhat comforting that Kit was more interested in showing off all the clothes he had purchased than talking about the growth inside his ass. If the doctor wasn't worried, and if *Kit* wasn't worried, then why the hell was *I* getting worried? That was my story, and I was determined over the next thirty-six hours to stick to it.

The night before the biopsy, I returned home from work and found Kit catching up on an old episode of *Elementary*—one of a handful of shows he watched without me. I didn't have anything against *Elementary*, per se. I just didn't have time for it. In this era of Peak TV, sacrifices and painful cuts had to be made.

I walked to the kitchen and noticed two unopened enema boxes on the counter—biopsy prep.

"I have to do one before bed," he told me, "and then another at 3 a.m."

I could tell by the inflection in his voice that he was dreading it. The pain from Wednesday's rectal exam had not yet dissipated, and now he had to shove more stuff into his ass.

He wrapped up his *Elementary* episode, grabbed one of the enema boxes, and disappeared into the bathroom. I, meanwhile, threw on my sleep sweats, hopped into bed with my iPhone, and scrolled through my Twitter feed. And then the sounds started. Even with the bathroom door closed, I could hear Kit moaning in pain. It caught me off guard. And scared me.

"Bodge, are you OK?" I yelled out.

"Yeah," he said, his strained tone belying his brave words.

The noises went on for forty-five minutes. Forty-five fucking minutes for *one* enema.

Eventually, the bathroom door opened and Kit—out of breath as if he had just run a half marathon—fell into bed.

"That was not fun," he exhaled.

As I leaned in to spoon him, he quickly pushed back. It was the first time in our almost thirteen years together that he had rejected my canoodle. "I'm sorry," he sighed. "I don't want to be touched."

I slinked back to my side of the bed, racked with sadness, helplessness, and fear. Eventually I fell off to sleep, only to be awoken by Kit's super-fun, aggressively upbeat, country-tinged iPad alarm at 3 a.m.

Oh, that alarm. Kit loved the irony of it. He *hated* getting up in the morning. And if you were in the unenviable position of having to be the one to *wake* him up, you had to be prepared to wear body armor. So the fact that he had downloaded history's most joyous alarm jingle to help wrest him from his slumber on a daily basis was both hilarious and quintessentially Kit. It never ceased to tickle me.

Until this morning.

Hearing that alarm filled me with dread. It meant it was time to administer Enema No. 2. It meant another hour of extreme discomfort for Kit. It meant another hour of me hearing him suffer while I lay there helplessly.

Kit took a deep breath and bounded out of bed, a man on a mission. I considered grabbing my headphones and watching an episode of *Girls* to drown out his suffering, but I just couldn't do it. I wasn't going to abandon him. We were in this together. So I scrolled through my Twitter feed and prayed to God that Round 2 would be less frightful than Round 1.

I don't recall if it was or it wasn't. What I *do* remember is the relief I felt knowing it was over when he came back to bed for the second time. I didn't attempt to canoodle him. Instead, I leaned over, kissed him on the cheek, and told him I loved him.

Two hours later, now 6 a.m., the alarm went off again. It was time to get ready for the biopsy appointment. Kit, not surprisingly, was slow to get out of bed. I let him hit snooze on the World's Cheeriest Alarm Jingle a few times, but at around six-twenty, I stopped pussyfooting around.

"We have to get a move on, Bodge," I announced.

Within fifteen minutes, we were out the door, in a taxi, and headed to Lenox Hill Hospital on the Upper East Side. We approached reception and I instinctually assumed control of the situation.

"Christopher Cowan is here for a 7 a.m. appointment," I announced, with Kit at my side. The pleasant-enough reception lady handed us off to another pleasant-enough lady who asked us a series of standard questions—full name, age, surgical history, allergies—all of which I answered for Kit. It gave me a purpose. And a little bit of control. It also gave Kit a breather after the rough night he'd just endured.

"Marital status?" she asked.

I hesitated for a second before declaring, "Single."

Without missing a beat, Kit interjected, "We already have a toaster."

That little crack—one of Kit's favorite go-to zingers—elicited a chuckle from the intake specialist.

We wrapped up the Q&A and Kit was taken away for surgery prep. I was told to hang back in the waiting room until he got settled in. I agreed only after confirming that I would be able to see him—and his doctor—before he was whisked off to surgery. Kit handed me his iPad and walked off with the nurse.

In less than ten minutes, the nurse returned and escorted me to the presurgical wing, where Kit—adorably decked out in a johnny and hairnet—was sitting. My heart melted. As I leaned in to kiss him, his surgeon, Dr. Samuel Voight, appeared. This was suddenly all moving very quickly.

"The plan is to get in there and get a closer look, take a piece of it and send it off for testing," the doc explained, very matter-of-factly and businesslike. "Christopher, you are going to have some discomfort afterward."

My mind started racing. My takeaway: He was going in looking for cancer. Cancer, cancer, cancer, cancer.

"There's also a chance you'll go in there and realize it's nothing serious, right?" I worriedly interjected.

Before Voight could respond, Kit shut my line of questioning down.

"Relax, Michael," he said with a twinge of irritation.

The doctor, picking up on my anxiety, looked me in the eyes and said, "We won't know anything until we get in there. I will come out and talk to you right after I'm done. In about an hour."

I didn't like the sound of any of this. But I put on a brave face for Kit, bent down to kiss him goodbye—did I mention how adorable and vulnerable and innocent he looked in his gown?—and slinked off to the waiting room.

It was still early—around 7:15 a.m. now—so the place remained relatively empty. There was a middle-aged Latino couple sitting nearby, glued to the television, which was playing the local morning news. I pulled out my iPhone and checked my email. First my work account. Nothing new since I had last checked in bed at home. Then my personal account. Also nothing new. I refreshed my Twitter feed a few dozen times. I kept close watch on the door, waiting for any sign of Voight. I checked my watch every five minutes, only to be reminded that *this was the longest fucking hour of my life.* As the minutes passed, my anxiety increased. I played out every possible scenario in my head, from the best case—"It looks like it's just a polyp!"—to the worst case— "It looks like a tumor!" I prayed a little. I reminded myself that the panic I was feeling was normal, given what had happened to my mother. I paced around the waiting room. I checked my email again. Still nothing new. Rinse. Repeat.

My God, what the fuck is taking so goddamned long?!

At around the seventy-four-minute mark I decided enough was

enough. I approached the reception desk, and before I could get a word out of my mouth, Dr. Voight appeared in the doorway.

"Hi, Michael. Come on back. Let's have a talk," he said, in an indecipherable, even tone.

I followed him down a corridor, through a room, and back to the same presurgical area from earlier. There was an empty bed and a chair. I went to sit down, but quickly changed my mind and remained standing and at eye level with the doctor.

"You should sit," he urged me, his earlier expressionless face giving way to something far more grim.

I sat down. And I braced for impact.

"I'm concerned about Christopher," he said.

In all the scenarios I had played out in my head, none of them had featured those four words. My body suddenly felt weightless, numb; I became light-headed. Nauseous. Shocked. Scared. I wanted to go back in time thirty seconds. Before those words had left his mouth.

It was happening again.

"The growth was a lot bigger than I anticipated," he continued. "And it had a hard texture. We took several pieces of it, so we will find out what it is. And we will treat it."

Kit has anal cancer. That's the message I was receiving. But all the WebMDing I had been doing on the Internet suggested that anal cancer was among the most treatable forms of cancer, despite the relatively recent high-profile death of Farrah Fawcett.

"Does he have anal cancer?"

"It may be. We won't know until the results come back. It may be something we've never heard of. Whatever it is, we will treat it."

"Can I see him?"

"Not yet. He's just coming out of it, and I need to go up and talk to him alone first. And then we'll come get you. Don't panic. Let's see what this is and then let's move forward."

My mind immediately went from *Kit has anal cancer* to *Kit doesn't yet know he has anal cancer but is about to find out all alone in a hospital bed with no one by his side to hold his hand or hug him.*

I took a seat in the waiting room and then immediately stood back up and started pacing. I locked eyes with the Latino couple from earlier, subliminally pleading with them to help me find my way out of this nightmare. This had to be a bad dream. The words "I'm concerned about Christopher" ricocheted through my mind. I wondered if Dr. Voight had arrived at Kit's bedside yet to deliver the ominous news to him. I didn't understand why I couldn't be there. Another wave of nausea hit me.

And then, out of nowhere, I was jolted out of my spiral of terror by the happiest, most lively explosion of music. I instantly recognized the tune. It was Kit's iPad alarm. And it was going off—in the middle of the pin drop–quiet waiting room. I had forgotten that I was still babysitting his device. I quickly flipped open the iPad cover, pressed my index finger against the home button, and shut it the fuck off.

I noticed it was 9 a.m.—Kit's traditional wake-up time. He'd neglected to adjust the setting last night. What I wouldn't give to go back in time to a morning when that alarm had signaled the start of a normal workday.

With the alarm crisis now in my rearview mirror, my thoughts returned to "I'm concerned about Christopher." Maybe those words weren't as scary as I was making them out to be? Maybe I had misheard him? Maybe this would still turn out to be much ado about something completely benign? I was momentarily comforted by the string of maybes, but my brain quickly reverted back to apocalypse mode. *Kit is going to die. Also, WHY AM I NOT WITH HIM RIGHT NOW?* I felt my blood begin to boil when suddenly, out of nowhere, there was music. Loud, happy, aggressively enthusiastic music.

It was Kit's alarm. And it was going off. Again. *What the fuck is happening?*

I furiously opened the flap cover, pressed the home button, and silenced it once more. It then dawned on me that hitting the home button was merely putting a Band-Aid on the problem. I was essentially hitting snooze. This was going to persist every five minutes unless I figured a way to shut the whole fucking thing down. But I didn't know Kit's password. He was very protective of his devices. The insecure part of me worried what exactly it was he was hiding from me. An affair with Todd? Or *affairs*? Grindr X-pics? Grindr chats? All of my worst-case scenarios involved Kit having sexual interactions with people other than me. The threat of infidelity felt positively quaint compared to the crisis we were now facing. But first I had to deal with a more pressing emergency—figuring out how to make this recurring alarm go away.

I ran my fingers around every inch of the iPad and found what I assumed was the *permanent* off button and jammed my finger on it *hard*. I prayed that would do the trick.

It didn't.

This insane piece of absurdist theater continued to play out for the next twenty minutes, to the point where I eventually just gave in and declared defeat. I passed the time just counting down the minutes until the next melodic assault. No one else in the waiting room seemed particularly perturbed by the noise.

I eventually noticed the time—it was past 9:30 a.m. I darted over to the front desk and demanded to be taken to his bedside. The receptionist asked me to hold on for a sec while she checked on his status.

"I can take you to Christopher now," the receptionist announced.

She led me around to a different corridor and into the huge recovery room, where beds were lined up as far as the eye could see. My eyes darted from bed to bed in search of my Bodge. We were a mere ten paces into the room when I saw Kit in the distance. He looked even more cute and vulnerable and innocent and lovable than he had before surgery, a by-product of the anesthesia, no doubt. He didn't appear nearly as worried as I had expected him to. Had Voight given him a more sugarcoated report, perhaps? Or was Kit just too drugged out to process it? In any event, I approached his bedside, kissed him on the lips, and uttered six words I never thought would leave my lips.

"Let's go home and get high."

3.

"I'm concerned about Christopher."

Those four words ricocheted in my head as we cabbed it from the Upper East Side back home to the West Village.

As we made our way down the FDR Drive, I noticed the city looked different than it had just hours before. The sun was out, but it was as if I were looking at the skyline through a psychedelic filter, like a scene out of *Battlestar Galactica*'s hauntingly stylized spinoff, *Caprica*. Maybe this *was* all just a nightmare.

I glanced over at Kit. He had positioned himself onto his right side to take the pressure off his sore ass. He was playing Candy Crush on his iPad mini. I replayed in my head what Kit said Voight had told him during their private postoperative powwow. "He said it was bigger than he was expecting, but that he would test it and we'd go from there. I'm not going to worry about it until I have to. There's still a chance it's nothing."

I *so* wanted that to be the case. But Voight's dire warning to me left little doubt that it was *something*.

I emailed my No. 2 at *TVLine*, Matt Mitovich, to tell him Kit's procedure was running late (which was a lie) and I would be taking the entire day off (which was true). I couldn't even remember what was on my schedule. And, quite frankly, I didn't care. My focus needed to be on Kit and *trying desperately not to freak the fuck out.*

The next six days were torturous. My mind was on a constant loop of denial and hopelessness and anger and frustration and confusion and . . . how the fuck could I focus on anything other than this?! Someone seriously needed to write a guidebook called *How to Survive the Week Between Biopsy and Diagnosis.*

Kit spent much of the weekend in bed, enjoying the side effects of his Vicodin, while I ran errands and went to the gym and tended to some *TVLine* work. I also immersed myself in the cult of WebMD. But I could find nothing on the anal cancer pages that sounded as scary as those four words had coming out of Dr. Voight's mouth.

Monday arrived and I dreaded the idea of going back to work. I loved my job. But the thought of chasing scoops and interviewing actors and writing my signature "Ask Ausiello" column as Kit's fate hung in the balance made me ill. But what choice did I have? If Kit could somehow muster up the strength to go to work—he was, after all, the one who could be dying—then so could I.

As I made my walk from the Times Square subway station to the *TVLine* offices on 45th Street and Sixth Avenue, I searched Google maps for the nearest church. Much to my surprise, there was a house of worship—Saint Mary the Virgin—nearby on 46th Street. Most of my workday strolls were confined to the area of 45th Street just east of Sixth Avenue, home to my go-to lunchtime spot, Pret A Manger. I rarely, if ever, ventured over to 46th Street. And even if I had, I probably would not have paid much mind to Saint Mary's.

Sandwiched between a Comfort Inn and Rosie O'Grady Bar and Restaurant, the church just blended into the street. Of course, the only church in Manhattan I had ever stepped foot in was the sprawling, world-famous St. Patrick's Cathedral, so I suppose anything would have paled in comparison to that.

I walked in and that signature incense-y church aroma instantly filled my nasal passages. I knew it well. It was the smell of guilt. I could practically hear God saying, "Oh, sure—*now* you come to church." And

I deserved the side-eye. I was a lapsed Roman Catholic. The last time I had stepped foot in a church anywhere was in 1998 for my brother David's wedding to one of my childhood besties, Pam.

I took a seat in the last pew and soaked in the scene. It was 10 a.m. on a Monday, so the place was virtually empty. The movements of the few people who were there echoed throughout the chamber. The church was much larger than the exterior would have led you to believe. I leaned forward on the padded kneeler, performed the sign of the cross, and promptly started begging.

"God, please let Kit be OK," I whispered, as a torrent of tears streamed down my face. "I will do anything you want. I will come to church every day for the rest of my life. Please, please, please don't let him die."

I then appealed to my mom.

"Mom, please, if you are up there, help me. I can't lose Kit, too."

And then my dad.

"Dad, I know we didn't always see eye-to-eye, but if you have any pull up there, I could really use a miracle."

After exhausting my entire list of dead relatives, and with tears and snot forming a puddle beneath me, I leaned back in the pew, collected myself, then got up and walked to work.

I repeated this ritual every day that week. Except on Wednesday, when I had to be at the office at the crack of ass to do an in-person, on-camera interview with Kristen Bell, an assignment that, under normal circumstances, would have had me foaming at the mouth with excitement. If there existed a Michael Ausiello TV Actress Hall of Fame, Kristen would be a member of the inaugural class right alongside Connie Britton, Lauren Graham, and, of course, Keri Russell.

My relationship with Kristen, much like with Keri, began when I started simultaneously covering and obsessing over her breakout TV series, *Veronica Mars*, which found Bell playing a gloriously snarky, Nancy Drew–esque sleuth. I used my platform at *TV Guide* to champion the low-rated UPN/CW detective series, which put me on Bell's (and series creator Rob Thomas's) radar. And then I leveraged all of that stored-up goodwill into scoring a cameo on the show, playing the lone male at a bachelorette party who embarrassingly has his underwear stolen right out from under him during all the revelry. Unlike the unfortunate *Felicity* debacle, this time around my scene *wasn't* left on the cutting-room floor.

Anyway, Kristen and I hit it off during those early *Veronica Mars* years and have remained buddies ever since. And now she was visiting my tony new *TVLine* offices for the first time to promote, of all things, the fan-funded *Veronica Mars* movie. A week before, when I'd finalized the scheduling with her publicist, I was bouncing off the walls in anticipation of doing this interview. Now I was dreading it. This wasn't just an interview with one of my favorite people talking about one of my favorite TV shows. It was an *on camera* interview with one of my favorite people talking about one of my favorite TV shows. I couldn't just phone this in. I had to be excited and enthusiastic and reverential because it was Kristen fucking Bell—all things that, a week ago, would've required no effort at all. But my every thought right now was of Kit.

I considered canceling the whole thing, but what would my excuse be? "My partner Kit had a biopsy five days ago and it's *looking* like it's incredibly serious and potentially life-threatening but we won't know for another day or so, so let's just call the whole thing off, k?" Oh, and I couldn't actually *use* that excuse because no one even knew this was happening and we couldn't risk telling anyone and having it get back to his parents because *we* needed to be the ones to tell them ourselves but *only* when it was established that it was incredibly serious and life-threatening because why the fuck would we want to get them worried about the possibility of losing their only child if this was all much ado about nothing?

Ultimately, I decided to go through with the Kristen Bell interview.

I arrived to work that Wednesday camera-ready—I played it safe with a black Banana Republic blazer, white collared shirt, and blue jeans. My mind boomeranged from thoughts of Kit possibly dying of cancer and my world crashing down around me to worrying about Kristen getting into and out of the office safely and without incident. Her publicist had emailed me the night before to ask if there was a way for Kristen to gain entry to the building unnoticed, as she had been swarmed by fans and autograph seekers at every one of her NYC press stops. I arranged with security to have her SUV pull into the garage under our building versus dropping her off at the curb. And from there she could just take the elevator to our offices on the twenty-fourth floor. This was uncharted territory for me. We'd had lots of talent pass through our offices, but it had never necessitated this level of cloak-and-daggerage. My gut was telling me this was probably just a case of celebrity handler overreaction. I mean, *I* considered Kristen Bell to be on the same level as, you know, Oprah. But she wasn't Oprah. On the slightly bright side, all the hoop jumping kept my mind, well, not *off*, but slightly adjacent to the Kit crisis.

I opted to wait outside our office tower to ensure that Kristen's caravan entered the correct building. I noticed a suspicious cluster of crazy loitering near the revolving doors that led to our lobby. There were two young-ish girls and one towering middle-aged guy, and they were armed with binders and folders and backpacks. The two girls seemed innocent enough, but the guy was fidgety and his eyes were darting around—like a hustler about to do a drug deal. His drug of choice being celebrity autographs.

I avoided making eye contact with them, but I was sure they could tell I was out there waiting for Kristen. The fact that I spent the next fifteen minutes with my eyes vacillating between my iPhone and the oncoming traffic was all the proof they needed that they were indeed in the right place at the right time.

I received a text from Kristen's rep that they were sixty seconds away, so I glided over to the garage door. I spotted what I assumed was her huge black SUV slowly heading down the street, and I walked briskly to the curb. The back window came down, and Kristen's publicist popped her head out and apologized for their tardiness. Meanwhile, out of the corner of my eye, I could see the Crazy Cluster approaching. I pointed the driver to the parking garage entrance, and as the vehicle made its way in, the imposing autograph dude realized what was happening and was not pleased.

"Kristen, don't be like that," he barked as the car swooped past him and into the building. "Kristen, don't believe the hype. You're just a TV star. You can take three minutes for your fans. Get off your fucking high horse."

I couldn't believe what I was hearing. And seeing. As I listened to this asshole berate my beloved Kristen, I became enraged and embarrassed and regretted ever thinking that her publicist was overreacting.

Once the SUV made it safely into the loading dock, the security guard started lowering the garage door. It was then that jerk-face realized he would be going home with a bunch of autograph-less Kristen Bell merchandise, and he angrily, viciously, nastily shouted, "*Cunt!*"

Wow, way to poison a perfectly beautiful word. And snap me back to reality.

In the wrong hands, "cunt" can be disgustingly misogynistic and hateful. But in the right hands, it can be the cherry on top of a low-fat ice cream sundae. I loved the word "cunt." Kit loved the word "cunt." For almost twelve years, we had batted the word "cunt" back and forth to each other like a light, shiny cat toy. We called each other cunts. We called Mister Scooch a cunt. We called *Downton Abbey*'s Dowager Countess a cunt. One year for Christmas I got Kit a *Cunt Coloring Book.* The word brought us immense joy. So to hear it used in such an ugly, violent, despicable manner—and toward someone I idolized, no less— was quite upsetting.

The SUV came to a complete stop inside the garage, and as Kristen made her way out of the car and toward me, I just shook my head in shame.

"Kristen, I'm so sorry."

"Please, I've heard worse," she said and shrugged, wholly unfazed. We embraced, exchanged some pleasantries, and I then led her and her army of publicists and groomers to the lobby elevators and up to *TVLine*'s offices on the twenty-fourth floor.

Our parent company, Penske Media Company (or PMC), had moved into Tower 45 (named after the street it was located on) about a year prior. It was a massive upgrade from our previous office setup, which was basically just one big room overrun by cubicles and shared desks and *way* too many people for such a small space. My boss Jay Penske's acquisition of the venerable showbiz trade *Variety*, coupled with the growth of current brands like *Deadline*, *Hollywood Life*, and, of course, *TVLine*, had necessitated a move to a larger space. PMC occupied the entire twenty-fourth floor, with *TVLine* and its four New

York–based employees situated near the center of the floor, by the main reception area.

One of the reasons I'd been excited to host Kristen was because I was super-proud of our new-ish digs. Since *TVLine* was a relatively recent arrival on the scene and essentially a start-up (even though it was backed by Penske), there was a perception in some circles that I worked out of my garage (that is, I would have if I'd lived in suburban New Jersey and owned a garage). Any opportunity to dispel that myth was a golden one.

Oh, and did I mention that my personal office was one of the biggest on the floor, second only to Jay's corner suite? I'd had offices at my previous jobs, but I'd never had an office quite like this one. Clocking in at a huge-by-Manhattan-standards three hundred square feet, my home-away-from-home boasted a huge wall of windows overlooking midtown Manhattan.

"My entire career was leading to this moment," I remembered deadpanning to Kit as we stood in the middle of the empty office looking out at the city, shortly before move-in day a year ago. And as excited as I'd been about my good fortune, Kit was even *more* excited. A large part of it was the happiness and pride he felt for me. But the other piece of it had to do with the fact that he had a fun new project to focus on. He brought his measuring tape and his point-and-shoot and documented every square inch of the place. He then retreated to his workspace at home and emerged hours later with a comprehensive layout and design scheme, complete with Internet screen grabs of furniture from CB2, as well as furniture he knew he could get on loan from his place of employ, Wyeth. Over the next six weeks, he was the CEO of Mike's New Office, ordering the furniture, lighting fixtures, carpeting. He presented John Birch, his boss at Wyeth, with a wish list of the specific midcentury pieces he wanted—including two Mario Bellini red couches and an Edward Wormley mahogany double-pedestal desk— all of which John approved. He then spent an entire weekend helping me curate, frame, and hang highlights from my fifteen-year career on the four walls. And in a retro-cool nod to the newsrooms of yesteryear, he affixed three large round clocks to the far wall and applied stenciling under each one that said, "New York," "Los Angeles," and, in a cheeky wink to *Buffy the Vampire Slayer*, "Sunnydale." When all was said and done, the office looked stunning. I was the envy of the entire company.

And now Kristen Bell was going to see it.

Of course, as with everything that week, the office now filled me with a sense of dread. The person whose blood, sweat, tears, and love had gone into building this beautiful nest might soon be ripped away from me.

Still, it was nice to hear the "Wow" leave Kristen's lips when she entered the office. She proceeded to poke around to check out all the little Easter eggs of my career. A personal thank-you note from J.J. Abrams for all my support of *Felicity*? Check. The T.R. Knight and Katherine Heigl covers of *Entertainment Weekly* for articles I wrote? Check. Photos of me and my favorite TV celebs, including a shot of Kristen and me from the 2013 Golden Globes after she tapped me on the shoulder in the back of the ballroom as she was sneaking out the back door to head home? Check.

Just as I was about to supply her with an answer to the complex question "What's with all the Smurfs?" (yes, Kit had given me "permission" to punctuate my office with a few tasteful pieces from my collection) my longtime producer/editor/cameraman jack-of-all-video-trades, Jason Averett, invited us to take our seats on the opposing red couches. Eddie the sound guy fastened Kristen and me with lavalier mics, a quick camera test confirmed that we both looked stunning, and . . . *action.*

I took a deep breath, in an effort to release some of the Kit-fueled nerves occupying every fiber of my being, mentally reviewed my questions, then launched into my introduction.

"I'm here with *Veronica Mars* herself, Kristen Bell. Kristen, welcome. So nice to have you here," I said with muted enthusiasm, which, lucky for me given my current mood, was sort of my signature shtick. It would've been extremely out of character had I hopped up on the red couch all Tom Cruise–like and started jumping up and down screaming, "OMG, Kristen Bell is *here*!!!!" I always approach my most beloved interview subjects with a sort of detached bemusement, primarily because, well, that's pretty much how I approach everyone I'm close to in my life. It's as if I'm saying, *I love you, but I'm kinda over you.* It's part built-in defense mechanism and part just my general personality. It has served me well. Plus, the talent seems to get a kick out of it. Denis Leary described it like this during a 2015 Comic-Con interview: "I just met you, but I already feel *so* sad that I disappointed you so much. Your judgmental vibes are hilarious."

I managed to get through the eight-minute Kristen interview without incident, despite only half-listening to her answers and suffering an extreme case of trauma-related dry mouth—the latter of which I only became aware of upon viewing the finished product. Every syllable that left my mouth sounded like it was coated in a layer of peanut butter and oil slick.

I escorted Kristen and her entourage down to the parking garage, gave her a big goodbye hug, and off she went.

Now back to my regularly scheduled nightmare.

Dr. Voight had told us to expect the biopsy results back as early as Thursday and as late as Friday, so I awoke Thursday morning feeling a mix of extreme dread and mild relief. The former because my worst nightmare might about to be confirmed. And the latter because there still existed a chance this could all be nothing.

It was beyond unsettling not knowing exactly how and when this potential bomb would be dropped. The likely scenario had Voight calling Kit at work at some point this afternoon, which seemed *way* too casual and informal a concept for what could end up being the most important phone call of his life. I considered just packing up my laptop and working from Wyeth all day, so I could be by his side when the call came through. I ultimately decided that having me and my cancer baggage swirling around him all day was probably not the best idea.

"Bodge, I will call you the second I hear anything," Kit assured me.

I reminded him for the twelfth time that I had terrible cell reception at my office, so it was best to ring me on my landline.

I spent much of the day staring at my phone. Every time it rang, a bolt of terror raced through my body. I tried to prepare myself for every possible worst-case scenario, thinking that if I imagined a specific outcome—for example, a hysterical and inconsolable Kit called to tell me he had Stage 4 cancer and was going to die—it would somehow make said outcome less likely to happen. Like, what were the odds that

I would envision a hysterical and inconsolable Kit on the phone tell-ing me he had Stage 4 cancer prior to him *actually* doing just that? I would need a crystal ball to predict such things. It was nutty logic, but it helped me pass the time.

As 3 p.m. approached, I was on the verge of a nervous breakdown. I couldn't focus on anything. So I called Kit.

"Anything?"

"Nope," he responded, not an ounce of worry in his voice. "We may not hear until tomorrow."

"I'm not leaving my desk," I assured him. "Call me the second you hear. I love you."

Less than an hour later, my phone lit up and I recognized Wyeth's phone number on the Caller ID. A jolt of fear shot through my body, I took a deep breath and picked up the receiver.

It was Kit.

"Voight just called," he said, his voice totally chill and carefree. I immediately felt a wave of relief come over me. Of all the scenarios I had played out in my head, a chillaxed-sounding Kit had not been one of them.

"I have a neuroendocrine tumor," he explained. "He said there's a 70 percent remission rate. He gave me the name of an oncologist."

My first thought: There was no mention of the C-word. My second thought, meanwhile, was . . .

"A neuro-what?" I asked.

"It's spelled N-E-U-R-O-E-N-D-O-C-R-I-N-E."

I grabbed a pen and paper and wrote it down. And then I put my machine gun of questions on full blast.

"Is it cancer? Did he say anything else? Did he sound worried?"

And Kit quickly waved his white flag.

"I told you everything I know," he insisted. "I have to run to that work event, so we'll discuss it when I get home. I love you."

"I love you, too," I replied. "Bodge, this doesn't sound so bad."

"I know," he said.

We hung up and I started typing N-E-U-R-O-E-N-D-O-C-R-I-N-E into Google.

"Neuroendocrine tumors are neoplasms that arise from cells of the endocrine and nervous systems . . . Many are benign, while some are malignant."

Many are benign. I liked the sound of that.

Embedded in the first batch of search results was an article about Steve Jobs, whose death from pancreatic cancer two years prior had shaken Kit to the core. He idolized the man. Unbeknownst to me until just this second, Steve's tumor was also of the neuroendocrine variety. Seeing that article pop up—and seeing the words "neuroendocrine" and "cancer" linked—was my first confirmation that Kit did, in fact, have a form of the C-word. But Steve's was in the pancreas, and that was always a terrible spot to get cancer. Kit's was in his ass. Could be an apples-and-oranges-type thing from a prognosis standpoint.

I dug deeper.

Medical terms I had never heard of, like "poorly differentiated," were coming at me left and right. I stumbled on a website for neuroendocrine tumor survivors with photos of happy middle-aged men and women who, with the help of modern advancements, had triumphed over the disease and were living relatively normal and happy lives. There was quite a bit of information on neuroendocrine tumors of the pancreas, liver, and colon, but very little on what happened when the disease was discovered in the anus or rectum.

I tacked the words "anus" and "rectum" onto my "neuroendocrine" search and Google called up a medical study.

"We report a rare case of neuroendocrine tumor of the anal canal and its poor prognosis," it read.

The words "poor prognosis" struck terror in my heart. I dug deeper, looking for a study that yielded a more positive outcome. That offered us some hope. But Google wasn't giving me any. Google was usually my friend. Not today. Everything I was reading contained a consistent message: Neuroendocrine cancer of the anus and rectum was almost always fatal, with a life expectancy hovering around one year. My face started to burn up. I felt dizzy. Nauseous.

"The best thing to say about this type of cancer is it's extremely rare," concluded one study.

Another study said neuroendocrine tumors were very responsive to some forms of chemo, citing an initial "70 percent regression rate," but then noting that the tumors—aggressive as they were—almost always grew back.

And then it hit me: Regression. Remission. Fuck.

That was likely the statistic Voight had quoted to Kit, and Kit had likely mistaken "regression" for "remission."

For the first time, the "I'm concerned about Christopher" was starting to make sense.

I noticed the clock—7 p.m. Nearly ninety minutes had passed from the time I hung up with Kit and launched my Google assault. I decided to climb out of the Internet rabbit hole I had dug myself into and go home. Kit was going to be at that work event for another hour or so, giving me time to figure out how much of my dire findings I should share with him.

And to pick up some wine. Google had failed me, but my other friend pinot grigio would not.

I tried to imagine what it was going to be like when I saw Kit for the first time since his diagnosis had been confirmed. Would I see him differently now? The hour I spent waiting for him at home felt like an eternity. I wondered whether he had done any of his own research.

I was sitting on the couch nursing my first glass of wine when he walked through the door. I felt like I was seeing a ghost. A dead man walking. Only he looked perfectly healthy, if a little tired.

"Sorry I'm late," he said, as he took off his jacket and emptied his pockets of his wallet and about six business cards of varying colors.

"What are those?" I asked.

"The event was a professional mixer for RIT students and alumni," he explained, referring to his alma mater, Rochester Institute of Technology. "I met some potential Wyeth interns."

He was out recruiting. He was planning for the future. It all felt so normal. It told me that he had *not* investigated his cancer diagnosis online. He was blissfully (or willfully?) unaware of how bad it was. He sat down next to me on the couch with the dinner he had picked up.

"I did some research," I alerted him.

"I assumed as much," he quickly responded. "Hit me."

"It's a form of cancer . . . It's the same kind of tumor Steve Jobs had."

"Seriously?" he replied. I could see the weight of it hitting him. "That can't be good."

"Voight told you there's a 70 percent remission rate?"

"Yes," he responded, confidently. "I even wrote it down."

He pulled out a piece of paper and started reading his scribble. I could see the words "70 percent remission" on there. Maybe Voight really had used the word "remission" instead of "regression." Maybe all the scary shit I'd been reading on the Internet was outdated. Maybe my cancer baggage was coloring how I was experiencing all of this. Maybe, maybe, maybe, maybe.

"What else did he say?" I asked. "Anything about the prognosis?"

"No. The only other thing he said was that he's going to put us in touch with an oncologist he works with. I think he said he's on the Upper West Side . . . What did the Internet say about the prognosis?"

"Not much," I quickly replied, laying the groundwork for my lie of omission. The alternative was my telling him that everything I had read online suggested he'd be dead in a year. And I couldn't do it. Partly because we still didn't have all the facts. But mostly because I just *couldn't do it.*

"It appears that this type of cancer is pretty rare," I told him. "So there wasn't a ton of information about it."

I sat back in the sofa, took another sip of my wine, and just focused on the maybes of it all. Then I cued up the previous Sunday's *Walking Dead*—one of our shared TV obsessions—on the DVR. I grabbed hold of his hand, squeezed it tight, and pushed play.

The next morning I promptly enrolled myself in Neuroendocrine Cancer 101. Dr. Dominic Abbott, the oncologist Voight referred us to, had decent reviews online, but there was no mention of his experience treating neuroendocrine cancer. My digital excavation turned up two key figures in the field of neuroendocrine cancer—Dr. Simon Barnes and Dr. Jeremy Cullen. I made appointments with them both. I also reached out to the granddaddy of all cancer centers—Sloan Kettering—and set up a consult there, too. I then coordinated with Voight's office to have Kit's biopsy results—and in the case of Sloan Kettering, the actual pathology slides—delivered to the respective oncologists. I started mapping out a detailed schedule for the following week, with two appointments set for Wednesday, another set for Thursday and the fourth and final one set for Friday. I ran the plan by Kit and without hesitation he signed off on it.

Also on Friday I sent a Facebook message to a former colleague of mine at *Entertainment Weekly*, Jeff Jensen, whose wife, Amy, was battling brain cancer. Jeff had eloquently, movingly, candidly chronicled their roller-coaster experience on Facebook over the past year. Kit and I had agreed to keep all of this on the extreme DL until we knew exactly what we were dealing with, but I desperately needed to talk to someone.

Within an hour of my messaging Jeff, he responded with his cell phone number. I closed my office door and immediately called him. I started the conversation by asking for an update on Amy's condition— Jeff's most recent post had shared some positive news that Amy's tumor was responding to a relatively new cancer drug called Avastin. Jeff explained to me that they remained hopeful that Avastin could become something of a long-term solution.

I then filled him in on what was happening with Kit. I immediately started to cry.

"I'm terrified," I confessed, letting my guard down for the first time since this ordeal started.

Jeff didn't offer me false hope or drop any cornball meditations like "Everything happens for a reason." He just listened as I unloaded two weeks' worth of fear and anxiety and helplessness and anger on him. He then urged me to call him anytime I needed to vent. It was just what I needed. I felt slightly less alone in this.

Over the weekend I lifted our agreed-upon cancer gag order again and called my younger brother, David, to fill him in on what was happening. Next to Kit, he was the family member to whom I was closest. He could be infuriatingly stubborn at times. And his frugality had been the source of much tension over the years. That said, David would do anything for me. And vice versa.

It was also over the weekend that I started thinking about tacking an additional appointment on to our packed oncology schedule next week. Only this one would involve a trip to city hall.

4.

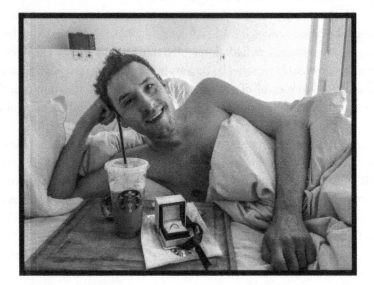

Kit and I had no interest in marriage. Even when gay unions had recently become the law of the land in New York, our position remained unchanged. Kit already, you know, had a toaster. And I didn't want to rock a boat that already had taken on a fair amount of water from bouts of infidelity and codependency and sexual dysfunction and pot use and just general malaise of being together for more than a decade.

Also, I had a profound fear of failure. Most of the major life decisions I had made carried with them a high probability of success. I didn't want a divorce to stain my "perfect" record.

But if the events of the past two weeks had crystalized anything for me, save for the fact that the Universe was totes evil and praying was a complete waste of fucking time, it was that Kit was *it* for me. He was my family. My best friend. My soul mate. My comedic partner. My travel companion. My cuddle buddy. My everything. I wanted—no, I *needed*—to enter into this scary, uncertain chapter not as his boyfriend or partner or longtime companion but as his *husband*.

And dammit, I was going to find a silver lining in this awful mess.

So I went online and filled out the marriage license application, and then optimistically updated the oncology schedule to include a wedding at city hall on Friday afternoon, immediately following our fourth and final appointment of the week, at Sloan Kettering. And then after work on Monday, I stopped by the jewelry store near our apartment to pick out the rings.

I knew exactly how I was going to pop the question—during our regular morning breakfast ritual, which basically involved me walking to Starbucks to pick up a Trenta-sized iced passion tea unsweetened with six Splendas for me, and a Tall iced chai skim latte with either a cup of classic whole grain oatmeal or some kind of Danish for Kit. (My main course—a dark-chocolate-and-sea-salt Kind bar—would be waiting back in the fridge at home.)

On this fateful Tuesday morning, I snuck off to Starbucks around 8 a.m.—a little earlier than normal since we had to be in Union Square by 10 a.m. for a CAT scan—and returned home to quietly assemble the pieces of my bait-and-switch wedding proposal plan on the kitchen counter. I was keeping one eye on the bedroom to make sure the recipient remained blissfully unaware of what was occurring just twenty feet from him. (He was, indeed, still fast asleep.)

I removed the Danish from the pink paper sleeve, replaced it with the ring box, and then positioned it in the corner of the large wooden cutting board that often doubled as a breakfast/dinner tray. (Welcome to New York City, where every household item serves a dual purpose.) I then added our beverages and my Kind bar to the surprise smorgasbord, made my way into the bedroom and parked it next to him on the bed. He was still fast asleep.

"Good morning, my love," I whispered as I planted a gentle kiss on his forehead. His eyelids slowly peeled back, he acknowledged my presence, and . . . then his eyelids promptly closed.

"Bodge, I have breakfast" was typically a card I'd play after numerous forehead kisses failed to yield my desired outcome, but, on this morning—with an MRI and CAT scan on the books and an engagement bombshell in the offing—there was no time for foreplay. And sure enough, the lure of a tasty treat and his favorite morning beverage was enough to get him to open his eyes, sit up, and take stock of the feast before him. I wondered if he would notice the unusually shaped Danish in the pastry wrapper, but he didn't. He was too busy sucking down a first sip of his beloved iced chai tea. A few seconds later, his eyes veered toward the wrapper and I could see a hint of curiosity register on his face. He poked at the bag—gingerly, as if worried something might jump out—and his suspicions were confirmed: something other than a Danish was inside.

"What is this?" he said, with a mix of fear and curiosity, before pulling out the ring box and opening it. He glanced up at me with a look of "Is this what I think it is?"

I took possession of the ring, grabbed his right hand, and . . . "Shit," I sighed. "Which one is the ring finger?"

"Oh, just give it to me," he demanded with mock irritation, before snatching the ring and slipping it on his finger. Much to my surprise, it was a pretty decent fit.

"Will you marry me?" I asked him.

He simultaneously chuckled and sighed. Meanwhile, as I nervously awaited his response, it dawned on me for the first time that he could say (*gulp*) no.

He looked up and deadpanned, "Oh, geez. You're marrying me because I have cancer."

It was funny because, well, it was true.

"It's more than that," I insisted, fighting back tears. "If anything good has come from this fucked-up situation it's that it allowed me to look past all of our problems—the pot, the lack of sex, my job—and realize that none of it matters. All that matters is that we're together. I want to be your husband. I want the doctors and nurses to know that the person by your side is your husband. And he would do anything for you."

I took a deep breath, looked into his eyes, and repeated the question at hand: "Will you fucking marry me or not?"

He cracked the sweetest smile and said, "Yes, Bodge, I will marry you."

I smiled, leaned in for a kiss, and then immediately filled him in on my plan to go to city hall Friday and get hitched immediately following our appointment at Sloan Kettering.

"I took care of everything," I assured him. "I went online, pre-registered, I know exactly where we need to go. Later today we'll go by the ring shop and get them sized, and hopefully get them back by Friday."

I then popped the *second* most important question of the morning.

"Speaking of the ring . . . do you like it?" I asked, hesitantly, before proudly declaring, "They're simple. And classic!"

"I don't have any problem with this ring," he declared. "You did good."

Mission. Fucking. Accomplished.

And then like a thunder bolt, it hit me: *I'm engaged. I'm going to be someone's husband.* Fat Mike from Roselle Park, New Jersey—or "Fudgepacker Mike," as John Valentine called to taunt me every day at the start of Mr. Bangs's Chemistry class, just loud enough so everyone could hear—was getting married to the man of his dreams.

And I couldn't tell anyone. Not yet, anyway. We had agreed to remain in radio-silence mode until we had concrete answers about the cancer. Answers we were mere hours away from getting.

I woke up the next morning with a strange feeling. Something called . . . optimism. It was just a twinge, but at this point I'd take a twinge. Maybe all the crap I had read on the Internet pertained to a worst-case version of this cancer, I thought. Maybe Dr. Barnes, the first of two neuroendocrine specialists we were seeing today, would reveal that Kit had a more treatable form of the disease. Maybe Kit and I would be able to grow old together as husband and husband. Maybe, maybe, maybe, maybe.

I ultimately had little control over how the day would turn out, so I exercised control where I could, beginning with the transportation. I arranged to have a car service pick us up versus waiting fifteen minutes in the freezing cold for a cab to turn down sleepy Jane Street. My go-to car service was Carmel, mostly because in those pre-Uber days they were one of the few non-taxi alternatives in NYC. What their drivers lacked in friendliness they made up for in promptness. The black sedan pulled up a few minutes before the scheduled pickup time of 9:30 a.m., and we hopped in and made our way to Barnes's East Side office.

I held Kit's hand in the backseat the whole way up. And then

I watched the pedestrians heading to work as if it were just any old Wednesday morning. They were probably thinking about what meetings and deadlines they had to knock out that day. Their most pressing concern at the moment likely involved whether they could make it all the way to the office without having to stop or even slow down, something that would involve a combination of jaywalking, good streetlight karma, and secret shortcuts. Perhaps they were also looking ahead to the weekend and what fun activities they had planned with their spouses.

I was jealous of them all.

Meanwhile, that strange optimism I had felt early this morning was slowly giving way to a more familiar feeling: utter and complete dread. It was hard not to feel like we were cattle being led to the slaughter.

We arrived at Dr. Barnes's office a few minutes before our scheduled 10 a.m. appointment time. The office occupied a retail space on the ground level of a six-story apartment building, with the entrance right off the street. It was rather modest and nondescript from the outside— not unlike a dentist's or dermatologist's office. I rang the buzzer and . . . crickets. I rang the buzzer again. Still more crickets.

"Maybe they're running late," I mumbled to Kit as I double-checked my watch. It was 10 a.m. on the nose.

"Let's record all of these appointments," Kit said to me, out of the blue. "That way we can review all of them at the end of the week and then decide who we want to go with."

"I don't have my device with me," I said, referring to the microcassette recorder I used at work to tape my talent interviews.

"Let me see your iPhone," Kit said, as he grabbed it out of my hand and began to fiddle with it. Sixty seconds later he showed me what he had just done. "You now have a voice memo app. Just click on it and hit record."

"Wow, I had no idea there was an app for that," I said, authentically amazed, as I often was, at Kit's technological adroitness.

Without missing a beat, he replied, "Yeah, well, you're very handsome."

We had stood there in the cold for a few minutes when a young woman approached holding a key in her hand.

"Good morning," she said, slightly exasperated. "Sorry to keep you waiting."

She unlocked the door and led us into the office, and . . . *Holy hole in the wall.* This place was tiny. And in a state of decay, like it hadn't been renovated since the turn of the twentieth century. My heart sank as I took in the scene, which instilled no amount of confidence.

I hovered by the disorganized reception desk, armed with my appointment sheet, while the office lady took off her jacket, checked the overnight voicemails, and just generally got settled in.

"Name?" she finally asked.

"Christopher Cowan," I replied on Kit's behalf.

"The doctor's not in yet," the receptionist said, barely making eye contact with either of us. She handed me a clipboard loaded with forms. "Please fill out this paperwork and hand it back to me with your insurance card."

The waiting room consisted of six mismatched chairs and a coffee table that looked like it had been purchased from the sales rack at Goodwill. The six dated, ripped, and soiled *People* magazines spread out on one of the end tables perfectly completed this depressing scene.

I took a seat, but Kit opted to stand next to me rather than endure the discomfort of sitting. As I filled out the paperwork, a few patients trickled in—all of them clearly over the age of sixty. And thin. And sickly-looking. The juxtaposition of these frail elderly individuals alongside my young, strapping fiancé was glaring. And maddening. Kit didn't seem to notice, his face glued to his iPad and his Candy Crush.

So. Much. Paperwork. But I was happy to unburden Kit of the tediousness of it. It also made me feel slightly less helpless. I only had to interrupt Kit's Candy Crush game twice—for his Social Security number and the name of his primary care physician. I knew the answers to the rest. I returned the forms to the receptionist.

"Has Dr. Barnes arrived?" I asked.

"Yes. He just got here. It should just be a few more minutes."

Eight minutes had passed when she summoned us into Barnes's office, a decent-sized yet ramshackle space that consisted of a huge old-person oak desk, two old-people chairs, and an old person's file cabinet. Old-people art dotted the walls.

Barnes was on the phone when we entered, and he motioned for us to take a seat. As he eased into the chair, I watched Kit's face to see if there was any wincing from pain. There wasn't.

I was trying to play it cool, but my anxiety was now at near-peak level. This unassuming man sitting before us had in his possession information that could destroy my life and end Kit's. I took some comfort in the casualness of Barnes's demeanor. The mere fact that he was tending to other business while we sat there signaled to the optimist in me that this wasn't as dire as I feared. It felt more like we were meeting with our accountant to go over our tax return.

Kit nodded in the direction of my iPhone, reminding me to cue up the app. I hit record and then stealthily placed it on Barnes's desk. I wasn't sure if I needed to ask him for permission to record the session. I erred on the side of "don't rock the boat."

He finished up his call and started rifling through papers on his desk. Kit and I waited patiently.

"I'm just getting settled," Barnes said to us. "I was at a conference this morning. You'll have to excuse me."

"Hopefully it was a conference on *neuroendocrine* cancer," Kit said, chuckling.

"Well, I'm part of the neuroendocrine tumor team at Cedars-Sinai . . ." He started to confirm what Kit had said. "So you're in the right place."

"Excellent," Kit said, with a mix of relief and hope.

"Are you two married or just partners or what?" he asked, continuing to flip through papers in a folder that I presumed pertained to Kit's case.

"Just partners," Kit responded.

"*Longtime* partners," I clarified.

"So, you found my name online?" he asked, shifting his attention back to us.

"Yes," I responded. "I searched for the best neuroendocrine specialists in New York. And your name came up."

"Take me through the timeline here . . . I'm not following," he said, clearly confused while looking over a piece of paper pulled from the file. "How did this start?"

"I've had IBS for many years . . . at least six years, if not more," Kit explained. "I had a bunch of tests, including a scope down my throat, a scope up the other end, no one found anything. That was maybe three years ago. And then about a month ago I presented with . . . blood in my semen . . . And then I went back to my primary care physician," he continued, "and he assured me that these were probably two separate things—the IBS and this blood in the semen. I also felt like I had a golf ball in my rectum. So he sent me to see Dr . . . um . . ."

"*Voight*," I interjected, reminding everyone but mostly myself that *I knew my shit.*

"Voight, yes . . ." Kit agreed. "And Voight did a DRE and confirmed that there was something in there. And then he ordered the biopsy. That was two or so weeks ago. And then we got the biopsy back and he said it was a neuroendocrine cancer. And then he sent us for the scans . . ."

"CAT scans," I interjected for clarity.

" . . . on . . . Tuesday?" Kit continued.

"Yep, yesterday," I confirmed.

"And, here we are," Kit concluded.

"Here we are," I confirmed, for no other reason than because I was nervous and scared and sometimes things came out of my mouth for no reason.

"So . . . which scans did you have?" Barnes asked.

Which scans did we have?! You're looking at the fucking folder, Grandpa was what I *wanted* to say. Instead, Kit and I just looked at each other, perplexed.

"It was in Union Square," Kit offered. "I'm not exactly sure what specific scans they were."

Kit added, "I believe Voight said they were just going to scan from the pelvis up. Since this is typically in a location above where I have it."

"The date on the scan is Tuesday, March 11," a perplexed Barnes said, reading from Kit's file. I wondered why he was so confused because we had just told him that the scan had been done on Tuesday. At this point it became clear that this was the first time Barnes had laid eyes on Kit's file. A long pause followed.

"So when did this Dr. Gingold come into the equation?" Barnes asked. "Was he the surgeon?"

"No," I snapped, barely able to contain my frustration. "Dr. *Voight* is the surgeon."

Kit chimed in, "I don't know who Dr. Gingold is. Unless that's someone Voight reached out to."

Another long pause followed as Barnes continued rifling through Kit's file searching for who-knew-what. I looked at my watch and ten minutes had now passed and I was still no closer to finding out if Kit was going to live or die. For the *next* ten minutes Barnes continued to ask us questions that a simple review of Kit's medical file prior to the meeting would've answered. I wasn't sure whether to be worried or relieved that this case seemed so unimportant to him.

Barnes proceeded to clarify Kit's cancer timeline. *Again.* He then reviewed Kit's pre-cancer surgical history, which included knee surgery and three procedures to correct a ptosis in his right eye. And I reminded Kit about the appendectomy he had undergone thirteen years ago—just two months after we had first met.

"Good memory," he said, cracking a smile, which confirmed to me that he was not nearly as wound up by Barnes's seemingly befuddled indifference as I was. I decided to take my cues from him and bring my annoyance level down a few notches.

"Do you have any flushing or diarrhea?" Barnes asked.

"Currently? No . . . it just feels difficult to make a bowel movement. What is flushing?"

"It's when your face becomes red . . . Any night sweats?"

"No."

"Any family history I should be aware of? Your mom and dad OK?"

"Yeah, Mom and Dad are fine. They're alive. They're hitting seventy. Gram's ninety."

"Are you having any pain now?"

"I have discomfort sitting for long periods."

"Where? In the rectum?" Barnes inexplicably asked.

No, in his head. *He has pain when he's sitting on his head* was what I *wanted* to say, my anger now building back up despite my earlier cooldown. Kit had already been diagnosed with a neuroendocrine tumor in his *rectum*. He had just complained of having pain *sitting down*. Do the math.

"Yes, in my rectum," Kit politely responded.

"Now, when you have a loose stool, what does it look like? Is it watery? Does it float? What color is it?"

"I would say my stools do *not* float," Kit replied, adopting a mock-professional tone that stood in stark contrast to the embarrassingly literally shitty subject at hand. "They are a normal color. They are sometimes . . . um . . . um . . . I don't want to say covered in *mucus*. But sometimes it just looks like there's some spit, or a saliva coating, for lack of a better term."

"OK," Barnes declared, sounding as if we were transitioning into the part of the meeting that actually fucking mattered. "I would like to examine you. Michael can, of course, be present."

"Um . . ." Kit interjected, worried that another painful DRE was in his near future.

Barnes picked up on this. "Would you like me to spare you a rectal exam?"

"Yes," Kit responded, instantly. "I would like to be spared that."

And then, out of nowhere, Barnes, with his eyes fixed on a page in Kit's medical file, said nonchalantly, "There's a description in the CAT scan report that you have some noduality in the lungs . . . Are you experiencing any shortness of breath?"

I wasn't sure what "noduality" was, but in spite of Barnes's carefree tone, it didn't sound good. When I had imagined all the ways we would get the news that Kit's cancer had metastasized to another part of the body, it was never dropped casually and abruptly fifteen minutes in. The room took on a sudden weightiness.

"No, there's been no shortness of breath."

I hesitated before asking the next, logical question, fearing the answer would involve the words "cancer" and "spread."

"What did the CAT scan show, exactly?"

"Oh!" Barnes exclaimed, as if suddenly realizing the point of this entire fucking meeting. "Let me grab my glasses."

Oh, this was exciting. Dr. Leo Spaceman's father was going to deliver the results to us in *real* time. It was like we were at the Emmys, only instead of finding out who was winning Best Drama Series we were going to learn if a man would survive.

"I'm working very slow this morning," Barnes stated, the first sensible, clear-minded thing he had said so far.

He started reading from the report. I braced myself in my seat, as if preparing for a crash landing.

I took a deep breath.

"There are multiple nodules adjacent to the inferior rectum, which are, presumably, related to the neuroendocrine tumor that was biopsied. As far as the chest is concerned, there are *multiple*—one to three millimeters each—pulmonary nodule densities. Given the multiplicity these are *worrisome* for metastatic lesions. There is a 2.7mm hypervascular nodule in the liver. This is also nonspecific. Both of those things are nonspecific. They would have to be looked at with the second scan. But the worrisome nature of this is that if you *do* have a primary tumor in the rectum, *could* it have spread to one area of the liver or the lung?

"The *good* news aspect of this," he continued, "is that with a neuroendocrine tumor, particularly what I see in the pathology report, it's very amenable to therapy. And rectal tumors that are neuroendocrine are much more amenable to therapy than are *agno*-carcinomas, which is the more aggressive type of tumor."

"So this *isn't* one of the more aggressive ones?" I asked.

"Neuroendocrine tumors are not aggressive," he said.

"So, if I'm understanding this correctly . . ."

"We have to decide where the tumor is coming from," Barnes declared. "That influences therapy. There happens to be good news here, even though this is a heavy thing to lay on you. It's a very *hopeful* situation, because there happen to be a number of different therapies that are coming to the forefront and are already here. So I just want you to take a deep breath. I know I told you that you have nodules in the lung that have to be explained. And I told you about the nodules surrounding the *rectum*. But there's treatment."

The frequency with which Barnes was referring to all the "good news" came as a huge relief, even though, logically, it stood counter to the *actual* information he was giving us, particularly with regard to the nodules in the lung and the liver. Also, Barnes's overall puzzlement should have signaled to me to take what he said with a grain of salt. But my mind was choosing to focus on the positive words and not the messenger. I also reminded myself that this was one of the foremost authorities in neuroendocrine tumor–age. If he said there was good news to be found here, why should I doubt him?

"Is surgery an option?" I asked.

"Surgery is an option once we identify the primary tumor," he said.

"And as far as the discomfort he is feeling when he sits down, what are the options in terms of alleviating that as we move forward so that he's not suffering?" I asked.

"Well, we have to treat that area," said Barnes. "That's why a rectal surgeon has to be involved."

"OK," Kit said, his voice completely light and carefree. "Sounds great."

As Barnes began to stand up, I sought out confirmation that this was not as grave a situation as the Internet had led me to believe.

"This sounds hopeful."

"*Oh, definitely,*" he said without an ounce of uncertainty.

"Oh, good," I said, completely and utterly relieved. "Because we came in here fearing the worst."

"Well, it's not exactly *good* news, but I'm telling you from my cat-bird seat, as a specialist in this particular area of oncology, it's one of the more treatable and even, potentially, curable conditions."

Kit and I looked at each other and smiled. I grabbed his hand and held it tight.

"Fantastic," Kit said.

Barnes showed us to an exam room where a pleasant nurse checked Kit's vitals and obtained some blood. I used this opportunity to sneak back into Barnes's office.

"Doctor, do you have a quick second?" I asked, discreetly closing the door behind me before waiting for a response.

"Of course," he said.

"Level with me—is this a terminal situation?" I asked, my voice trembling.

"Absolutely not," he replied, matter-of-factly. "As I said, it's not a *good* situation, but there have been a lot of advances in this area."

"You have no idea how relieved I am to hear you say that," I sighed. "I made the mistake of going on the Internet, and some of what I read was horrifying. I feel like we have a chance."

I slinked out of his office and back to the exam room, where Kit was laughing it up with the nurse. There'd been a weight lifted off of him. And me.

We left Barnes's office with a spring in our step and a new hopeful outlook. Once we hit the pavement, I embraced Kit. And then I burst into tears.

"I was so scared I was going to lose you," I said, sobbing.

He hugged me tight and replied, "You're not getting rid of me that easily."

PREVIOUSLY ON . . .

As promised, Kit called me the next morning with the coordinates for our art excursion. I could count on one fingerless hand the number of times I'd been to any kind of art exhibit, unless you considered the animation art gallery at New Jersey's Woodbridge Mall an art exhibit (the Friz Freleng–signed limited-edition cell of Tweety antagonizing Sylvester with a water gun that I coerced my grandmother into buying me remains one of my most prized possessions). Suffice it to say, I was going to be a fish out of water, which scared me a little, considering Kit and I were still in the "first impression" stage of our courtship. Of course, if I could spend five years pretending to know how to play baseball, I could bullshit my way through one measly art show.

We met outside a gallery on West 24th Street and the butterfly quotient upon seeing Kit again remained in the stratosphere. But I kept my cool. I didn't want to seem *too* eager and tip the power balance in his favor. As it was, I worried the gay police were going to issue me a citation for trespassing outside my league. Kit paid the entrance fee as I soaked up the scene. It was moderately crowded, mostly with young, smartly attired couples looking all obnoxious, serious, pretentious, introspective. They were ready to be *enlightened*.

Kit and I walked over to the start of the exhibition and stood silently as we read the artist statement, which basically told us that we would be seeing a series of color portraits of "women confronting middle age" by famed photographer Cindy Sherman. I flashed Kit a look of, "OMG, this is *so* totally right up my alley," and I *think* he bought it.

He proceeded to the first portrait—just as advertised, it was a peculiarly distorted image of a middle-aged woman—and I was . . . already bored out of my fucking mind. *How many more of these are there?* was what I *wanted* to say. But I *couldn't* say that. I could feel Kit watching me, judging my response to the art. So I followed him past portrait after portrait and acted like these broads were speaking to me. Which basically meant I just studied Kit's reactions to the pieces—an occasional head tilt, an eye squint here and there, a knowing smile—and promptly copied them. I wanted Kit to know that I was picking up what Sherman was throwing down. That not a single nuance was lost on me.

And then, a curveball!

"What do you think of this one?" Kit inquired as we stepped in front of the sixth or seventh portrait.

Fuck! I wasn't prepared for a pop quiz!

"It's . . . um . . . haunting," I replied. "So very, very *haunting*."

"How so?"

Seriously?! A follow-up? It was hard enough for me to come up with one adjective. Ugh. I looked at the photo again, searching for something else to say about this aging spinster before me.

"She looks . . . sad," I said, as sweat began to form on my brow. "And lonely."

And just then, I noticed a mischievous twinkle in Kit's eye. This fucker was enjoying watching me squirm. He knew I was out of my element.

I then asked him, "What do *you* think?"

"I'm not really feeling it," he said and shrugged, much to my relief and slight embarrassment. "She's had better shows."

We departed the gallery soon after, and once out on the street, I shared with Kit my true feelings about the exhibit, confessing, "I wasn't crazy about it, either, but I think you knew that."

Kit smirked. "There's something you should know," he said. "I take all of my second dates to see art."

"So . . . this *was* a test?!"

"This was *absolutely* a test," he confirmed, gleefully and unapologetically.

"Well . . . did I pass?"

He pulled out his little black book, but instead of telling me what he was jotting down, this time he remained silent.

"*What are you writing?!*" I asked as I tried to sneak a peek. He pulled the book away and then tucked it back into his pocket.

"*Buh, buh, buh,*" he interjected, raising a finger in the air. "That's for *me* to know."

And just like that, my concerns over my art stupidity began to ease. Kit seemed oddly charmed by my greenness. And my ill-fated attempt at a cover-up. It was almost as if I had passed the test by failing.

Kit suggested we take advantage of the crisp fall weather and go for a walk through Central Park, an idea I jumped at because I knew we'd be near his apartment, which likely meant there was another feverish make-out session in our future.

Sure enough, after a forty-five-minute stroll past such Central Park staples as the Sheep Meadow preserve, high-end tourist food trap Tavern on the Green, and John Lennon memorial Strawberry Fields, we retired to Kit's apartment and promptly attacked each other with our tongues. Within thirty seconds we were rolling around on his bed kissing, touching, grabbing, moaning. My heart was pounding as I reached my hand under his shirt and explored his lanky but toned swimmer's build of an upper body, slowly making my way up through the wisp of hair on his chest. As he lay on top of me, I could feel the full weight of his six-foot-three, likely 190-pound or so body on me—this was not a small man. And judging by the bulge piercing his khakis, everything about Kit was big.

"Home Wrecker"–size big.

Kit was also wending his way around my decidedly smaller frame, spending an inordinate amount of time feeling up my hairy, muscular legs, which, as luck would have it, were my best assets. All those years getting chased by bullies, combined with my adult obsession with running, had given me killer gams. I had my fair share of body issues, but they did not extend to my legs. And Kit was clearly attuned to this.

As his hands worked their way north, Kit managed to penetrate the extra layer of security—the skintight tank top that I had placed under my sweater—just long enough to realize my abdomen was not nearly as shredded as my calves. Luckily, his hands breezed past my jelly belly and set up shop on my chest, specifically my nipples. An attempt to completely lift up my shirt was blocked by yours truly.

"We should probably slow down," I suggested, halfheartedly.

"Says who?" Kit replied, playfully, as he rerouted his hands to my nether region. "*He* doesn't seem to want to slow down."

But *he* was writing checks my fragile self-esteem couldn't cash. At least not on Date No. 2.

"I don't want to have sex now," I informed him as I jammed my tongue in his ear. "Don't get me wrong—I *want* to have sex with you right now. But . . ."

But Kit was getting dangerously close to coming face-to-face with Fat Mike. And I was panicking.

Although I had spent only seven years of my life obese, they were a painful, psyche-altering seven years of mockery and shame and Ho Hos. By the time I entered high school my five-foot-ten frame was carrying around 250 pounds and all the bells and whistles that came with it. Multiple fat rolls? Check. Double chin? Check. Buried-penis syndrome? Check.

Back-to-school shopping became pure *Zero Dark Thirty*–level torture. My mother and I would always go to the same store—a mom-and-pop clothing shop called Grandview, right in town. Every year, I'd walk in just praying they'd have my sizes—forty-two-inch-waisted pants and XL tops. Even when they did have pants big enough for me, I still always purchased ones with elastic waistbands, for extra room and comfort. Which meant that yes, I was one of the few teenagers in the tristate area who didn't own a single pair of jeans. It was all khakis and parachute pants.

My father tried to shame me into losing weight by forcing me to bring our scale down from the bathroom and weigh myself in front of the entire family at the dinner table. But that little trick only succeeded in making me feel more shame, which, in turn, led to more overeating. Why eat a Big Mac and a large fries when I could eat a Big Mac and a large fries *and* a six-piece Chicken McNuggets? Why just devour an entire bag of Doritos while watching *Falcon Crest* when I could melt a jar of Cheez Whiz in the microwave and pour it over an entire bag of Doritos? Why consume just three slices of pizza when I could have *five* slices of pizza plus two mozzarella sticks and a few squares of garlic cheese bread?

By tenth grade, my classmates had given me the nickname Grimace—because I had roughly the same physique as Ronald McDonald's big, purple sidekick. I dreaded passing the fast-food joint when we were all being bused here or there on class trips. I also dreaded taking my shirt off in public places—swimming pools, school locker rooms, etc.—because I didn't want anyone to see my stretch marks. And, naturally, I also loathed having my photo taken. My single worst photo ever was snapped on a class trip to Washington, D.C. I had won an essay contest along with several of my classmates, and the prize was a week in D.C. as part of some group called Close-Up. Ironically, an actual close-up might have been more merciful than the shot in which I posed alongside our local senator in a black-and-white *horizontal-* striped shirt. I looked like a pregnant zebra.

It was February 23, 1990, at roughly 7 p.m.—a little more than one year after my mom's death—when I decided I was tired of being fat. I was sitting at my maternal grandma Ronnie's dining room table getting ready to devour a piece of my Carvel ice cream cake. I had just turned seventeen and weighed 255 pounds. I paused for a moment before taking my first bite and made a promise to myself: After I eat my birthday cake, it's over. The Fat Mike era was coming to an end. And this birthday cake would be its swan song. And it was.

The following day, I went to our local Acme supermarket and purchased myself a thirteen-ounce can of SlimFast vanilla mix (plastic shaker and measuring cup included) and for the next year I had a shake for breakfast and a shake for lunch, followed by a sensible dinner. By the time I graduated high school in June, I had dropped 60 pounds. And as I neared my senior year at the University of Southern California, by which point I'd replaced SlimFast with vegetarianism and running, I shed another 40, putting me at 160 pounds, a weight I have more or less maintained to this day.

But I had never fully exorcised Fat Mike. Although I had no shortage of confidence when fully clothed, I became plagued with insecurity every time I caught a glimpse of my naked body in the bathroom mirror.

Needless to say, Fat Mike took some of the joy out of sex. It was tough to be fully present with your partner when you had one eye on your ribbed tank top to ensure it was properly concealing your imperfect tummy.

Fat Mike didn't stop me from having—or taking some pleasure in—sex, whether it was the rare one-night stand or the even rarer steady boyfriend (of which I've really only had one; his name was Charlie and we were together for three years before amicably ending things due to irreconcilable ennui about sixteen months before I met Kit). And to date, no guy had ever shrieked in horror upon seeing me in my natural state. But, hey, there's a first time for everything!

And I really did not want that first time to be with Kit.

Back to our date: Kit assured me that he could wait. And wait he did. For two long, blue-bally weeks, during which it seemed like he was enjoying, almost welcoming, this odd, foreign concept of abstinence. In the meantime, our connection deepened and our spark intensified.

On the occasion of our sixth date, our game of "just the tip" began to transition into "Just the whole dang dong." At the same time, Kit was gaining the upper hand in his ongoing battle with my wife beater, his frisky fingers tugging at it as if to say, *Lemme see what you've been hiding under here.*

Sound the alarm! Security breach!

I forcibly grabbed his hand and restrained it behind his head, feebly, clumsily attempting to make it look like I was getting rough with him. It backfired, as he broke free from my grasp and started lifting my body's cotton armor. I shooed his hand away again, before reluctantly, mortifyingly confessing, "I'm a little insecure about my tummy."

And with those seven words, Kit knew my deepest, darkest secret.

He moved his hand back to my midsection, only instead of lifting my tank he reached under it. He placed his hands on my belly and he just . . . left them there, never breaking eye contact with me. I felt exposed. And vulnerable. And embarrassed.

But I also felt safe.

Safe enough that by Date No. 7 I was having sex with Kit completely naked.

And by Date No. 9 I even let him turn on a light.

It was around Date No. 12, roughly four weeks after our orbits had first collided at Webster Hall, that Kit would utter the words "I love you." Well, he didn't actually utter them as much as he shouted them in the middle of an orgasm.

He quickly backtracked on that declaration, blaming it on his heightened emotional state (read: the mind-blowing sex). I lightly teased him about his coitus-fueled outburst, before confessing that I, too, had been having L-word thoughts (although I managed to keep mine suppressed while climaxing). But we both agreed that it was too soon to be crossing that particular threshold after just one month of dating. Kit suggested we get our feet wet with *I love you*'s illegitimate brother.

"If you mouth the words 'olive juice' it *looks* like you're saying 'I love you,'" he explained to me as I rested my head on his chest. He then offered to do a demonstration.

"Holy shit," I exclaimed, marveling at how right he was. It totally looked like Kit had just said he loved me—without actually, you know, saying he loved me.

"OK, your turn." Kit smiled.

I followed his lead and mimed the words "olive juice" right back at him. And then he mouthed them back at me. And then we repeated this silly exercise a dozen more times, giggling like two sixteen-year-olds who had just cheated their way to a perfect score on the SATs.

It was also during this eventful pillow talk session that we expressed a mutual desire to be each other's B-word. It certainly felt like we were boyfriends, but it was nice to know we were on the same page in terms of making it official. There was also a practical component to it: We were already having unsafe, condom-less sex, although before doing so we had done a careful review of our STD histories.

As we lay there cuddling, I couldn't help but begin to imagine a future with (my new *boyfriend*!!) Kit. I knew it was early days, and there was still a ton we didn't know about each other, but I had never been this excited about a guy before. I wanted to spend every hour of every day with him, even if that meant sacrificing time with my friends (poor Matt was forced to wing it without his wingman) or my family (fewer Red Lobster Sundays with my grandmother and Aunt Joan).

So, in addition to hanging out at Kit's place on weekends, I started sleeping over during the workweek, which meant having to lug a duffel bag filled with a change of clothes to and from the office, in addition to my work backpack. It also meant recycling the same two or three outfits. To my colleagues at *TV Guide*, it probably looked like I had begun living out of my car.

Luckily, Kit and I were highly compatible sleep mates—neither of us snored and we both respected each other's bed boundaries, although Kit's octopus-like tentacles often made their way past the invisible median. I pretended to be annoyed by the intrusion, although, secretly, I loved waking up with *my cute boyfriend's* body parts all over me. It spoke to how comfortable he was with me.

The fact that I needed to report to work almost two hours before Kit meant that he was always asleep when I left in the morning. As a result, I perfected an Ethan Hunt–like ability to get fully showered and dressed without making a peep. I did not want to do anything to jeopardize my sleepover privileges!

Of course, inevitably, accidents happened. Like the morning my belt buckle made contact with Kit's desk as I was preparing to loop it around my waist. That was followed immediately by my backpack tumbling off of his chair and crashing onto the floor. The force of the near-simultaneous explosions caused Kit to spring up like half of an unmanned seesaw, only it wasn't Kit so much as it was his evil, fire-breathing twin.

"This. Has. To. Stop. *Now!*" he roared, as I stood there trembling, my half-fastened belt swaying in the wind. And then, as if someone had flipped a switch on the nape of his neck, his body fell back onto the mattress and he resumed sleeping.

I stood there at the foot of his bed, still in shock at what I had just witnessed. Who the fuck *was* that? My fear was quickly replaced by fury at his spectacular overreaction. I fastened my belt, threw some clothes into my duffel bag, picked my backpack up off the floor, and flew out of his apartment like a pissed-off bat out of hell, doors slamming behind me. And if my noisy departure didn't send Kit a power-fully passive-aggressive message, perhaps the absence of my customary "good morning" note on his nightstand would drive home to him how steaming mad I was.

As I walked to the Sixty-sixth Street subway station, my anger intensified. A little fear started to creep back in, too. What if the amazing man that I was falling in love with was, in reality, a short-fused psychopath? It was hard not to feel like the other shoe was dropping, shattering our entire four-week whirlwind romance in the process.

I resolved not to initiate any contact with Kit for at least twenty-four hours. If my late parents' dysfunctional relationship had taught me anything, it was that the silent treatment could prove to be a most lethal weapon in the aftermath of a fight.

At around 10:30 a.m., just as I was getting ready to hit publish on my daily online news roundup, my office phone rang. It was Kit's number on the caller ID. *This should be interesting.*

"Hello," I grumbled.

"Good morning," Kit exclaimed, jovially, the horn-honking in the background confirming to me that he was likely en route to the subway from his apartment.

"I'm mad at you," I fumed.

"Uh-oh," he exhaled. "What'd I do?"

"You honestly don't remember what happened this morning?"

Crickets.

"I honestly don't," he confessed genuinely, before sheepishly adding, "Oh, wait . . . did I yell at you?"

"Yes," I confirmed, fighting back tears. "I dropped my backpack on the floor and you *tore* into me."

"Shit. I'm sorry," he sighed, his voice decidedly less cheery. "What did I say?"

"You screamed 'This has to stop!' as if it was the last straw or something. I feel like I try so hard to be quiet when I leave . . ."

"Mike, there's something you should know . . ." Kit muttered, all cryptic-like, my internal panic meter rising. "I kind of have Morning Tourette's."

I thought I'd misheard. "You have *what*?" I replied, stupefied.

"Morning Tourette's," he repeated. "Basically, I'm a dick before 10 a.m. I once reduced an ex to tears for making too much noise while I slept."

"That's not a real condition," I countered. Relief started to set in as it became clear that Kit felt like a total and complete shit. Also: "Morning" and "Tourette's" were just funny when paired together.

"I'm really sorry, Mike," Kit continued. "I'm not myself in the morning."

"I'm going to occasionally make noise while you sleep," I explained. "I don't want to be in constant fear of getting yelled at."

"I will try to keep the Tasmanian Devil under control," he replied, supersweet and contrite. "In the meantime, can I make it up to you with dinner tonight?"

And just like that, my anger was gone. My boyfriend was back.

"Yes, you can," I said. "And you can also buy me some peanut butter frozen yogurt afterward."

"Deal," he said, before adding, "Olive juice, Mike."

"Olive juice, Kit," I replied.

We hung up and I merrily hit publish on my morning news column.

Kit and I learned more new stuff about each other over the next couple of weeks as we continued to wade through the mostly fun discovery phase of our relationship. For instance, I learned that Kit's artistic interests included an obsession with fonts. He learned that I liked to pick the feathers out of pillows and then lightly graze my skin with the pointy tip. I learned that the serious girlfriend he'd had in college, Beeba, remained one of his closest, dearest friends. He learned that the acting bug had bit me between the ages of twenty-five and twenty-eight, during which time I costarred in nearly a dozen New Jersey community theater productions, including classics such as *Six Degrees of Separation* and *Biloxi Blues*. I learned that he was racked with anxiety during certain social situations and developed a symptom wherein the cuticles on his fingernails became itchy. He learned that I collected Smurfs as a kid. I learned that he had a quite a stockpile of sex toys. He learned that I *still* collected Smurfs. I learned that he was self-conscious about his droopy left eyelid, partly because he had inherited it from his doppelgänger dad. He learned that, no, seriously, I *still* collected Smurfs. And I would come to learn that Kit was not OK with it. I was, in fact, about to find out just how *not* OK with it he was.

5.

Filled with all this newfound hope and optimism, I texted my brother David with news of Dr. Barnes's upbeat prognosis as Kit and I made our way downtown for our second appointment of the day. It was literally the first piece of good news we had been handed since this whole mess had begun and I was excited to share it.

We were next scheduled to see a Dr. Cullen, whose office was in the heart of Union Square, at 11 a.m. Like Barnes, Cullen was—at least according to the Interwebs—among NYC's foremost neuroendocrine cancer specialists. It was a super-niche field, so it came as no surprise when Cullen announced within seconds of our meeting that he and Barnes were buds.

"He's a very accomplished oncologist who knows a lot about neuroendocrine cancer," he said of Barnes.

Cullen, a slightly younger, thinner, and more focused version of Barnes, approached the sink and began washing his hands. The setting of the meeting was an exam room as opposed to an office, which sent off digital rectal exam (DRE) alarm bells in my—and, I was sure, Kit's—head. I checked my iPhone to confirm the audio app was on and recording. It was.

"Christopher, as I was telling your brother when I spoke to him by phone last week, I—"

"I'm actually his partner," I interjected.

"Oh, I'm sorry—as I was telling your *partner*," he awkwardly corrected himself. "The pathology report seems to be telling me that your neuroendocrine tumor is an angrier form," he continued. "It doesn't mean that it's traveled anywhere, but it puts it in a somewhat different category than what we usually talk about with regard to neuroendocrine tumors or carcinoid tumors. But there is treatment."

Translation: Neuroendocrine cancer, itself something of an anomaly, had a rare and nasty sibling.

Cullen went on to cite the suspicious "tiny little" nodules in the lung and liver that Barnes had alluded to, although he seemed considerably less worried about them, saying, "I think we can assume they're probably nothing." *Phew.*

"Dr. Barnes seemed very hopeful," I continued. "Do you agree with that assessment?"

Cullen hesitated for a second, before uttering a quiet yet resolute "Yes."

All told, the Cullen appointment was another check in the win column. I texted my brother David—"Doc. No. 2 said same as Doc. No. 1. Lots of hope."—as we left the doctor's office in search of some lunch. We decided to grab a bite at Kit's old professional stomping ground, Così.

I gave Kit my order—hummus and veggies on multigrain bread and a large fountain Diet Coke with extra ice (my Così usual)—while I went in search of an available table. We were in the thick of Manhattan's weekday lunch crush, so the seating pickings were slim. I spotted an unoccupied standing table right up front and immediately staked my claim to it. It boasted a nice view of bustling Union Square *and* Kit didn't have to endure the pain of sitting. The universe was handing us wins left and right today!

As I waited for Kit to arrive with our grub, I took a deep breath and attempted to mentally navigate the awkward transition from our cancer-filled morning to . . . lunch at Così. I took in all the hustle and bustle, young professionals making the most of their lunch hour. Not a care in the world. I had been one of them just ten days ago. Ah, those good old pre-cancer days, when Kit and I would pop into a Così after work and talk about our respective days or maybe finalize the weekend itinerary (naps, snacks, naps, dinner, more naps) or perhaps continue planning the African safari that had been on the back burner for years.

To paraphrase one of Liz Lemon's most iconic catchphrases, I desperately wanted to go back to there.

Kit arrived with our lunch.

"Is this OK?" I asked him of my choice of table.

"It's perfect," he said. "I wasn't going to sit anyway."

As I prepared to take my first bite, I decided to surprise Kit with some more good news about our Morning of Optimism. A cancer gift, if you will.

"So, when you were getting your blood drawn at Barnes's, I snuck back into his office and asked him point-blank if your cancer is terminal," I recounted to Kit, who was going to town on his Così club sandwich. "He said without hesitation that it wasn't."

"Really?" he responded, his mouth half-full.

"Really," I confirmed.

It felt OK to share with Kit my Internet-fueled fears about his condition now that two oncologists who also happened to be *neuroendocrine specialists* had ruled many of them out. If today's promising prognoses proved legit, there was a real chance we'd get to live out our dream of retiring to Hudson, New York, and opening the world's coolest pop and pop shop.

Just as I began to wrap my arms around the visual of an octogenarian Kit trying to steer customers *away* from the Smurf section of our store, another thought popped into my head: Now that Kit seemed to have a real shot at beating this thing, maybe I should look into a prenup. I mean, what if he beat cancer and, in the process, developed a whole new outlook on life—one that no longer included me but rather someone more chiseled and with fewer sex hang-ups and whose vision for a perfect Sunday involved spending three hours in Home Depot picking out backsplash tiles? And then, upon finding this person (who may or may not be a certain interior decorator named Todd), he divorced me, took half of my fortune and rode off into the sunset with his fancy human upgrade, leaving me alone with a depleted bank account and nothing but my *Grey's Anatomy* scoops to keep me warm at night?

And, just then, as I stood across from Kit at Così, a lightning bolt of shame struck me down for thinking of money at a time like this. It was followed quickly by a burst of relief because, my God, I was freaking out over a scenario wherein Kit lived long enough to divorce me, take my money, and marry someone else. That was a massive step up from where I had been just six hours ago.

Just to be safe, while I was at work that afternoon I shot our real estate attorney, Lisa Gabler—who had represented us in the sale of our apartment the past August—a quick email casually inquiring whether prenuptial agreements fell within her purview. There was no harm in asking and potentially getting the ball rolling should our next two oncological appointments confirm the rosy outlook painted by the first two. Lisa had no idea Kit was sick, let alone that we were engaged, so my email at worst would give her momentary pause, versus outright scorn and judgment. But wait—she'd eventually hear about his illness. And then she'd remember my out-of-the-blue email query, do the math, and realize that, holy fuck, this shit-heel client of hers was worried about protecting his medium-sized fortune while his fiancé was fighting for his life.

I immediately regretted entertaining such a thoughtless, disgraceful, base line of thinking. And then making matters worse by leaving a paper trail. I was a heinous human being.

On my way home from work that night, I decided to make my shame spiral complete by burying my guilt under an XL cake batter-flavored, carob chip–soaked frozen yogurt at 16 Handles.

As I neared the shop, I noticed I had a voicemail. Maybe it was Crown Jewelers telling me our resized rings were ready to be picked up.

Nope, it was Jennifer from Dr. Abbott's office. "I'm calling to see if we can move your appointment tomorrow from one o'clock to noon.

The doctor wants to make sure he gets enough time with you and Christopher," she said.

My crisis antenna stood erect. Our initial appointment had been for an hour. He needed *more* than an hour? This was the oncologist to whom Voight had referred us, so it dawned on me that he might be "concerned about Christopher," too.

Fuck.

I texted Kit about the time change, but I didn't divulge the reason behind it.

Thursday morning arrived and we showed up at Abbott's super-swank Upper East Side office for Consultation No. 3. The fortysomething doc had a commanding presence and a firm handshake and oozed authority and confidence. He was the anti-Barnes.

Kit and I took a seat, and I cued up the audio app on my iPhone, discreetly clicked record, and rested it on his desk.

"This is an extremely serious situation you're in, Christopher," Abbott said solemnly, as I felt the blood drain out of my body.

"OK," Kit nervously responded. I reached over to grab his hand and squeeze it tightly.

"You have an extremely aggressive form of neuroendocrine cancer. The tumor in your rectum is enormous. It's the size of a fist—it doesn't surprise me that you're having so much discomfort sitting—and it's growing fast. As a result, the treatment we are recommending is also very aggressive. It's a combination of two chemotherapy drugs, cisplatin and etoposide. It's a powerful mix and, I have to be honest with you, Christopher, it's going to be rough on you. In addition to nausea and vomiting, you will feel extremely fatigued. Food will taste differently. You will lose your hair. We have to go at this thing with everything we've got."

I squeezed Kit's hand harder. The harsh reality of the situation was hitting me: *Kit will suffer. I will* watch *Kit suffer.*

This was all really happening. Again.

As Abbott continued to lower the boom Dr. Phil–style on us, his laundry list of horrors hitting my ear like Charlie Brown white noise, I turned my head to the right and looked at Kit. I noticed that he was as white as a ghost.

It was clear that Abbott and I were both waiting for Kit to say something. Anything. I wondered what his first words would be. Would he inquire about the chemo and the pain? Would he ask when he'd start losing his hair?

Finally, Kit spoke.

"What does this mean for my job?" he innocently asked, as my heart broke into a million fucking pieces. "Will I be able to work while I'm getting chemo?"

"I don't think that will be possible," Abbott responded.

"How long will I be out?"

Kit's love for his job and the people with whom he worked was never clearer to me than in this moment. All of the horrible shit he was being told . . . and what concerned him most was being away from Wyeth.

"I think you should plan on being out for at least a few months," Abbott said.

"What about surgery?" I inquired.

"Surgery is not in the cards," Abbott responded, not an ounce of uncertainty in his voice. "The tumor is too big. He would be decimated."

Abbott was contradicting pretty much everything both of New York's premier authorities on neuroendocrine cancer had told us yesterday, while also confirming much of the scary shit I had read on the Internet.

"Doctor, can I beat this?" Kit asked hesitantly.

"I believe you can," Abbott said. "You are a young, healthy guy. Those things are very important. And these drugs have proven very amenable to your kind of tumor. I am optimistic. And there's possibly a radiation component after chemo."

And just like that, the clouds parted just a smidge and a little hope shined through. Kit still had a fighting chance.

Before we left, the doc introduced us to the main chemo coordinator, a pleasant-looking woman in her thirties who gave us a tour of the "chemo suite," which was basically one large room with a series of recliners and IV drips. The first red flag immediately went up.

Where the fuck are the beds? was what I *wanted* to say. Instead I politely asked "Are there any beds?" with the concern in my voice palpable. "There's no way he is going to be able to sit down for that length of time."

She hesitated for a moment and then slowly reached inside her presumably tumor-less asshole and pulled this gem out: "The recliners can extend pretty far back . . ."

"That's not going to work," I interjected, bluntly. "He has a tumor the size of a fist in his rectum. He needs a bed. He needs to be able to lie on his side."

I was annoyed that this was something we had to explain to her. I realized this cancer was rare, but was Kit really the first patient to walk through these doors with an XL rectal tumor? Was this *really* such an unusual request?

Apparently, it was.

"We could see about bringing a bed in here, I suppose," she said, rather unconvincingly.

And just like that, this place's stock began to plummet. We left the appointment feeling positive about the doctor, but decidedly negative on the facility itself. Suddenly, tomorrow's Sloan Kettering consultation was looking like our last—and perhaps only—hope.

It was now lunchtime, and we decided to do something unusual for us: grab a bite at our favorite Mexican restaurant—Benny's Burritos—in the middle of a workday. Benny's was right down the street from our West Village pad, but we'd been frequenting it long before we'd moved into the hood. When we lived in midtown, we often made "special" trips down here—"special" because we rarely ventured outside our comfortable three-block Hell's Kitchen radius for dinner—in the hopes that we would score a prime seat in the dive's outdoor sidewalk seating area. Better to gawk at the cute boys coming to and from the Equinox next door. The vegan burrito was also pretty yummy.

It was early March and chilly, so we settled for a window seat inside. We did that couple-y thing where we looked at the menu even though we knew *exactly* what we were getting. While we waited for the server to take our order, we conducted a postmortem on the Abbott appointment: Awesome doctor who clearly knew his shit and had a concrete plan? Check. A hospitable and comfortable chemo suite that could accommodate Kit's unique pain issue and in which we could see ourselves spending much of the next month holed up? Nope.

In that moment, a wave of sadness passed over me as we sat at our favorite restaurant talking about cancer. This was our depressing new reality. And then Kit did a very "Kit" thing. He looked at me all serious-like for five seconds and then asked for my iPhone. I handed it to him and he turned the camera function on. (Kit was between iPhones—he was waiting for the new 6 model to come out.) He then began taking pictures of me. I couldn't imagine why he wanted to capture my sad self, but I didn't resist. I never felt more loved and special than when Kit photographed me.

He then handed the camera back to me, and as I was about to tuck it away in my pocket, I did a *not* very "Mike" thing.

I turned the camera on him.

I rarely did this because I never felt more insecure than when I was taking photos in Kit's presence. It was like trying to perform a monologue in front of Meryl Streep. But I saw something in him—perhaps it was the same thing he had just seen in me—that demanded to be photographed. My sadness suddenly gave way to soul-crushing guilt as I snapped photo after photo and really *looked* at him. Why didn't I do this more often? Why didn't I notice him—like *really* notice him—the way he did me when the camera was in *his* hands? It had taken cancer to get me to do something as basic as pay real, close, special attention to Kit. I started to cry. I put my iPhone down. And then we ordered lunch.

Afterward, we paid a visit to Crown Jewelers around the corner to check on our resized rings (Kit's ended up being a little too big, while mine was a smidge small). The clerk delivered the disappointing news that they wouldn't be ready in time for our wedding tomorrow and fetched us a temporary set that wasn't nearly as simple and classic but that fit us perfectly. Not ideal, but, for the purposes of the ceremony, doable.

As we exited the store with makeshift rings in hand, Kit formally registered his disappointment, sighing, "I don't like that we're going to get married with rings we have to give back."

The alarm sounded at 6:30 a.m. Our fourth and final oncology consult at Sloan Kettering was at 8 a.m., and I had allotted extra time to get ready because *it was our wedding day!* Schedule-wise, I figured we'd be finished at Sloan at 10 or 11 a.m. at the latest, leaving plenty of time to tie the knot before city hall's marriage bureau closed at 3:45.

Kit spent his first fifteen fully awake minutes with his nose buried in his tiny closet debating what to wear. He had always been very fastidious about his wardrobe. Kit was one of those hateful creatures that could put on a pair of jeans and a T-shirt and still be the hottest, smartest-looking guy in the room. He nonetheless devoted an inordinate amount of time choosing what he was going to wear on any given day, and that was especially true this morning. He tried on at least four different jacket-pant combinations before settling on a dark blue corduroy blazer, bright pink sweater, matching collared shirt, and blue jeans.

He looked so handsome. Two weeks of being poked and prodded and operated on hadn't diminished his hotness quotient in the least.

"I want to look nice for my wedding photo," he said as he fixed his collar in front of the giant, leaning mirror in the bedroom.

"You look very dapper, Mr. Ausiello-Cowan," I cooed.

"I think you mean Mr. *Cowan-Ausiello*," he retorted.

Wardrobe-wise, I opted for something slightly more subdued (read: safe and boring and curve-disguising)—a large gray Banana Republic sweater over a blue-checkered shirt.

I started packing a bag for the busy day ahead. Among the items in my satchel: a folder with my notes about the Sloan appointment, our temporary rings, and a printout of the email from the city clerk's office containing our marriage certificate confirmation number. I peeked out the window to see if our Carmel car had arrived; it had. Kit, meanwhile, was on his hands and knees frantically looking under our couch for something.

"Bodge, the car's here," I impatiently told him. "What are you looking for?"

"Here they are!" he exclaimed with relief before standing up, opening his hand and revealing two of the black plastic spider rings we won at that Atlantic City arcade just a few weeks earlier. "Scooch was batting them around the apartment last week."

I just looked at him, bewildered and bemused.

"I'm not getting married with rings we have to return," he said.

It was adorable and absurd and oh-so-very Kit. I gave him a skeptical glare as if to say, *We can discuss this later*—as he buried the rings in his pocket and we headed out the door.

Our appointment was at Sloan's midtown headquarters, or "Outpatient *Pavilion*" as they cloyingly referred to it in the literature. It was a fucking cancer center, not a shopping mall.

Traffic was horrendous, basically stop-and-go the entire way. And our Carmel Car Service "chauffeur's" herky-jerky driving style only made things worse. He dropped us off at the corner of 53rd and Third and I reluctantly paid him for making us both irritated and nauseous.

As we approached the entrance, a distinguished-looking gentleman wearing a Sloan Kettering jacket and cap held the glass door open and cheerily exclaimed, "Good morning, gentlemen." *Oooh*, Sloan had its own doormen/greeters. Nice touch.

We entered the lobby and . . . well, I'll be . . . it looked like a fucking pavilion. A bright, shiny, modern pavilion. We moved with the herd past the main security desk, where Kit grabbed a handful of Purell from the nearby dispenser, and proceeded up the elevator to the sixth floor.

The elevator dropped us off in front of a swank reception desk, which rested in the middle of a sprawling waiting area filled with chairs and sofas and benches and art and plaques and waterfalls and coffee and sunlight.

It was peaceful. And orderly. *And there was a snack station!*

"I'm here with Christopher Cowan," I informed the young, female receptionist as Kit left to find a comfortable couch where he could lie on his side. "We have an 8 a.m. with Dr. Michelle Davis."

"How do you spell his last name?" she asked, her fingers ready to click the appropriate keystrokes.

"C-O-W-A-N," I relayed.

"Yep, I see him here," she said, her eyes on her computer screen. "You're all checked in. Please have a seat and listen for your name to be called."

"Thank you."

At this point, without having even met Dr. Davis, Sloan Kettering had zoomed past Dr. Abbott—and certainly Drs. Cullen and Barnes before him—as my top choice. I wasn't sure where Kit's head was at, but mine was crushing hard on Sloan K.

I looked around the waiting room in search of my husband-to-be. I finally spotted him stretched out on one of the sofas lining the huge windows overlooking Third Avenue, his nose once again buried in his iPad. I took a seat next to him.

"This place is pretty nice, huh?" I asked him.

"Definitely better than that shame-hole Barnes called an office," he zinged, shifting his position.

"You OK?"

"Yeah, just a little extra pain this morning," he said with a wince. "That car ride didn't help."

I sat back and took in the surroundings. The surprisingly crowded, for 8 a.m., waiting room boasted a wide array of age and ethnic groups, although it appeared that we were once again the youngest people there. Regardless, I felt comfortable. Safe. Hopeful.

I stood and alerted Kit that I was "going to get the lay of the land," borrowing an expression my dad would use on the first day of literally *every* one of my childhood vacations. "Do you want something to drink?"

"I'll take a cup of water," he said.

I moseyed on over to the snack station and began poking around. There was a big basket filled with saltine and graham crackers; an under-the-counter fridge replete with various juices, chilled spring-water, hot coffee, and tea (but no Diet Coke, sigh). I grabbed Kit his cup of water, stuffed a few packs of graham crackers in my pocket, and returned to our couch.

"Thanks, babe," he said as I handed him his water. I pulled the graham crackers out of my pocket and gave him a big toothy smile as if to say, *They got snacks, Bodge!*

"Someone likes this place," Kit said, an air of amusement in his voice.

As I took my seat and started emotionally devouring graham cracker after graham cracker, I checked in with God to make sure He had our backs this morning. *Please send us off to our wedding with good news*, I silently pled.

As the clock approached 8:45 a.m., Kit noticed I was getting antsy. We were, after all, on a *relatively* tight schedule. "I'm going to see what's up," I informed him as I began to stand.

"Relax," Kit said. "Let's give it fifteen more minutes."

"OK," I said, nodding as I sat back down.

Over the next fifteen minutes, I noticed Kit spending more time looking up at the reception desk than he was playing Candy Crush. This was the part of the Kit-and-Mike anxiety dance in which he gradually absorbed my restlessness and paranoia to the point where we were both one big anxiety powder keg waiting to explode. As the clock struck 9 a.m.—less than seven hours until the marriage bureau closed—I sprang to my feet and approached the reception desk. And because the universe just loved to fuck with me, would you believe that was precisely the moment the words "Christopher Cowan" reverberated through the vast waiting area.

"Here!" Kit shouted, as in the distance a young woman made her way through the maze of sofas and chairs following Kit's voice. She spotted both of our hands raised in the air, smiled, and approached.

"I'm sorry for the wait," she said, genuinely. "You can come with me."

We stood and followed her back through the maze, through a door, and into a bland corridor.

"How are you both doing today?" she asked cheerily. Her sunny attitude was comforting. Maybe she had seen Kit's file and was excited about all the good news Dr. Davis was going to be giving us today?! A boy could dream.

"A little anxious," Kit said.

"But hopeful," I interjected.

"Well, you're in good hands with Dr. Davis," she assured us, as she ushered us into a nondescript room, one that had a desk, an exam table, a few chairs, and what looked like a private bathroom. "Dr. Davis will be in shortly."

She closed the door behind us, and Kit slowly climbed onto the exam table, positioned himself on his side, and fired up his Candy Crush. I started snooping around the room, opening drawers, peering behind cabinets.

About five minutes passed and there was a knock at the door. In walked a petite, thirtysomething woman with shoulder-length blond hair and wearing a white lab coat. She was extremely pretty and put together. Under the lab coat she was wearing a skirt-and-blouse combo that looked like it had just been pulled off the rack at Barneys. I was not a shoe person but was fairly certain that those heels had been ripped off of Carrie Bradshaw's feet.

She didn't look like a doctor. She looked like someone who *played* a doctor on television. She perfectly rounded out the utopian view of Sloan I'd adopted ever since I'd walked through that entrance.

"I'm Dr. Davis," she said, with the most sumptuously soothing and compassionate tone I had ever heard, as I stealthily hit record on my audio app.

Kit and I were both smiling. We'd just met this woman and we were in love. We were choosing Sloan Kettering as our treatment center, I quietly decided.

"Christopher, I'm just going to give you a quick exam," she said, soothingly. "Can you sit up?"

"Yes," Kit said, matter-of-factly, as he scooted to the front of the exam table. It was as if Dr. Davis's aura of utter perfection instantly eased his ass pain. She pulled out her stethoscope and placed the resonator over his lungs.

"Take a deep breath for me," she instructed him, and he inhaled and exhaled. She moved the metal disc to the right side of his chest. "And again." She then repeated this exercise with the disc on his upper back. Inhale, exhale, rinse, repeat.

"Your lungs sound good," she said. "Are you able to lie on your back?"

"Sure," Kit said, as he stretched out on the table.

"I'm just going to apply some pressure to your abdomen, let me know if it hurts," she said, as she dug her hand into him. Was she feeling around for additional tumors? Regardless, Kit was tolerating it perfectly. "OK, great. Thank you. You can sit up. Or you can go back to lying on your side."

"Yeah, the biopsy inflamed the area and it's tough to sit for long periods," Kit explained.

"The other oncologists we saw said the chemo should relieve that pretty quickly," I noted to Davis.

"That's true," she confirmed. "The trouble with this kind of cancer though is that it grows back quickly. There are different types of neuroendocrine tumors and yours is what we call a *high-grade* neuroendocrine tumor, which is extremely aggressive."

I felt the hope and optimism in the room begin to evaporate. And I desperately tried to contain it before it was too late.

"Those oncologists also said that between chemo and radiation there's a lot of hope here," I told her, my voice taking on a sudden alarm.

"The problem is, the tumor is already at an advanced stage," she said.

And then Kit stunned me by asking her, point-blank, "What stage are we talking?"

Prior to this, there had been minimal discussion of staging. We'd never asked, and the only time it had come up—with Dr. Abbott—we'd been told that this type of rare cancer didn't lend itself to traditional staging. I tensed up and just stared at Dr. Davis, waiting for her reply. It came quickly and without hesitation.

"Stage 4," she said, her air of sunshine and happiness now replaced by darkness and dread. I looked at Kit and his face suddenly became bright red. He smiled nervously, spontaneously letting out an "OK..."

Dr. Davis saw us both reeling. "I'm sorry," she said.

"Bottom-line this for me, Doctor," Kit said, barely able to contain his swelling panic. "What are we looking at here?"

"You mean in terms of time?" she asked.

"Yes," he said.

"We don't like to give numbers. Our patients are not numbers..."

"Please, Doctor," Kit interjected.

Dr. Davis hesitated, before carefully replying, "About a year."

I grasped the corner of the desk, supporting myself so my knees didn't buckle. I looked at Kit. I saw the shock invading every pore of his body. I felt it invade mine, too. Was this what an out-of-body experience was like? Because I suddenly felt as if I were looking down on someone else's apocalypse.

Dr. Davis continued to talk, but I couldn't hear a word she was saying. Kit began to sob. "I need a minute," he cried out. "Please give me a minute."

Dr. Davis nodded her head and exited, closing the door behind her.

I rushed to Kit's side, as he stood up from the exam table. "I need a minute," he repeated, only now it was directed at *me*.

"I am not leaving you, Kit," I exclaimed. "Please don't ask me to leave you."

"*I need a minute!*" he screamed, before escaping to the examining room's private bathroom. He shut the door. And then it started. The wailing. The most horrible sound I had ever heard in my life. I started frantically pacing around the room, alone, trying to figure out how I could tweak the space-time continuum by just five minutes so we could go back to life before a doctor at New York's premier cancer center told us that Kit would be dead in a year. Kit continued to bawl. I began to fear for his safety, that he might somehow harm himself. Everything was spiraling out of control. I had to do something. I raced from the room, reluctantly leaving Kit all alone, and rushed to Davis at the nurses' station.

"Dr. Davis, please come back in the room," I begged. "Please give Kit some hope. He's really upset. I'm scared. Please. There *has* to be some hope."

The resignation on her face told me that there was no hope to be had, but she nonetheless returned to the exam room, just as Kit was exiting the bathroom.

"I'm OK," he assured us, his eyes bloodshot.

"Christopher, everyone is different," she said. "And the year time frame is a *range*. It could be more than a year."

It also could be less was what I *wanted* to say.

Dr. Davis's pep talk left something to be desired, but at least the temperature in the room had cooled off. I was not currently worried that Kit was going to hurt himself. I was now back to worrying simply about him dying of cancer in twelve months.

"If you *do* decide to receive treatment here, I would like to start as soon as possible," Dr. Davis explained. "I can have our chemo nurse stop by and talk you through what to expect, and he can also give you a tour of our chemo suite. I'll give you guys time to discuss it."

Dr. Davis exited and closed the door behind her.

"Hey, this is *one* doctor's opinion," I assured him (and me). "Remember what Abbott said—this is a rare cancer. It's not surprising that there are differing takes on the prognosis."

"I can't believe this is happening," he cried, as I feared him heading for another meltdown.

"We got this, babe," I insisted, as I grabbed his hand and looked in his eyes and started to cry. "You're not alone. We're in this together. I love you."

We hugged. We then agreed to hear what the chemo nurse had to say. Despite Davis's dire death threat, Sloan K still seemed to have a lot going for it.

There was another knock at the door and in walked an impeccably styled, slender, five-foot-seven Asian man in his early thirties. His bright red bowtie matched his socks, which instantly set off my gaydar. He introduced himself as Will, his deep and masculine voice subsequently confusing my gaydar. Regardless of his sexual orientation, he was upbeat, friendly, and pleasing to the eye. He went over the chemo regimen, cisplatin and etoposide, which was the same cocktail Abbott had recommended (I found the consistency comforting).

He handed us a folder filled with information about side effects and whatnot. He then took us for a tour of the chemo suite, which blew Barnes's and even Abbott's out of the water. It even had beds.

Will escorted us back to the examining room and gave us a few minutes to talk privately.

"What do you think?" I asked Kit.

"I think this is where I'll be getting my chemo," he replied, nary an ounce of uncertainty. "I prefer Abbott as a doctor, but this place is just on a whole different level."

I preferred Abbott, too. He had given it to us straight, but he had also given us some hope. Davis was essentially forfeiting the game before it even began.

"If only we could bring Abbott over here instead of . . ." I began to say.

". . . the Grim Reaper," Kit cracked, referring to Davis.

It was comforting that even amid what had to be one of the most traumatic hours, if not the *most* traumatic hour, of his life, Kit's wicked sense of humor shined through. I planted a kiss on his lips and then checked my watch. It was approaching 11 a.m. Our window to get married was beginning to close. Maybe it was for the best? I'd been hoping to glide into city hall on a wave of optimism. It was clear that was not going to happen. It was also clear that it was more important than ever that we get married that day. The idea of going home with this grim prognosis *and* a failed marriage attempt was too depressing to even contemplate.

"How are we doing on time?" Kit asked.

"We're going to need to be on our way in about an hour."

"We'll be out of here in an hour," Kit said resolutely.

Will returned, and we informed him that after a week of oncology speed dating we had decided to proceed to first base with Sloan Kettering. He escorted us back out to the waiting room and instructed us to listen for one of the young interchangeable office assistants to call our name so we could schedule our chemo sessions. The waiting room was packed now, which meant the seating options were few and far between. The couches were all taken, so we reluctantly grabbed the only two vacant chairs in sight.

"This OK?" I asked. Kit nodded, as he carefully glided into the chair, tilting his pelvis to take the pressure off his ass.

Sitting directly across from us was an adorable-looking elderly African-American couple. The husband was busy people-watching, while the wife was flipping through a magazine. It was impossible to tell which one of them was there for treatment, because aside from the natural frailty that came with being in their late seventies/early eighties, they appeared to be perfectly healthy. They hadn't said a word to each other since we'd sat down, but I'd already determined that they'd been together for a long time.

Under normal circumstances, Kit and I would have looked at each other with endearment and said, "That'll be us in thirty years." But if Davis's End of Days prognosis was to be believed, that would never be us. I was looking directly at the future I would never have with Kit. Our Hudson, New York, fantasy would remain just that. It took everything in me not to burst into tears.

I then looked over at Kit, expecting to find him playing Candy Crush. But he was not playing Candy Crush. He was looking straight ahead at the elderly couple, too. And he was *sobbing*.

"I need to go to the bathroom," he said, his voice so heavily anguished I could barely make out the words. He left his iPad on the chair and made a beeline for the nearby bathroom. Before the door swung shut, I heard him begin to shriek. The sound drove a knife straight through the center of my heart.

I noticed that the wife was now looking up from her magazine and staring directly at my tear-drenched face. She remained silent, but I felt the compassionate vibes she was emitting. I wondered if she realized how lucky she was to have made it into her twilight years with her soul mate.

Kit returned from the bathroom, his pace slower than when he'd walked in. The redness around his eyes was now more pronounced. He looked beaten down.

"I want to sit somewhere else," he whispered to me as he picked his iPad up off the chair. I quickly grabbed my bag and followed him, stealing one more glimpse of the elderly couple as I went. I loved them. But I also hated them.

As we began to search for a pair of seats with the fewest number of emotional triggers, one of the female Sloan bots shouted, "Christopher Cowan." She invited us to take a seat at one of the half-dozen intake stations attached to the main reception desk, and we proceeded to schedule the first two chemo rounds, both of which required one seven-hour stint in the chemo suite followed by two weeks off. Davis recommended starting ASAP, so we booked the first round for Monday morning.

It was now approaching 12:45 p.m. We had to motor. We exited Sloan and hurriedly hailed a taxi to city hall. Come hell or high water, we were getting to the church on time.

6.

It was roughly one-thirty when the cab pulled up in front of 141 Worth Street. As I paid the $16 fare, I noticed a young, traditionally attired bride and groom getting photographed on the front steps. They were surrounded by a half-dozen or so smiling friends and relatives. It began to hit me. I was getting married. I was getting fucking married. But before I was able to bask in the joy of that reality, Dr. Davis's three-word grenade, "About a year," exploded anew in my head. If only the cancer of it all could have just gone away for the next two hours.

We raced past the happy couple half-blocking the entrance and barreled into the city clerk's building. We entered two wrong interior doors before arriving at the correct destination—the marriage bureau. I was immediately wowed by the Grand Central Station–like atmosphere. The place was humungous. And mobbed with couples of every color and gender and size and age and ethnicity. Some of the duos were fully decked out in traditional garb; others looked as if they were going back in time thirty years to their senior prom at the Newark Airport Hilton (as someone who attended two proms in New Jersey, one of them at the Newark Airport Hilton, I'm allowed to make that joke). Others—like us—looked ready for Sunday brunch in the West Village.

The sheer volume of the crowd worried me. I saw every couple as an obstacle to our getting married before 3:45 p.m. The good news: There was no line at the check-in counter.

"Hi, we're here to get married," I aggressively informed the middle-aged gentleman behind the desk.

"Do you have a confirmation number?" he asked with annoyed indifference.

"I do," I said, flashing the printout of the confirmation email before him.

He handed us a small ticket, not unlike the tiny slip of paper you pull out of one of those red dispensers at the deli counter. Ours read "C834."

"Wait until your number is called," he said, gesturing to the digital board at the center of the room.

I decided to risk the inevitable eye-roll and sigh by asking, "How long would you say the wait is?"

He begrudgingly scanned the room, looked at his watch, and responded, "Hard to say. At least an hour."

OK, that was not so bad. That put us at 2:30, which still gave us an extra hour to play with. I had additional questions—like, *What exactly happens when our number is called?* and *Do we immediately exchange I do's upon receiving our marriage license?* and *Is there a special line for people dying of cancer?*—but I decided it was probably best to quit while I was barely ahead.

Kit and I proceeded into the bowels of the room and found some empty wall space to lean on. And we just took in the scene. The joy. The excitement. The flashbulbs. The happiness. The hope. I wanted so badly to play in that same euphoric sandbox. But I couldn't. All I could think about was the death sentence Kit had been handed just hours ago. I attempted to give myself the same pep talk I had delivered to Kit back at Sloan: It was one doctor's opinion. Dr. Barnes had thrown around the word "curable." Dr. Cullen said those nodules were "probably nothing." Dr. Abbott had been "optimistic." Dr. Davis had represented the other, more dire end of the spectrum. But there *was* a spectrum. That was my story and I was sticking to it.

With Kit busily typing what I presumed was a work email on his iPad, I fetched us a late lunch at the hot dog stand that I had noticed when the cab dropped us off. I grabbed Kit a dog with mustard and extra sauerkraut and a bottle of water, and myself a Diet Coke and a soft pretzel. The only food I'd eaten today had been a Kind bar and some Sloan Kettering graham crackers, so I could afford a carb splurge.

As I returned with our sustenance, I noticed the "C" row on the digital board was nearing the 800s. We were 834. I texted Nina Boesch—one of our nearest and dearest friends, who earlier this week had agreed to be our witness-slash-photographer—with an update on our whereabouts.

We had met Nina six years earlier at a Fourth of July fireworks viewing party thrown by mutual friends Kate and Patrick on the roof of their Park Slope, Brooklyn, apartment building. I was intrigued by her very noticeable German accent as well as the burgeoning cottage industry she had carved out on the side in which she took discarded MetroCards, chopped them up into tiny pieces, and turned them into mosaic-like art. It helped that she had a wickedly inappropriate sense of humor. I knew this because she was only mildly put off when, within thirty minutes of meeting her, Kit accused Nina—the sweetest, most open-minded, philo-Semitic person on the planet—of being the secret love child of one Adolf Hitler. We also *loved* her love of New York. Her immigrant backstory—she had parlayed a one-year stint in a German young professionals exchange program into a whole new life, during which she graduated from the prestigious Rhode Island School of Design—was inspiring. She was now employed as a Web developer at one of NYC's top design firms. As we began to see her more frequently, at brunches and Super Bowl viewing parties and whatnot, she started inviting us to join her on her myriad NYC adventures. Like walking the entire thirteen-mile stretch of Broadway in one spring afternoon. Or attending a fundraiser on the floor of the New York Stock Exchange. When Kate and Patrick relocated to Portland, Nina became ours.

Nina was one of a very small group of people who knew what was happening with regard to the cancer *and* the wedding. The fact that we had invited her into this small club and chosen her to be the sole guest at our shotgun nuptials spoke to how big a part of our lives she had become.

Within ten minutes, Nina arrived, camera in hand. She was beaming.

"It's your wedding day!" she exclaimed, before giving each of us a hug.

"Thank you so much for doing this," Kit said to her.

"I'm so honored that you asked me," she said, genuinely. She then inquired, "How did it go at Sloan?"

"Don't ask," Kit said, cryptically.

"Oh, no," Nina said.

"We're calling the doctor the Grim Reaper," I informed her, while shaking my head as if to say, *Please don't press any further.* Nina worriedly nodded, confirming that my message was received.

The three of us anxiously watched the digital board, and as the number ticked closer to C834, we inched closer to the "C" window. Ready to pounce.

And at 2:36 p.m., as the board changed from C833 to C834, pounce we did. In fact, the C833 peeps—a young Puerto-Rican couple—barely had a chance to vacate the lane before we rushed the counter. The middle-aged Caucasian lady behind the glass greeted us pleasantly, as I handed her my email confirmation.

"I'm going to need both of your IDs," she said, as Kit and I forked over our driver's licenses. She looked at her computer and started typing away.

"Christopher, where were you born?"

"Camp Hill, Pennsylvania," he responded, adopting his "professional" voice.

"And Michael?"

"Elizabeth, New Jersey," I told her, adopting my embarrassed voice.

"Will you both be keeping your last names?"

Kit and I looked at each other, smiled, and responded in unison, "Yes."

She continued typing.

"The marriage license costs thirty-five dollars," she informed us. "How will you be paying?"

Wow. You couldn't get a decent pair of *socks* in Manhattan for $35. What a bargain.

"Credit card," I responded, as I handed her my black American Airlines Visa card, the points from which I intended to put toward the airfare for the African safari Kit and I were planning. She took the card and I shot Kit a look that said, *This is all moving so quickly and easily and cheaply.*

She ran the card, I signed the receipt, and she handed over the marriage license for us both to sign. I scanned it quickly before applying my signature. I felt a sudden onset of butterflies seeing the words "Marriage License" above the names "Michael T. Ausiello" and "Christopher E. Cowan." I passed it over to Kit to sign.

"Where do we go now?" I asked the lady behind the glass.

"Are you having your ceremony here?"

"Yes."

She handed us a piece of paper titled "Marriage Ceremony Information."

"Wait twenty-four hours and then return with your marriage certificate," she said.

Um . . . *Whatchoo talkin' about, Willis?* was what I *wanted* to say. I shot Kit and Nina a panicked look.

"We need to get married *today*," I stressed to her, without explaining that the reason we couldn't come back in twenty-four hours was because the marriage bureau was closed on the weekend, which put us at Monday and Kit started chemo on Monday and who knew what fresh hell awaited us *after* Monday and besides we *really* needed to come out of this day with a win.

"You need a judicial waiver for that," she informed us. Oh . . . that was all? Phew. Easy peasy. One quick question: *What the fuck is a judicial waiver?!?* was what I *wanted* to say. Instead, I cleared my throat and calmly inquired, "What?"

"If you want to get married today, you need to go across the street to 60 Centre Street and get a judge to sign what's called a judicial waiver."

I looked at the time. It was now 2:45 p.m.

"You close at three-forty-five, yes?" I asked.

She nodded.

"Are we going to make it back here in time?"

She glanced at her watch, gave us one of those *You're fucked* expressions, and said, "You better hurry."

I stared at Kit. "Are we doing this?"

Without hesitation, Kit said, "Less talking. More running."

And with that, the three of us raced out of the marriage bureau, dodging brides and grooms and brides and brides and grooms and grooms left and right. Kit was moving at such a fast clip that I almost felt the need to remind him that he had a fist-sized tumor in his asshole.

We made it out onto the street, and it was clear that Kit, who was valiantly leading the charge, had no fucking clue what direction to head on Centre Street. The lady had said "across the street," but in *what* direction? As Kit began sprinting north, with me and Nina in tow, I imagined his infamous *Cannonball Run*–themed iPad alarm music blaring in the background. He took notice of a street number, stopped in his tracks, paused, and screamed, "Other direction!" He started running south and we followed right behind him.

I looked at Kit, and there was a childlike excitement and sense of purpose in his eyes. It reminded me of the time we were at the front of the line to get into the Magic Kingdom one year earlier, just as they were opening the park gates at 9 a.m., and we raced through the desolate Main Street ahead of thousands of other frenzied tourists, most of whom, like us, were heading to Space Mountain.

Kit spotted a cop and asked him where 60 Centre Street was, and the officer pointed across the street to the unmissably massive, globally iconic, hexagonally shaped, heavily pillared, granite structure—aka the New York Supreme Court Building. Oh, shit scrotums. *That's* 60 Centre Street? That's the kind of building that requires six layers of security to penetrate—*four layers more than we currently had time for.* Also, why was the seemingly mile-long marble staircase leading to the entrance teeming with so many people?

As I got closer, I noticed huge Panavision-y cameras and fancy lighting and boom mics and a smattering of important-looking millennials brandishing walkie-talkies.

Ugh. It was a film shoot.

"Excuse me, what's going on here?" Kit queried one of the bystanders.

"I think *Law & Order: SVU* is shooting an episode," the obvious tourist responded, excitedly.

Kit and I exchanged a look, the subtext of which was basically *Seriously?!*

The three of us made our way past the herd of looky-loos before being blocked by one of the power-tripping, walkie-talkied millennials, who ordered us to stand down. Kit was having none of it.

"We have to get inside now or we won't be able to get married today," Kit pleaded.

"It will just be a few more minutes," the bouncer responded. "Thank you for your patience."

I looked past *Law & Order*'s guard dog and noticed the cameras weren't even rolling. The crew was merely setting up for the shot.

"This is bullshit," I groaned to Kit. "They're not even shooting."

That was all the confirmation Kit needed. "Let's go!" he shouted, as he pushed past the perimeter and started rushing up the cascade of marble stairs, Nina and I right behind him.

"*Stop!*" the bouncer yelled as we zoomed past the production and toward the front entrance. Nina started hysterically laughing at the absurdity of it all, which made Kit laugh. Which made me laugh until I remembered, you know, the cancer stuff.

Once we were inside the rotunda, it took us a few minutes to get through the security line and head up to the judge's chambers on the third floor. We entered the modest-sized office—the waiting area of which was empty—and approached the nonthreatening-looking man in his forties standing behind the counter.

"Hi, we need to get married today and we need a judicial waiver," I said with palpable angst, as I placed our marriage license before him.

The gentleman, who was obviously operating at about ten speeds slower than me, idly looked up at the dusty clock hanging on the wall.

It was a few minutes past three. "The judge is done for the day," he informed us. "He leaves at around three."

"We were told we had until *three-forty-five*," I replied angrily.

"That's when the *marriage bureau* closes," he clarified. "The judge works different hours."

I looked at Kit, my eyes welling up. We were fucked. Just as I was about to wave the white flag and declare that today's marriage ceremony was simply not meant to be, Kit said, "We have extenuating circumstances."

"Oh, *do* you," the gentleman responded, somewhat playfully. "What exactly are your *extenuating circumstances?*"

"I was just diagnosed with cancer," Kit informed him. "I start chemo on Monday, which is why we need to get married today."

The clerk looked at the two of us with a mix of suspicion and concern. I looked at him with a mix of *Fuck yeah* and *My fiancé just shut this shit* down.

"It's true," I interjected in an effort to allay any misgivings he might have. "We literally just came from Sloan Kettering."

"I'm very sorry to hear that," he said, looking back up at the clock, which now read 3:08 p.m. "Let me see what I can do."

He disappeared into a back room, and without missing a beat, Kit turned to us and proudly, unapologetically declared, "I just played the cancer card."

He was making cancer jokes. This tenacious and resilient and remarkable man standing before me, the one who just hours ago had learned that he might have less than a year to live, was making cancer jokes.

The clerk returned a few minutes later with good news. "You're all set," he said as he handed us the signed waiver. He then looked at Kit and genuinely added, "I wish you all the best."

We both profusely thanked him for his kindness and compassion and, most of all, his assistance. We then revved up our internal accelerators and made a beeline for the elevator. It was now 3:24 p.m. We had T minus twenty minutes before the marriage bureau closed up shop. Once in the lobby, we raced for the exit and . . . before we could feel the sun on our faces, we were stopped cold.

Law & Order: Mother Fucking SVU struck again.

"We're in the middle of a scene, please wait here until we give the all-clear," a different, female walkie-talkied millennial ordered us.

"I'm sorry," Kit interrupted, his patience for any remaining obstacles officially at zero. He charged past the perimeter and announced to the entire crowd, "We have a wedding to get to!"

Before I had time to fully appreciate the brazenness of his actions, I was running to play catch-up. As we raced down the steps, I heard what I believed to be a perturbed director bellow, "Hold please! Reset!" And then I realized *SVU*'s bouncer had not been fibbing. They were, indeed, in the middle of shooting a scene this time. Or at least they *had been*. I caught a fleeting glimpse of the actors lining the staircase. I didn't immediately recognize them. I began to question whether this was an *SVU* production after all. Regardless, I felt badly for fucking up their shot. But not as badly as I would have felt if they had gotten their shot and we had missed our wedding.

With Kit continuing to lead the charge, we cleared the steps, bounded back across the street to the marriage bureau, and were reunited with the middle-aged gentleman at the front desk. It was now 3:35 p.m.

"We're back," I declared with nervous excitement. "We have our judicial waiver. We're ready to get married."

He handed us a new ticket number, A172.

"We're OK with the time, right?" I asked. "The place isn't going to shut down at three-forty-five?"

"As long as you receive a ticket before three-forty-five, you're good," he assured us.

"*Thank you*," I said as I turned to Kit and smiled. "We made it."

Holy shit testes. To quote my favorite line from *Muppets Take Manhattan*, "Extra. Extra. *Somebody's getting married!*"

We proceeded over to the area near the four chapel rooms. The crowd had thinned considerably. The board read A150, and I felt my emotions ramping up as the reality started to hit me that in less than fifteen minutes I was going to take one of the biggest steps of my entire life.

As the counter steadily climbed to A172, I felt myself approach high doh. The tears were now streaming down my cheeks as I envisioned what it would be like to marry the man of my dreams only to watch him slowly, painfully slip away from me. Kit saw me struggling to hold it together. "It's starting to hit me," I informed him.

"Don't you back out now," he deadpanned.

Not a chance, I assured him, telepathically. I was all in. I was a fucking *basket case* at the moment, but I was all in. I'd never been so sure of anything in my entire life.

My breakdown was temporarily interrupted by one of the circa 1980s New Jersey high school prom brides, who was having a meltdown of her own about twenty yards away. "I can't believe you are doing this to me on my fucking wedding day!" she shouted into her cell phone. "You knew *exactly* what time you were supposed to be here. Don't even bother coming. I *hate* you, Mom!"

Kit, Nina, and I shot each other a "Gotta love New York City?" look, before my attention returned to the rising numbers on the counter . . . A168, A169, A170 . . . I felt a rush of gratitude toward the Universe for compelling me almost thirteen years ago to snap out of my 9/11 malaise and attend that Gay Sports Ball at Webster Hall.

A171, A172 . . .

"Ausiello-Cowan!" a man shouted.

Kit and I simultaneously shouted, "Here," as the man behind the counter handed some paperwork to a no-nonsense, petite brunette woman who had clearly cranked out a million of these today alone and was ready to get her weekend on.

"Follow me, please," Ms. Jaded McJadedson ordered us, before leading us into one of the nondescript chapel rooms. Our designated room was completely empty save for a podium and a generic, emotionless, ugly-yet-colorful watercolor painting hanging on the wall. She took her place behind the podium and, before Kit and I were even in our positions, asked, "Do you have rings?"

"Yes," Kit replied, reaching into his jacket pocket, pulling out the plastic spider rings from Atlantic City, and placing them on the podium.

"We have special vows . . ." I interjected, my voice cracking because I was already a blubbering mess.

"You can recite those after I leave," she said curtly, as she noticed the spider rings and did a double take. And then a triple take. And then a quadruple take. And then she . . . cracked a smile.

"We are gathered here today to witness the exchanging of marriage vows between Christopher and Michael," she began. "If there is anyone present today who knows of any reason that this couple should not be married, let them speak now or forever hold their peace."

Kit and I turned around and looked at the only other person in the room, Nina. The three of us laughed.

"Please face each other and join hands," she continued, as Kit placed his iPad under his armpit and grabbed my clammy hand. "Do you, Christopher, solemnly declare to take Michael to be your husband?"

"I do," he said, his eyes beginning to water.

"Do you promise to love, honor, cherish, and promise to keep him for as long as you both shall live?"

Fuck, I had forgotten about that line. Sigh.

"I do."

"As a symbol of your promise, please place the ring on his finger."

Kit picked up one of the spider rings and slid it on my finger. Ms. Jaded McJadedson was now beaming. She then turned to me.

"Do you, Michael, solemnly declare to take Christopher to be your husband?"

"I do," I uttered through a torrent of tears and snot.

"Do you promise to love, honor, cherish, and promise to keep him for as long as you both shall live?"

Ugh, there it was again.

"I do."

"As a symbol of your promise, please place the ring on his finger."

I picked the remaining spider ring off the podium and placed it on his finger.

"By the powers vested in me by the great state of New York, I now pronounce you married," she concluded. "You may seal your vows with a kiss."

Kit and I met each other halfway and kissed.

"Congratulations," she said, her frown still firmly planted upside down. "All the best to you both in the future."

She handed us the marriage certificate and exited. I wiped my tears and turned to Nina. "You mind giving us a few minutes?"

"Not at all," she replied. "Just come get me when you're done."

I hadn't prepared any vows, preferring instead to talk off the cuff—a decision I was slightly regretting at the moment. Regardless, I informed Kit that I'd go first.

"We've had our ups and downs over the past thirteen years, but I always knew you were *it* for me," I began, sobbing. "I knew you were the person I wanted to grow old with. I don't know what the future holds for us, and I'd be lying if I said I wasn't a little scared. But you're stuck with me now. I love you with all my heart, Kit. And I'm so proud to be your husband."

Kit, who was now a blubbering mess as well, fired up his iPad. "I wrote my vows, but I'm not sure if I'll be able to get through them," he said, his voice cracking.

"I knew immediately," he began, before pausing to compose himself. He attempted to go on but stopped. "I can't," he said. "Please . . ." He handed me the iPad.

I took the deepest of breaths and started reading his vows aloud.

"I knew immediately after we met that you were the one. The last thirteen years haven't always been easy, but we always find our way. I love you. I love us. We are in this together and now it's official. Nothing can say what you mean to me. You are my best friend and I can't imagine my life without you."

I rested the iPad on the podium and we wrapped our arms around each other. And sobbed.

"I love you, Kit," I cried.

"I love you, Mike."

I didn't want to let go of him. I *couldn't* let go of him. We stood there in the tightest of embraces for what felt like two or three minutes. Kit eventually pulled back, wiped my tears, and kissed me.

I brought Nina back in, and we proceeded to pose for a half-dozen photos with our marriage certificate. I tried my best to crack a smile, but I was still an emotional wreck. Kit, however, was smiling widely and excitedly.

We exited the chapel and took a few more photos in the main room and on the front steps before we hugged Nina goodbye. Kit and I were now standing alone on the corner of Worth and Centre, figuring out what came next.

"Cab it home?" I suggested.

"Let's walk," Kit replied, surprising me yet again. The sun was still out and the temperature was a chilly but comfortable fifty-three degrees—certainly walkable weather. I had figured Kit would be ready to collapse from mental and physical exhaustion at best, moderate rectal pain at worst. Full disclosure, *I* was wiped out.

"You sure?"

"Let's start," he said, cautiously. "See how far we get."

And just like that, he grabbed my hand—one of the tentacles of his spider ring lightly grazing my palm—and we began to make our way due north toward our West Village abode.

On the bright side, a long walk afforded me an opportunity to catch my breath and process the wild eight-hour Tilt-A-Whirl ride we had just climbed off. On the downside, processing the past eight hours was a daunting prospect. I found myself immediately missing the frenzy. As stressful and emotional as it all had been, it had left little time for me to be alone with my thoughts. The marriage stuff in particular had been a perfectly timed distraction coming out of the Sloan appointment. Now all the noise was gone.

As we strolled through the southern tip of the Financial District, a section of the city that was mostly foreign to me, my thoughts drifted to one of my favorite pastimes: daydreaming about my future with Kit. Whenever we found ourselves exploring a new neighborhood—whether it was Manhattan or while on vacation in San Francisco or Portland or Seattle or Austin—we'd fantasize about putting down roots there. But before my brain could entertain the idea of our buying a loft in one of the myriad industrial-looking buildings this far downtown, I heard Dr. Davis whispering in my ear, *Psst. He'll be dead soon, stupid. Time to start coming up with some new dreams.*

Twenty or so minutes passed and we were now entering the heart of Tribeca. I checked in with Kit to gauge his stamina and pain level. He assured me that he was hanging in there. It was at this moment that two things dawned on me: We hadn't spoken the entire walk so far, and this had been our longest uninterrupted period of hand-holding on the streets of New York. It felt good not to care what anyone thought.

Oh, and I was a married fucking man.

As we invaded SoHo—a neighborhood that had played host to our first official post–Webster Hall date at Corallo Trattoria, many a birthday dinner at The Dutch, monthly weekend shopping jaunts to Camper and Cole Haan in search of the perfect shoe, Kit's hair salon Aveda on West Broadway, his beloved place of work (the Wyeth showroom on Spring Street)—I started mourning the life we were leaving behind. And . . . tears. I found myself wondering where Kit's head was at during our uncharacteristically silent journey north, but I decided not to interrupt his peaceful state with an interrogation.

We were now approaching the West Village. Kit's pace had slowed down, as had mine. We started discussing the evening ahead. First up, a much-needed nap. After that, maybe we'd invite a few friends over to toast our nuptials.

We dropped by our favorite liquor store to pick up some booze before swinging by the local chocolate shop to snag some tasty treats. As I planned the night's quaint gathering in my head, I imagined how different things would have been if we had just subtracted cancer from the equation. Maybe we would be headed to a real wedding reception, complete with fun, offbeat but impeccably coordinated outfits; an elaborate flash mob scored to Lady Gaga's new song "Gypsy" that involved the entire wedding party but was, of course, led by me and Kit; and goodie bags featuring select Pretty Bitter items, maybe a Smurf or two, and, just to fuck with everyone, a fake voucher for a free all-expenses-paid cruise to the Greek islands.

As we entered our apartment, armed with two bottles of prosecco and a bag of dark-chocolate nonpareils, we were greeted by our best man, Mister Scooch. Exhaustion quickly overtook us and within two minutes we were both spooning in bed. Because my arms were wrapped tightly around Kit's chest, I noticed immediately when his breathing began to accelerate. I quickly realized it was because he was crying.

"Bodge . . ." I whispered to him as I clutched him tighter. He started crying louder, breathing heavier . . . He turned his body around to face me. I braced for another Sloan-level breakdown.

He attempted to communicate to me, but he was so distraught I could barely make out the words. "Kit, I can't understand what you're saying," I said. "Calm down."

"It takes me months to find a pair of glasses I like," he screamed in anguish. "And all I have is one week to find a doctor to . . ."

He paused to catch his breath.

"*I don't want to die!*" he wailed as he rested his head on my chest. He attempted to speak more, but his hyperventilating body was making that tough. He found a way to get the words out. "I'm going to fight as hard as I can . . . but if I can't fight anymore, promise me you will live for both of us. *Promise me*, Mike."

The expression "hell on earth" had never felt so apropos than in that very moment. Listening to the love of my life painfully, tearfully expressing a passionate will to live just hours after being told he had terminal cancer, and then following that up with a plea for me to live on his behalf, was so excruciatingly painful that I can't find the words now to accurately describe it.

I wanted out of this nightmare. Enough was enough.

As Kit soaked my T-shirt with his tears, I joined the emotional breakdown already in progress. I knew he was waiting for me to respond to his request. But I couldn't give him what he wanted.

No, I will not fucking live for you. Because you are not dying. And if you do *die, I'm going with you. Because a world where you are dead and I am alive is not a world I'm interested in being a part of* is what I *wanted* to say.

Instead, as I cradled him in my arms, my brain went rogue and sent a signal to my mouth.

"I will, Kit. I promise."

7.

Kit and I had our weekend getaway prep down to a science. Just before 10 a.m., I'd head to the National Car Rental office perpendicular to Port Authority to retrieve our vehicle while Kit stayed behind in the apartment, hunting and gathering all of our road-trip essentials: E-ZPass tag, requisite USB car-syncing stereo cords, assorted Target returns, etc. He also used the time to ensure that Mister Scooch had enough food and water to keep him nourished and refreshed during our absence; otherwise we'd find an obnoxious cunt of a cat when we returned.

Once in possession of my temporary wheels, I'd drive to the apartment to retrieve my trusty copilot, calling or texting him when I was five minutes out so he could begin making his way down to the street and avoid getting the tardy man's stink eye from yours truly.

As I turned the corner onto Jane Street in our rented sedan on this inauspicious Saturday, there was Kit standing at the bottom of our brownstone stoop like a puppy dog leashed outside a Starbucks anxiously waiting for his human companion to appear (if Kit had a tail, it would almost certainly have been wagging furiously). Almost thirteen years and sixty some-odd excursions in, I still got the warm and fuzzies upon seeing Kit waiting for me at the curb, partly because *holy shit he was so fucking handsome and he had chosen ME* and partly because it signaled the start of a new adventure.

However, as I approached Kit on this particular morning—roughly twenty-four hours after Sloan Kettering's foremost oncological Grim Reaper had lowered the boom on us—I felt a rush of sadness as the full weight and purpose of this weekend's getaway set in. The fact was, this time, we weren't en route to the Jersey Shore to play Skee-Ball at Frank's Family Fun Center, followed by dinner at the Shrimp Box. We were also not driving to upstate New York to fraternize with the rescued pigs, cows, and goats at the Woodstock Farm Animal Sanctuary. Heading to Maryland to visit my brother David, sister-in-law Pam, niece Lanie, and nephew Will? Nope, not that either. Traveling to Kit's hometown of Millersburg, Pennsylvania, with a trunk full of jumbo blue IKEA bags lined with gifts of every shape and size for our traditional weeklong Christmas visit at his parents'? [*Family Feud* "X" buzz sound]

Well, we *were* heading to see Kit's parents in Millersburg. But it was to inform them that their only child—their pride and joy, their reason for living—had a devastatingly rare and lethal form of cancer that could kill him within a year.

I pulled to the curb, popped the trunk, and watched as Kit loaded in our bags. He then opened the passenger door and let out an enthusiastic "Hi, *huzzzzzband.*"

I gave myself a moment to enjoy how magnificent that word sounded coming out of Kit's mouth before responding with a smile, "Hello, my husband."

Kit plopped the E-ZPass disc on the dashboard, connected my iPhone to the car stereo, then began a minutes-long struggle to find a comfortable sitting position. After attempting several different poses, he reclined his seat all the way back and rested his entire body on its side, facing me. It was agonizing to look on helplessly as he fought to do something as basic as sitting down in a car.

"There we go," he said, letting out a big sigh as he settled into his not-at-all-comfortable-looking position. "That should do the trick."

I leaned in and kissed him on the lips—my subtle way of reminding him that his struggle was my struggle—before stepping on the gas.

Our traditional route out of the city since moving to the West Village six months ago—Jane to Washington to Spring to Varick to the Holland Tunnel—would take us directly past Wyeth's SoHo showroom (which was now open on Saturdays, albeit only from the rich people hours of 11 a.m. to 5 p.m.). It crossed my mind that a quick visit with his work family—to whom Kit had been giving regular, slightly truncated medical updates (i.e., they knew he had cancer but didn't know how bad it was)—might give Kit a little emotional boost on this day of dread.

And an emotional boost for Kit was an emotional boost for me. And I *really* needed an emotional boost. I was a newlywed who was about to become a widower, and in three hours, I would have a hand in destroying the lives of two of my favorite people on the planet.

"We're going to pass right by Wyeth . . ." I reminded Kit. "We're not in any huge rush if you want to drop in and say hello."

"Let's do it," Kit responded without hesitation, as he eyeballed the car's digital clock, which read 10:40 a.m. "The store doesn't open for another twenty minutes, but someone will be there."

As a result of an ongoing gas-line replacement project in the neighborhood, huge swaths of the street outside of Wyeth were barricaded, which made locating a parking spot a challenge. I found an illegal slice of concrete across the street and pulled in.

"I'll wait here," I informed Kit.

"I won't be long."

"There's no rush," I assured him, foregoing my traditional *You've got five minutes we're on a schedule hurry hurry hurry!* neuroses. "Take all the time you need, Bodge."

Kit snapped his seat into its regular upright position and slowly climbed out of the rental. In the rearview mirror, I watched him lightly jog toward the entrance and ring the bell (it was one of those fancy stores with a doorbell to prevent riffraff—i.e., anyone with less than $10 million in liquid assets—from wandering in off the street).

It was roughly four years ago that Kit, getting restless from a ten-month stretch of unemployment, had responded to a super-sketchy-sounding help wanted ad on Craigslist for a temporary gig "photographing furniture in SoHo." He walked into the interview armed with high skepticism and low expectations and walked out with a job.

Within three months, he had become an expert on midcentury furniture, with names like Hans Wegner, Finn Juhl, and Edward Wormley falling off his tongue as if they were first cousins. And his simple, striking, classic photography of such iconic pieces as Wegner's Papa Bear Chair and Juhl's Architect's Desk—images that received prime exposure on the quasi-eBay-for-millionaires site known as 1stdibs—had become the talk of the niche high-end furniture industry. Kit's passion—his gift—had always been still-life photography (he hated the lack of control inherent in human subjects), and Wyeth afforded him the opportunity to tap into his superpower like never before.

Within a year, Kit was essentially appointed Wyeth's creative director/brand ambassador. He also emerged as one of the company's top salespeople, making him even more indispensable in the eyes of his quixotic, painfully shy boss, John Birch, whose extreme fussiness and legendarily high standards rivaled Kit's own extreme fussiness and legendarily high standards.

For the first time in his life, Kit was in the employ of someone he not only respected but revered. To Kit, John was a design god. He loved working for him, learning from him, just being around him.

As I sat there looking at the storefront, I recounted all the times I had excitedly marched up to that front door and peered through the frosted glass hoping to catch a glimpse of Kit gliding across the floor assisting a well-heeled client or ever-so-slightly rearranging a piece of furniture to complete some tableau in his mind. I would then ring the bell and anxiously, excitedly wait for him to get close enough to the door to notice it was me on the other side. Once eye contact was made, his face would light up and he'd mouth the word "What?!" before opening the door and greeting me with a kiss. Those precious seconds between ringing that doorbell and locking eyes with Kit were among my favorite seconds ever. He loved having me there just as much as I loved being there.

Sometimes I would show up unannounced at the end of the day, either to take him out to dinner or to just enjoy a glass of rosé with coworkers Missi, Dakota, Julie, Evan, and Tiffany (a common post-closing ritual at Wyeth). And if he was still working, I was more than content to park myself on some $100K sofa and continue watching Kit do his thing in the place he loved with the people he loved. (And if I was really lucky, I'd catch a glimpse of one of Wyeth's A-list clients, like Jennifer Aniston or the Olsen twins or Steven Spielberg.)

After he'd spent years trudging through unhappy work experiences and squandering his immense talent, it made me happy, relieved, and proud to see Kit ascending to his professional peak.

Only to now watch him get ripped away from it.

Was his brief visit this morning a quick hello or the start of a long goodbye? With Dr. Davis's dire prognosis ringing in my ear, I couldn't help but fear it was the latter. And the prospect that Kit might have already put in his final day at Wyeth was just too much for me to bear. And I started sobbing. And I continued sobbing for ten straight minutes, finally stopping when I saw the front door open and Kit walk out. Among my goals this weekend was to avoid letting Kit see me lose my shit.

As he approached the car, I noticed he wasn't alone. He had friends. In one hand he was clutching a plush vintage Nauga monster doll and in the other he was cradling a Kay Bojesen–designed wooden monkey, two signature Wyeth accessories Kit had long coveted. The monkey, in particular, was a favorite of his. John had about a dozen of them embedded throughout the store—sort of like a *Where's Waldo?* for the 1 percent—and Kit had taken great pleasure in finding fun little spots for them to hide out. The monkey was like Wyeth's unofficial mascot (a very, very, very expensive mascot). This was the first time I was seeing it out in the real world, and in Kit's hands no less. My heart skipped a beat.

"Wedding presents!" he declared upon opening the car door. He positioned his treasures in the backseat, as if they were our children. He then whipped out his camera and started taking pictures of our new passengers.

"John was there?" I inquired.

"Yep," he responded, adjusting the toys' positioning before snapping away a few more pictures.

"And he just gave you these?"

"Yep," Kit said, grabbing one last photo before sliding back into his seat, searching for the same sideways position as before.

As I took stock of our two new additions in the backseat through the rearview mirror, I was unable to hold back the tears. So much for me suppressing my meltdowns around Kit.

"What did you tell everyone?" I asked.

"I said I'm starting chemo Monday and will likely be out for a few weeks." Kit paused before solemnly adding, "They know it's serious."

I wiped my tears, planted a kiss on his lips, and shifted the car into drive.

We were barely on the Jersey side of the Holland Tunnel when Kit pulled out of his duffel bag our plastic white salad bowl and a package of his beloved Boogie Wipes (a relatively new product invented as a gentler Kleenex alternative for kids battling colds, which, as Kit discovered through trial and error, doubled as a gentler toilet paper alternative for adults battling Stage 4 rectal cancer).

"You may have to bear with me shitting in the car," he sheepishly informed me. "I have to seize the moment when and if it comes. I'm sorry."

The idea of Kit shitting inside a salad bowl while in the passenger seat of a moving vehicle was not nearly as upsetting to me as Kit feeling shame or embarrassment for having to shit inside a salad bowl while in the passenger seat of a moving vehicle. Our new normal was changing by the minute and I had no choice but to just fucking roll with it.

"Please don't apologize," I responded, somewhat angrily. "We're married now, Bodge. I'm pretty sure that means you can shit next to me in a car."

Kit, meanwhile, shifted our literally shitty conversation to a figurative one.

"What are we going to tell my parents?"

One of the blessings of the disorientingly wide array of opinions we'd received—from Dr. Barnes's decidedly rosy outlook to Dr. Abbott's brutally honest yet modestly optimistic stance to Dr. Davis's apocalyptic forecast—was that we had a smorgasbord of truth to play with. I had my own personal opinions about each of the prognoses—namely, that

Davis's dismal prediction was likely the most in line with reality, based on my own covert Internet research and the general strength of the Sloan Kettering brand. But I tried to convince myself that was all they were—my opinions. It was entirely possible my cancer baggage was coloring my perspective, causing me to put more stock in a worst-case scenario. The Universe tricked me into having hope that my mom and dad would overcome their own health battles, and fuck if I was going to be fooled for a third time. Maybe I was reflexively gravitating toward the path of least optimism so I didn't have my heart torn out again?

I decided to keep this internal tug-of-war to myself. As I saw it, Kit needed to be armed with as much hope and optimism as possible as he headed into battle next week, and that meant downplaying the Davis of it all.

It was a helpful mindset to be in as we made our way to Millersburg. I wanted to do anything possible to spare putting his mom and dad through the same emotional trauma Kit and I had endured at the hands of Davis. The thought of sitting his parents down and telling them that this time next year their son might very well be dead was too painful to even entertain.

But this was not my decision to make. Up until now, Kit had been playing it very close to the vest with them on the information front, and he ordered me to do the same. He had been OK with our telling them—via speakerphone and with nary a trace of angst in our voices— that a growth had been found and sent off for testing. And despite their calling and emailing us practically daily asking if the results had come in, Kit had kept stalling. He had felt it best that we drop the C-word to them in person.

But we had yet to discuss *how* exactly to drop it.

"We need to pull the Band-Aid off slowly," Kit continued. "It's going to be hard enough for them to hear that I have cancer. I think we just tell them it's rare and there's not a lot known about it, which is why there's a wide range of opinions. One doctor said I can beat it, another said I'm facing the fight of my life."

"And that's all true," I assured him. "It's not like we're lying."

"They're going to be devastated regardless," Kit sighed. I could see him through the corner of my eye fighting back tears.

"Maybe we tell them the good news first," I suggested.

Kit wiped a tear cascading down his cheek before agreeing. "Yes. Definitely. You packed the marriage certificate?"

"Yep," I confirmed.

There was no doubt in my mind that word of our nuptials would be received positively by his mom and dad—something you would've had a tough time convincing me of almost twelve years ago in the wake of my tense first meeting with Marilyn in Kit's hospital room following his appendectomy. In the ensuing decade-plus, Kit's mom and dad had become something of PFLAG poster parents. They had embraced Kit's sexual identity as lovingly and unconditionally as they had embraced the man he loved. I felt like a member of the family because they *made me* feel like a member of the family. They spoiled the shit out of me and I loved it.

Prior to any of our visits, they stocked up on my favorite beverages—namely Diet Raspberry Snapple and Diet Coke—while also preparing a plethora of vegetarian/healthy options to supplement the traditional Pennsylvania meat and grease-soaked offerings on throwback-minded Kit's food and beverage wish list. And to underscore just how comfortable I was with them, I wouldn't think twice about giving them shit if the Snapple or soda they purchased was past the expiration date. (As I educated them early on, the aspartame in diet beverages spoils after six months, sullying any/all flavor—hence the importance of checking the sell-by date.) I loved how shocked and appalled they'd both get when I informed them that their local, dusty, hundred-year-old mom-and-pop supermarket—which probably received one fresh shipment of Snapple and Diet Coke a decade—had sold them outdated product.

I thoroughly enjoyed being around Bob and Marilyn, probably even more than Kit did, since my relationship with them didn't carry with it thirty or forty years of baggage. To wit, Kit greatly appreciated having me around to run interference with his mom, who, upon greeting us, always had a million questions about what we'd been up to. I loved that she had such interest in our lives, but it pushed all of Kit's anxiety buttons. He had major interrogation-phobia, a likely result of a lifetime spent hiding his sexuality. So even the most innocent and casual of inquisitions caused him to shut down.

This was why, early into our relationship, I was prone to walking on eggshells whenever I needed to extract information out of him. I eventually developed certain tricks that turned my fact-finding missions into something of a playful game. My most successful strategy involved showing up at Kit's bedside in the morning with his favorite Starbucks breakfast and, just as he was biting into his Danish, sheepishly calling a "Morning Meeting." Those two words signaled to Kit the arrival of a possibly serious discussion that would likely include a string of questions ("We need to decide what we're getting your parents for Christmas") and maybe a grievance/concern or two ("If you're going to wear my shirts, please hang them back up in the closet when you're done"). He appreciated the heads-up, even if the words "Morning Meeting" triggered a Pavlovian eye-roll. It was akin to a parent turning a fork full of spinach into an airplane.

Really, Kit's parents were two of the lowest-maintenance people I'd ever met. They wanted to see us as often as possible, but they never nagged us about it. And when we *did* visit, they gave us zero grief when, mere seconds after greeting them with a hug, we marched right upstairs to the spare bedroom to take a six-hour nap.

More than anything, it was nice to have a home base, to feel like I belonged somewhere. My brothers had their own wives and kids and traditions, leaving me to feel like something of an outcast. But ever since 2002, the year I'd attended my first Cowan Christmas, I felt like I had a family of my own. And I was so grateful.

As we continued to cruise along I-78 en route to Pennsylvania, Kit—who in addition to being my copilot also functioned as the car's official deejay—scrolled through my iTunes library and, without any prompting from me, teed up my newest obsession, Lady Gaga's *Artpop*. Mother Monster's latest album had received a mixed-to-tepid reaction from critics and fans alike, but this dyed-in-the-wool fan couldn't get enough of it. And I'd made Kit listen to it enough times that he was practically addicted by proxy. We already had tickets to the Madison Square Garden stop of her *Artpop* Ball tour that spring. Hopefully, by then, the chemo would have shrunk Kit's tumor to the point where he could attend comfortably.

Over the next forty-five some-odd minutes, Kit kept busy playing games on his iPad while I drifted off into *Artpop*-land, occasionally tuning out the cancer noise assaulting my brain long enough to get lost in (and occasionally butcher) the lyrics. By the time the final track, "Applause," began, we were closing in on Harrisburg, which meant we were closing in on our traditional Target pit stop.

Not only was Target one of Kit's favorite retail chains from a design/branding perspective, it was also among his most rewarding shopping experiences. It blended three of his favorite things: clean lines, big aisles, and good bargains.

Kit required *at least* an hour of Target shopping time—long enough to roam every aisle in search of the essentials (toothpaste, Magic Erasers, Orbit bubble gum), the elusive stealth sale (a ten-pack of ballpoint pens we didn't need for only 50 cents!), the dreaded-by-me, throw-caution-to-the-winds gamble (new lamps for the bedroom!), and—my favorite—a surprise or two for yours truly (typically a piece of clothing, like a sweater with a slimming pattern, a retro *Star Wars* T-shirt or super-cozy, canoodly pajamas).

Our typical Target routine looked like this: We entered the store, grabbed shopping carts, and went our separate ways before meeting at the cash registers to conduct a formal review of our items. I was almost always done about thirty minutes before Kit. Lucky for me, every Target was equipped with a fountain soda machine and a healthy assortment of magazines, so I had plenty to do to pass the time as I nervously awaited the arrival of his overflowing cart. When at long last he'd appear, I'd wheel my cart over to his and we'd compare our items to weed out any overlap (typically toiletries, which represented most of what I'd pick up). Then Kit would cautiously take me through the gamble pile—stuff he knew I'd veto but figured he'd give a shot anyway, like an accent table for the dining room, or a throw rug for the foyer, or yet another scratching post for Mister Scooch to defiantly thumb his nose at. I'd typically respond to each of these items with an eye-roll and some variation of "Seriously, Kit?!"—triggering a "Come on, pretty *please*" response from him. In the end, I'd almost always cave because Target Kit was another one of my favorite Kits, and the truth was, he'd probably get home, decide it didn't quite match the décor, and throw it in the return pile anyway. With the negotiation portion of our Target dance complete, we'd search for whichever register had the shortest line or the cutest, hopelessly straight cashier, split our orders roughly down the middle so that we were both shouldering a fair amount of the fiscal burden (because we were one of those long-term couples that kept their finances separate in order to maintain some semblance of independence), and check out.

Today, as we pulled into the parking lot, Kit's enthusiasm was markedly more muted. I wondered how much of his traditional full hour of allotted shopping time he would end up using. What *did* a person get at Target the day after being told he had only a year to live?

"I'm just going to bop around a bit," he said upon entering the store. "I won't be long." Kit commandeered a shopping cart while I opted to leash myself to the fountain soda machine in the Target Café for a much-needed Diet Coke. I'm typically in autopilot mode before my body has its first taste of fountain Diet Coke. And Target, much like Chipotle, had mastered the perfect mixture of syrup and carbonation. (At the other end of the spectrum, 7-Eleven and Subway had the worst.) My mouth was salivating with anticipation.

The café line moved quickly and, before I knew it, I was filling my 32-ounce cup with Diet Coke from the self-service machine. I slapped on the lid, slipped in the straw, and took the telltale first sip. And the verdict was . . . chemically saporous. I found myself longing for the pre-cancer Target days when Kit would hover over me at the soda machine, waiting to test my freshly poured Diet Coke, and, after doing so, declare—via an orgasmic, Mike-mocking tone—"Mmm, good mix. Good mix."

I took a seat and promptly began marveling at the alternate universe playing out in front of me wherein people were merrily shopping without the imminent death of a loved one hanging over their heads. I desperately searched for a woebegone face in the crowd, hoping to spot someone experiencing a similar End of Days crisis as mine. I fixated on the suburban soccer mom sitting across from me, alongside her perfect-looking husband and two perfect-looking children eating their gross-looking Target hot dogs. Back in the olden, pre-apocalypse days, Kit and I would be jointly cruising her husband, with one of us— likely Kit—whispering to the other, "Hot for daddy?"

Kit's shopping spree lasted a historically-low-by-Target-standards fifteen minutes. He checked out and met up with me in the café, armed with just one heartbreakingly small, sad bag of loot (way down from his usual ten or so). Before I even inquired what was inside, he pulled out two big blocks of multicolored stationery, each clear plastic cube containing two hundred note cards and envelopes, twenty-five for every color of the rainbow and then some. All told, four hundred of the brightest, cheeriest, happiest-looking note cards I'd ever seen.

"They were on sale—five bucks apiece," he bragged. "I figure we can use them to write thank-you notes."

Jesus. Despite everything he was going through and was *about* to go through, he managed to *still* find the best bargain in Target. And it spoke volumes about his optimism—and maybe his denial—that he had purchased enough note cards to carry us through retirement. His resilience and spirit and perseverance filled me with such love it took everything in me not to throw my arms around him and beg him to promise me that we had a lifetime of Target runs ahead of us. Instead, I contained the emotional tsunami swelling inside me, save for an errant tear or two, and proceeded to the soda machine to refill my cup. We then made our way out to the car.

As we approached the car, Kit asked me to pop the trunk 'cause he needed to get something out of one of our bags. He didn't say what. Only once we were settled in the front seat did I notice he had grabbed his pot paraphernalia (i.e., one-hitter, lighter, and pouch containing the weed).

"Before we get to Millersburg, I'm going to need to stop somewhere and take a hit," he informed me, matter-of-factly.

Two weeks ago, before Dr. Voight declared he was "concerned about Christopher," such a sentence would've made my blood boil. It also would've surprised me, considering that after nearly two years of escalating tensions over Kit's increasing pot use, he had signed off on some new, extremely rigid parameters put forth by me. Basically, he was not allowed to get high in my presence or bring pot into my/ our apartment. I was forced to set such strict boundaries because he was miraculously able to find the tiniest loophole in all of my previous requests. ("You said I couldn't *smoke* weed at home. You didn't say I couldn't *inhale* it through a vaporizer.")

Now I had zero qualms about Kit's getting high. In fact, since the moment he'd come home from the hospital following his biopsy, I'd been encouraging it. In what felt like a nanosecond, pot went from being my sworn enemy to one of my dearest, most dependable friends. Yes, it had put me through hell the past two years, but, ironically enough, if Kit hadn't already been such an expert, he wouldn't have been heading into this emotionally terrifying, physically painful journey with a proven palliative tool under his belt. I still hadn't fulfilled the hospital bedside promise I'd made him two weeks ago to break my pot cherry, but I had a feeling that day was coming.

In the meantime, I had my wine.

I for *sure* needed wine to get me through these next twenty-four hours, and it just so happened that there was a strip mall in Halifax, Pennsylvania, the town neighboring Millersburg, that contained a liquor store *and* enough deserted parking lot for Kit to get baked in relative seclusion. As we approached said shopping plaza and neared some of the childhood touchstones that held special meaning for Kit (and now me), I wondered what Pennsylvania's open-container laws were. The thought of Millersburg existing *without* Kit was so torturous it necessitated some type of brain-numbing substance.

Kit had a love/hate relationship with his hometown. Like an ex he could never quite get over, Millersburg simultaneously captivated and haunted him. There was always a tinge of pride in his voice when he described its smallness, vis-à-vis his customary "It doesn't have a single traffic light!" I always read it as "Yep, I grew up in the middle of nowhere, and I got *out*!" For Millersburg, and its modest size, was the root of a lot of angst.

Being different—gay, artsy, font-obsessed—in small-town eighties America had its challenges. "There are no secrets in Millersburg," Kit often lamented to me. "Everyone knows everyone." But as he grew older, and his life got bigger, Millersburg's diminutiveness became its biggest selling point in his eyes. And it was what drew him back.

As we drove through Halifax, we passed the first landmark—

Sorrento's Pizzeria, home of Kit's favorite submarine sandwich since he was old enough to eat. (The secret to their hoagies' success, he informed me early on, was the homemade bread.) And, as we entered Millersburg, the markers started hitting us rapid-fire. There was the Susquehanna riverbank at which he spent many a summer searching for curious-looking rocks and signs of wildlife with his friend Jen (not to be confused with his Florida-based BFF, also named Jen). There was the secret spot under the bridge trestle where he would hang out with his then best friend, Scotty. The post office trash can that he saw as a treasure chest (for inside it, there were often discarded catalogs full of shiny new things to covet). The five-and-dime (now a beauty parlor) he visited every day after school to buy candy with the money he made returning his classmates' lunch trays (he charged a dime, which, not-so-coincidentally, was exactly the amount of change that was left after they paid for their 90-cent meals). The restaurant at the Millersburger Hotel where he worked as a host. The CVS where he took a job as cashier/candy-aisle stock boy to pay back his dad after he wrecked their car (he proudly proclaimed that it was the most stunningly staged and curated candy aisle CVS had ever seen). His grandmother's house, the site of many a backyard fish fry. Kit's childhood home, the left side of a duplex house, which his parents still owned and rented out. And lastly his parents' current home, a beautifully restored 1850s Georgian Colonial that held nearly as many memories for me as it did for Kit.

"Turn here," Kit advised me, leading us away from his house, over the train tracks and back toward the river. His beloved, deserted trestle bridge was now in spitting distance. "Pull over. You can keep the car running. Just give me five minutes."

I put the car in park and watched as Kit grabbed his camera and one-hitter before hopping out and walking briskly under the modest bridge, toward the riverbank. He disappeared from view.

I immediately felt an overwhelming urge to shut the car off and race after him, partly because I didn't want to be left alone with nothing but my thoughts. And partly because I didn't want him to do anything stupid, like pull a Virginia Woolf and fill his jacket pockets with rocks before walking slowly into the river.

I rolled the window down to listen for a cathartic wail, or maybe some gentle weeping. But all I could hear was the sound of the flowing river, an occasional bird chirping. I took a deep breath, closed my now tear-soaked eyes, and just listened to Millersburg.

Upon opening my eyes, I saw Kit walking toward the car. He didn't look like someone who had just had an emotional breakdown. There were no rocks falling out of his pockets. In fact, as he climbed back into the car and I saw him up close, his face was resolute, not despondent. He leaned in, kissed me, and said, "Let's do this."

Roughly twenty minutes later, we sat Bob and Marilyn down in the living room and we did it. There were no violent breakdowns. No ambulances were called to the scene. There was just quiet shock. And deep sadness. And lots of tears. And no shortage of jokes from Bob about Kit hitting the jackpot by marrying me without a prenup. That was followed by some hugging. Which was followed by some more crying. And then Kit put his Genius Bar cap on and retired to the dining room table with his parents to figure out why their two-year-old iMac kept crashing. I, meanwhile, ventured upstairs to take a nap.

8.

It was now Monday, we were back home in the West Village, and Kit—his first chemo appointment mere hours away—was scouring our kitchen cabinets. He was looking for "The Lurker." He was focusing his search on the bottom cupboard that he'd tagged as his own private "junk drawer" since I moved in last August. Among the items inside: his favorite candy (Swedish Fish, Lemonhead, Root Beer Barrels, and Chick-O-Sticks), a smattering of iWhatever cords, a half-dozen 50-cent-off Boogie Wipe coupons (did I mention that each pouch contained an adhesive coupon on the underside of the opening flap and my adorably thrifty husband was determined to accumulate enough to score a free pack?), miscellaneous camera equipment, a hard drive or two, and a mass stash of random novelty items, among which, he now believed, was "The Lurker."

I pointed out that it was possible "The Lurker" was hiding out in his man cave in Williamsburg, but he insisted otherwise. "I remember putting it in here," he said.

It was on our way back from Millersburg yesterday that Kit had experienced his "Lurker" epiphany. Mere moments after declaring that the best way to flip the bird right in cancer's ugly face was to give his XXL rectal tumor a name, he recalled a trinket he had picked up at San Diego Comic-Con two years prior. (I'd begged him to take a few days off from Wyeth to join me at the annual geekapalooza to build out/decorate *TVLine's* greenroom, aka the first stop some of TV's biggest A-listers would make before convening in the adjacent studio for an on-camera interview with yours truly. Kit used one of the lulls in the schedule to brave the nerd-drenched convention floor, and returned an hour later with the most Kit-like collection of keepsakes: a T-shirt featuring a cartoon rendering of a burly daddy bear wearing nothing but a blindingly pink Speedo; a retro, circa-1970s poster promoting 3-D "approved stereo vision" glasses for home television viewing; an artsy-looking limited edition *Muppet Show* print—a gift for me!—and, as I vaguely recall, the aforementioned Lurker figurine.)

Kit hereby resolved to call his tumor "The Lurker." Now he just had to find the namesake figurine, something he had been too tired to do when we got home late last night, hence the search-and-recovery operation currently under way this morning in our teensy kitchen. The seeming urgency behind the mission perplexed me, but mostly I was just happy he was keeping his mind focused on something other than his fast-approaching three-way at Sloan Kettering with etoposide and cisplatin.

While he was emptying the contents of the cabinet onto the kitchen floor, I was on the sofa tearfully polishing off a draft of history's most bittersweet Facebook post: a joint announcement alerting our family and friends of both Kit's cancer diagnosis and our subsequent shotgun nuptials. When I first pitched it to him last week, Kit was initially against the idea of broadcasting his plight on social media. His social-media presence was pretty much limited to about a dozen monthly Instagram posts, primarily consisting of pictures of random objects he encountered around the city (a lonely salt shaker on a restaurant table, a tattered umbrella abandoned on Eighth Avenue following a rainstorm) and cat porn (NSFW close-ups of Mister Scooch's naughty bits). He wasn't crazy about having something so personal become so public. But even more than the privacy invasion, he worried people would pity him, a fate *worse* than death in his eyes.

So, over the weekend, in between Diet Coke runs on I-78, I slowly, tenderly attempted to chip away at his doubts, holding up my former *EW* colleague Jeff Jensen's moving, eloquent, candid, inspiring Facebook updates about his wife Amy's battle with brain cancer as an example of the good that can come from sharing one's story. The friends and family members who followed Jeff on Facebook seemed genuinely grateful for the updates, as difficult as some of them might've been to read.

I also had my own selfish reasons for wanting to go public. The months ahead were no doubt going to be exponentially more difficult than the past three weeks (and that's saying something, since the past three weeks blew massive amounts of chunks), and the thought of having a regular cheering section on Facebook was tremendously comforting. And, on a practical job-related level, it would save me from having to explain to my work associates—publicists, producers, etc.— one by one why I'd been, and would continue to be, slow to respond to their emails for the foreseeable future. Also, perhaps as a result of my fifteen years working in media and seeing the harm that can come from poor communication, I wanted to be in control of the messaging.

Heck, I just wanted to be in control of *something*.

So, about an hour into our drive home yesterday, Kit reluctantly agreed to let me chronicle his cancer fight on my personal Facebook page, provided he got to vet the posts before I pushed them live.

"Here it is!" Kit exclaimed from the kitchen, before bounding over to the couch and reintroducing me to "The Lurker." I instantly remembered him for what he was: a classic toy soldier reimagined as a campy, glow-in-the-dark B-movie monster. The two-inch figure was enclosed in a sealed, clear wrapper and affixed to a hot pink label emblazoned with the comic book–fonted words "The Lurker." The overall vibe was silly and smart with just a hint of terror. It was, holy fucking shit, *Kit*!

Kit then walked over to the accent table next to our high-backed, red-cushioned IKEA chair, grabbed the ceramic middle-finger statue he'd so proudly procured at Atlantic City's foremost 99-cent store, and positioned it in the middle of our coffee table. He then placed The

Lurker directly in front of the middle-finger statue. Talk about clear and concise messaging, not to mention a beautiful symbol of cheeky defiance.

As I looked at the darkly comic art installation on the coffee table before me, I *got* now why Kit had been so determined to debut it before we left for Sloan. He was flipping cancer the proverbial bird, and he was doing so on Day 1 of the war. Dr. Davis's dispiriting, demoralizing diagnosis be damned, my husband was in it to win it.

With the Lurker diorama assembled, I asked Kit if he was up for reading and (hopefully) approving the first dispatch of our Facebook Cancer Diary. I could see him mentally shift gears before hesitantly saying, "OK." He took the laptop, placed it on the kitchen counter, and started reading.

Michael Ausiello
March 24, 2014 •

Some big news to share—some of it good, some of it less so. Let's get the crappy news out of the way first.

Two weeks ago, Kit was diagnosed with an extremely rare, rather aggressive, high-grade neuroendocrine cancer. Because it's such an unusual form of this disease, there is little in the way of data about prognosis, but his doctors at Memorial Sloan Kettering are hopeful that an aggressive chemo cocktail will melt away the fist-sized tumor currently nestled in the lower part of his gastrointestinal tract.

Treatment begins today and continues through Wednesday (all of the outpatient variety), and then, after a three-week respite, the three-day-on, three-week-off cycle continues. This could go on for anywhere from three to four months.

One variable: Docs detected two tiny nodules in his lungs that could be related to the primary tumor. They're too small to biopsy, so his docs are taking a wait-and-see approach on that front: If the nodules vanish during chemo, then it's obvious there has been spread. And if they stick around, it's probably unrelated. Again, the goal is for the chemo to wipe away any/all of the cancer. Surgery is being billed as a last resort, so we'll cross that bridge when we get to it.

Kit, meanwhile, has Gallows Humored his way through every step of this process. If attitude is half the battle, he's going to kick cancer's ass. (BTW, we have dubbed the tumor "The Lurker," so please refer to it as such in any correspondence.)

As Kit's Chief Information Officer, I will continue to keep you posted on his condition. In lieu of get-well gifts, please send positive energy/vibes out into the Universe.

And now for the good news . . .

After a 13-year courtship, Kit and I are officially husband and husband!

Immediately following the final pre-chemo appointment at Sloan Kettering on Friday afternoon, we hailed a cab to city hall and tied the knot in front of our good friend, witness-for-hire, and impromptu wedding photographer Nina Boesch. Pre-cancer diagnosis, there were no bigger marriage cynics than the two of us. I mean, we wanted the RIGHT to marry, we just had no interest in EXERCISING that right. But it's funny how life's little curveballs can shift one's perspective. I'm officially married to my best friend and soul mate and I feel like the luckiest guy in the world. In lieu of gifts, please send positive . . . JUST KIDDING WE'LL TAKE GIFTS!*

* Please do not send gifts. It was a joke. We don't need another toaster.

As he made his way through all 420 words, I sat there silently on the couch, glancing over at him every few seconds to study his body language in an attempt to get a sense of how it was hitting him. I wondered if he'd noticed that I'd written around the fact that his tumor was in his rectum. If he asked me about it, would I admit that I'd dodged that particular detail as a way of protecting him from the hateful bigots out there who would look at a gay man getting booty cancer as some kind of cosmic retribution? The more worrisome question: Was it my own deep-seated internalized homophobia that caused me to sidestep the very significant role his ass was playing in this story? And, by doing so, was I sending a subliminal message to the world that his cancer *was* brought on by his sexuality and not, you know, the *actual* culprit: terrible fucking luck?

Also, was he having second thoughts about going public with his plight now that he was actually *reading* the dispatch? Or, perhaps even worse for this writer, was he instead going to ask for a wholesale re-write? Was I good at penning two-hundred-word news stories about the latest *Grey's Anatomy* cast shakeup, but god-awful at writing about my husband?

Despite a couple of subtle, contemplative sighs, Kit finished reading the draft as emotionally composed as when he'd started. He picked the laptop up off the kitchen counter, handed it back to me on the couch, and much to my relief, said, "It's perfect."

Then, while he retreated to the bathroom to get showered, I took a deep breath and mentally prepared to make Kit's cancer diagnosis real and official and a matter of public record, thus shattering whatever tiny glimmer of denial-fueled hope I might have had that this was all just a giant fucking nightmare I was going to wake up from. I dragged into the post a few Kit-approved wedding photos that Nina had emailed us, and I clicked Post. And then I waited.

Thirty seconds went by and there was a grand total of zero comments. A minute went by and that number had increased to . . . actually, it was still zero. Where were all my warm viral hugs, dammit! I refreshed the browser hoping maybe it was just the slow Wi-Fi, and, just like that, a big comment cluster appeared. A dozen or so heart-felt messages, all expressing elation about our marriage and shock and sadness—and support—over the cancer piece of it. I hit refresh again and another dozen comments showed up. And the number kept growing. I began to cry as I took in the love. I also felt an enormous weight lift off of me now that the secret was out.

I closed my laptop, walked to the entrance of the bathroom, and alerted a still-showering Kit that the news had broken and the love was pouring in. I then informed him that I was heading out to make a late-morning Starbucks run.

"You're uje?" I asked.

"No. Oatmeal today, please," he replied.

"You got it. Back in ten minutes."

It actually took twenty on account of my swinging by the (*brace for a fast-approaching storyline twist!*) jeweler to retrieve our freshly sized wedding bands that I'd been notified were ready for pickup (via a voicemail left for me on Saturday, right around the time Kit and I were dropping the C-bomb on Marilyn and Bob).

Upon walking back into the apartment, I dispensed with any of the pomp and circumstance that had accompanied last week's stealth proposal, found Kit tying his shoes in the bedroom, and took his hand.

"I've got something for you," I whispered as I slid the ring on his finger. It took a second to clear his big-ass knuckle before safely arriving at its destination. I planted a kiss on Kit's smiling face before informing him, playfully, "*Now* you're mine."

"Me next," he gleefully replied, as I handed him the ring box containing my band. He scooped it out, took my hand, and I let out a quiet sigh of relief as it glided up my chubby finger. A perfect fit. He kissed me before retrieving his camera to snap some pics of our newly bejeweled digits. During the impromptu photo shoot, the rings lightly grazed each other, letting off the most magical "clinking" sound. Kit and I instantly looked at each other in wonderment, like we'd just accidentally mixed chocolate and peanut butter and invented Reese's. Our marriage had an official soundtrack.

It was odd seeing, and feeling, a ring on my finger. Save for the four days in high school when I'd sported my senior class ring, foolishly thinking it would make me look cool and maybe-possibly lead to a reduction in the number of "fudgepacker" slurs hurled in my direction, I had never owned or worn a ring before. It would definitely take some getting used to. One thing was for sure: It felt really nice looking over and seeing the identical ring on Kit's hand. We were now a confirmed unit.

Our Carmel town car was due to arrive in five minutes, so I grabbed a bag from the closet—in this case a Netflix-branded tote the streaming giant had gifted me and my fellow journalists with at some press event—and started packing for our inaugural Sloan stint. Actually, Kit started handing me stuff and I just tossed it in. Boogie Wipes? Check. Chargers for Kit's iPad and my laptop? Check and check. The latest issue of *Entertainment Weekly* with *Game of Thrones* on the cover? Check. A change of clothes in case Kit puked all over what he was wearing? Check.

I mentally hit the pause button as I imagined the chemo-related horrors that awaited Kit. I flashed back to Dr. Abbott's plain-spoken, Dr. Phil–style warning about the horrible side effects of the purposefully aggressive drugs (the same cocktail Davis had since recommended) and I became light-headed. I had, thankfully, over the course of our almost thirteen-year relationship, witnessed Kit suffering only a handful of times: the lead up to and aftermath of his appendix surgery; the night he learned that his accountant had accidentally mailed copies of his 2012 tax returns to his old apartment on 68th Street and directly into the hands of his now bitterly estranged roommate Kirby; and our plane ride back from Puerto Rico during which an unruly six-year-old was kicking the back of Kit's airplane seat during the entire three-hour flight while his useless discipline-averse mother did nothing.

Looking back, I'm pretty sure I was in more pain than Kit during each one of those ordeals. The sight of him in dire straits released some kind of chemical in my brain that turned me into an emotionally wrought basket case who had to do anything in his power to make his pain go away, including, in the case of the aforementioned airplane imbroglio, prying open the airplane's emergency exit door and hurling that hyperactive, prepubescent demon spawn out into the open air mid-flight as his passive, shoulder-shrugging mother looked on (you may've read about that incident in the news).

What was it going to be like to see Kit *truly* suffering?

I snapped out of my fear spiral as a matter of self-preservation and because we were on a schedule. Before heading for the door, I eyeballed on the couch the vintage Nauga monster doll that Kit's boss John had gifted him—picture the Abominable Snowman from *Rudolph* only much smaller and bluer—picked him up, and squeezed him into what little space was left in the tote, his large jagged-toothed grin peeking out the top.

"Why are we bringing him?" Kit huffed, his "*way* too cutesy" alarm no doubt blaring in his head.

"Good luck charm," I responded, abruptly, signaling to him that there was no room for negotiation.

Kit flashed me a disapproving look, just so he was on record as having not supported my decision to bring a stuffed animal (albeit an effen expensive stuffed animal) to Sloan with us, before we walked down the stairs and out onto the street to our Carmel car.

With lunch hour approaching, the traffic was predictably hella-cious as we made our way to Sloan's midtown *pavilion*. Kit and I both kept busy refreshing Facebook to read the latest comments. I saw Kit soaking up all the good vibes pouring in, and I felt relief that my largely self-serving gambit appeared to be working out pretty well for him, too.

I temporarily moved away from Facebook to scan my work email for only the fifth time since I woke up this morning. In the pre–Kit cancer era, I would've checked it about three times that number already. I was still posting the occasional casting story and "Ask Ausiello" column, forwarding tips along to the staff, and weighing in on big-picture decisions here and there. But generally, my highly capable No. 2, Matt Mitovich, was running the show. And believe me, if you're ever forced to temporarily step away from a business you created, in order to be with your spouse during a life-or-death health crisis, you should be so lucky as to have a Matt Mitovich in your corner.

Matt and I had jump-started our respective publishing careers six-teen years before at a Northern New Jersey–based soap opera maga-zine called *Soaps In Depth*. He was something of a unicorn among *SID*'s junior staffers in that he was not fresh out of college (he was in his thirties), he was neither female nor gay (a straight man writing about Erica Kane? pshaw), and, last and most importantly as far as I was concerned, he could *write*. His raw copy required no editing, and he possessed impeccable news instincts that rivaled my very own impec-cable news instincts. Since I was the magazine's senior news editor, he made my life exponentially easier.

So, naturally, when I made the leap to TVGuide.com after three years at *SID*, Matt was promoted into my post. And when an editor position opened at TVGuide.com several years into my gig there, my superiors wisely acted on my strong recommendation and poached Matt. And I stood back and watched with pride as his profile in the industry grew. And when I made the leap to *Entertainment Weekly* in 2008, Matt, as he had at *SID*, slid into my shoes and became TVGuide .com's leading purveyor of scoop.

It went without saying that Matt was the first call I made when I decided to walk away from my dream job at *EW* and accept Jay Penske's generous offer to launch a consumer TV news site. If *TVLine* was going to reach its full potential, I needed Matt by my side. And if I was going to maintain some semblance of a life outside of work, I *really* needed Matt by my side. Luckily, Matt instantly said yes.

Now three years into *TVLine*'s life, Matt was already running the day-to-day operations of the site. And he was surrounded by a veritable journalistic dream team (if I knew anything about baseball I'd liken them to some historically great Yankees lineup). Said all-star lineup included my former *EW* colleagues Michael Slezak and Vlada Gelman; another onetime *SID* writer, Kim Roots; and up-and-comer Andy Swift. *TVLine* could not have been in better hands, and I could not have been more grateful.

It helped that my current boss was Jay "family first, work second" Penske, a man who'd offered to charter a private jet to fly Kit and me home to Millersburg last weekend so Kit wouldn't have to sit on his ass in a car for three-plus hours (an offer we graciously declined on account of Kit insisting his ass was perfectly fit for car travel). A man who had come to know and love Kit personally through, yes, his connection to me, but also through his and his wife Elaine's affinity for midcentury furniture. Jay's discovery during his scouting of me that my partner worked for Wyeth had been the icing on the Ausiello cake for him. When I informed him last week by phone that Kit had cancer, he broke down, before offering any and all resources at his disposal to ensure that I could give Kit my undivided attention. He also offered whatever financial assistance we might need, although I reminded him that Kit had long been enjoying Penske Media's kick-ass, low-copay benefits as my domestic partner and, now, my husband. (Wyeth had many pretty

things, but a benefits package to rival Penske's was not one of them.)
The fact that Kit and I didn't have to worry about how his cancer fight
would be paid for was tremendously comforting and not something
we took for granted.

As we neared Sloan, Kit put down his iPad and I could see him
looking at his ring in the sunlight. He took out his camera and silently
snapped a few photos. He then grabbed my hand.

"I'm sorry you're going through this again," he sighed.

My heart sank.

"Please don't ever say the words 'I'm sorry' to me again," I said
sternly. "About anything."

"Unless it involves one of your heinous farts," I added. "But even
then I'll probably let you skate by."

We arrived at Sloan and proceeded to the sixth floor. Kit found a
seat as I walked to the front desk. "I'm checking in my *husband* Christopher Cowan," I announced to the receptionist, accentuating "husband"
because (a) we were here, we were queer, we were betrothed—get used
to it, and (b) it was my first time introducing anyone as my "husband"
so, naturally, I was going to lean into the word a bit.

My husband, Christopher Cowan. My *husband*, Christopher
Cowan. I couldn't imagine those words ever getting old.

Points for the receptionist, my still-bold-for-2014 declaration didn't
even cause her to flinch. I loved the fancy, progressive Sloan Kettering!

"Great, I have him all set here," she replied. "Go ahead and have a
seat and they'll call your name out when they're ready."

"I just want to confirm that he's getting a bed, not a chair," I added
casually.

"Hmm . . . let me check. Those usually fill up first," she responded,
setting my blood to a light simmer as she scanned her computer. "I'm
not seeing anything in the system about a bed, but I can let the staff
know that that's your preference."

"It's not my preference," I said, my blood now approaching a low
boil. "It's a *necessity*. I was assured he would get a bed. We were *promised* a bed . . ."

"Unfortunately, it's impossible to *promise* . . ."

"He is not able to sit down in a chair," I interrupted, slightly startled by the resolute, unrelenting Michael who had taken possession of the conciliatory, confrontation-avoidant Michael. "Dr. Davis assured us that he would get a bed. He has a rectal tumor the size of the Death Star." (Yes, I exaggerated a bit; so sue me.)

"I will let them know," she replied calmly and, to her credit, compassionately.

I attempted to settle myself down before joining Kit; the last thing he needed was to catch wind of the unfolding behind-the-scenes drama. Unfortunately, he could spot the smoke billowing out of my ears a mile away.

"What happened?"

"Nothing."

"What happened?"

"Just making sure they have a bed for you."

"I'll be OK," he assured me. "I can lean back if I need to."

"I got this," I snapped. "You are not sitting in a chair for four hours. Period."

I managed to talk myself off the ledge by the time one of the nurses announced "Christopher Cowan" and led us into the chemo wing. I could feel my pulse quicken as I waited to see if she was going to escort us to one of the semiprivate rooms with a chair or one of the semiprivate rooms with a bed. Eh, fuck the suspense. I needed to know now.

"I just want to confirm that he's getting an actual bed and not a chair," I said calmly.

"Unfortunately, our beds are currently full, but our chairs can recline . . ."

"He *needs* a bed."

"Hey, it's OK," Kit assured me in a calming tone, as the nurse led us to the "infusion chair" that had apparently been earmarked for Kit.

"No, it is not OK. We were promised a bed." I turned to the nurse, tears running down my cheeks. "He has a *rectal* tumor. It hurts for him to sit down for five minutes let alone *four hours*. He needs a bed. We were promised a *bed.*"

As I unloaded on the nurse, Kit began to position himself in the chair to prove to me that he could do it. But his wincing and gasping as he attempted to find a comfortable position only strengthened my case.

"OK," the nurse finally said upon being presented with Exhibit A (i.e., Kit suffering in front of her face). "We'll find him a bed."

She walked over to the nurses' station and conferred with her colleagues. I tried to eavesdrop, but all I could hear was whispering. Within two minutes, she returned.

"Follow me," she said.

I wiped my tears, and Kit and I followed her down the row of semi-private chair-only cubicles and into . . . a glorious private room with a door and a bed and a window. I was overcome with relief. *This* was why we had chosen Sloan. This room right here.

"You guys will be in here today," the nurse said reassuringly.

I could see the relief on Kit's face. We both thanked the nurse.

As Kit took off his shoes and got settled into that beautiful, gorgeous, sumptuous bed, I took a moment to savor the victory. While the events of the past three weeks had clearly foreshadowed the hands-on role I would take in Kit's medical care, this morning's chair-gate brouhaha had firmly established *how* I would tackle my job as caregiver: ferociously, passionately, and with zero tolerance for bullshit. And it felt good.

It felt good to fight for something without worrying about my emotions getting the best of me or how I'd be perceived or what the possible blowback would be. It felt good to love someone so much that literally nothing was as important as making sure that person was safe and comfortable and protected.

With my guard safely down and Kit settled into his bed with his iPad, my mind shifted to his parents back home in Millersburg, no doubt wondering and worrying how things were going. They'd expressed a desire to travel back with us to New York to be here for Chemo: Round 1, but Kit put the kibosh on that. There was no way in hell he was going to reserve his mom and dad ringside seats to his showdown with chemo. Plus, he reasoned to them, he was in good hands with yours truly. I, in turn, assured them I would barrage them with frequent updates.

With that promise fresh in my mind, I grabbed the Nauga monster out of the Netflix tote bag and rested it in front of Kit on the bed. I then whipped out my iPhone, my desire to take a photo unmistakable.

"No," Kit protested. "No cancer photos."

"Just one to send to your parents," I pleaded, before adding, "I won't post it on Facebook. I promise."

Kit sighed, put down his iPad, held the doll close to his chest, and gave me the biggest, sweetest, bravest smile.

PREVIOUSLY ON . . .

CHRISTMAS IN LITTLE ITALY
WITH SANTA
NEW YORK CITY
DECEMBER 9-22 2001
BIG CHAIR PHOTO 800 929-0066

Turned out my love of the miniature Belgium-born humanoids known as the Smurfs was *Kit's* Morning Tourette's–like aha moment. He knew I was a Smurfs fan. But he didn't know the depths of my fanaticism, which dated back to one spring afternoon in 1982 when, while walking home from elementary school with my best friend and neighbor Lynda Szwedo, she whipped out a two-inch blue-bodied female gnome on roller skates and changed my life forever.

"It's a Smurf," she declared.

"Oh, like the cartoon," I replied, referring to NBC's recently launched Saturday-morning series, which had failed to catch my interest during a brief sampling several weekends ago.

Lynda proceeded to explain that Gift Expressions, the card store in our neighboring town of Union, New Jersey, that just so happened to be next door to the Acme supermarket where my mom did all her food shopping, carried dozens of these little blue treasures. "I have about ten already," she bragged.

I exerted a fair amount of childhood energy coveting cool stuff

Lynda owned that I didn't, couldn't, or wasn't allowed to have myself (see also: backyard swimming pool, Barbie dolls, long flowing locks tailor-made for braiding). But as I held in my hand Lynda's gliding female Smurf (who I would come to learn had her own name, Smurfette), I decided that, partly for competitive reasons and partly because this twinkling nymph was just too fucking cute for words, I, too, was going to start a Smurf collection. And it was going to be the biggest Smurf collection in all the land. Certainly bigger than Lynda's.

So, that weekend, after I helped my mom load the groceries into her car, I dragged her next door to Gift Expressions to begin my Smurf expedition. Within seconds of walking into the modest thirteen-hundred-square-foot shop, I spotted this bright yellow spinning hexagonal tower on the counter next to the register. It was labeled "Smurfs Collector's Center," and behind the six Plexiglas-protected compartments were dozens of Smurfs assuming all kinds of poses and professions. There was a doctor Smurf. A clown Smurf. A nerdy-looking bespectacled Smurf. A Smurf brandishing an apple. A pointing Smurf. A sitting Smurf. An old man Smurf who, for possibly attention-whorish reasons, eschewed his tribe's traditional white Phrygian-ish hat for fire engine red. I was entranced by the sea of blue. I wanted them *all*. And not just to put Lynda's collection to shame. I was genuinely smitten.

"You can buy one," my mom informed me.

Just one?" I sulked. "Come on, *Mom*."

"*One*," she maintained, as she flashed the sweet sixtysomething female sales clerk a smile. "They're not cheap, you know."

She was right. As the price tag affixed at the top of the tower read, they were $1.50 apiece—not an insignificant chunk of change. So I drank up my glass half-full and began to slowly rotate the case, studying each and every figurine as I went. If I was allowed only one Smurf, you better believe I was going to make it a good one.

After four minutes of painstaking deliberations—just as my mom reminded me that there was a gallon of Breyers Neapolitan ice cream melting away in the trunk—I alerted Grandma Gift Expressions that I had made my selection.

"I want this one," I indicated enthusiastically, pointing to the grinning Smurf clutching a bouquet of flowers in one hand and a wrapped present in the other.

"Ah, Birthday Smurf," she remarked, approvingly. But instead of retrieving the Smurf from the case, she ducked down below the counter for a few seconds before reappearing with the exact figurine I had requested in her hand. *What the what?* She had a secret stash of duplicates under the counter?! This made the experience all the more magical. It was as if the Smurfs inside the official collector's case were sacred and not to be touched. I found the process of Smurf buying as thrilling as the acquisition itself.

I skipped out of Gift Expressions with my Birthday Smurf in hand, and I was already plotting my return to snatch my runner-up pick, Hamburger Smurf.

The following Saturday morning, I parked myself in front of the TV in our family room at 9 a.m. and watched the Smurfs cartoon on NBC from the perspective of a collector. And a program I'd initially greeted with indifference now had me on the edge of my seat. Then, later that day, I returned to Gift Expressions with the $1.50 I'd earned from cutting coupons for my mom and took possession of my Hamburger Smurf. Within two weeks, my collection had grown to six. Within a month it had eclipsed Lynda's dozen. Gift Expressions had become my second home, so much so that I was on a first-name basis with shopkeeper Rose.

The Smurfs craze, and my subsequent obsession, eventually faded by the late eighties, by which time I had amassed upward of seven hundred pieces, which included not only figurines but mushroom houses and stuffed plush and mugs and posters and scratch-and-sniff stickers and Christmas ornaments. Rose eventually turned the prime counter real estate over to the Smurfs' far inferior undersea successors, the Snorks. But in a wonderfully full-circle gesture, she ended up selling me the rotary Collector's Center for the bargain-basement price of $5.

After a ten-year Smurf sabbatical—during which I ensured my precious, safely stored-away collection didn't fall prey to the dreaded *Star Wars* action figure curse whereby they would get unloaded at the family garage sale or, worse yet, tossed in the trash by a reckless parent during an especially aggressive run of spring cleaning—the advent of eBay in the mid-nineties reawakened my now nostalgia-tinged infatuation. I spent hours combing the nascent auction site in search of those figurines that had escaped me as a kid, like the elusive "Surprise Bag" or the "I Love NY" Smurfs. I was determined to fulfill the promise I'd made to myself on that fateful stroll with Lynda Szwedo in 1982 to literally Have. Them. All.

With printed-out checklist in hand, I started attending toy shows and flea markets on weekends. I was once again receiving Smurf-related gifts from my family at Christmastime. I was no longer the kid collecting Smurfs. I was the *adult* collecting Smurfs, a label I wore like a badge of honor. I embraced the fact that the Smurfs were *my* thing. The thing that made me unique. The thing that set me apart.

The revived hobby also doubled as therapy, in that it transported me back in time to the innocent early eighties, before my mom got cancer, before John Valentine started calling me a fudgepacker in Biology class, before my masturbatory sessions started producing a sticky white residue. If ever I was feeling anxious or scared, I closed my eyes and imagined myself eagerly bounding into Gift Expressions with a dollar bill and two shiny quarters burning a hole in my pocket. It remains my happy place.

My ultimate goal? To create a Smurf shrine that takes up an entire room, one that mixes elements of a store and a museum. But until I'm wealthy enough to own a home with a spare bedroom or a finished basement, or a small sliver of a sumptuously curated gift/furniture boutique in Hudson, New York, I will just make do with more modest transitory Smurf shrines, like the one I haphazardly created in my one-bedroom, fourth-floor suburban New Jersey walkup apartment in Bloomfield.

The one Kit was about to lay eyes on for the first time.

It was on a Saturday in early December 2001 when Kit first stepped foot on my turf. I was cautiously eager for him to get a window into my blue-colored world. Up to this point, he had seemed charmed by my distinctively kitschy taste, and there was a shitload of kitsch waiting for him behind my front door.

Kit appeared OK at first as he silently, methodically entered my apartment's small foyer, which featured a motley smattering of ceramic Smurf statues both store-bought and handmade-by-my-mom, haphazardly interspersed with a few random Disney-themed tchotchkes on the unit's built-in shelving.

He then sauntered into my bathroom, flipped on the light, and took stock of my Friz Freleng limited-edition cell hanging over my toilet, the still-labeled toiletries scattered about my sink, the Kmart shower curtain, the Christmas-themed hand towel marking the approaching holiday, dust bunnies in every corner. I could feel the judgment emanating from every pore of Kit's being. His silence spoke volumes, the overriding theme being "He *lives* like this?!"

His subtle shade turned to overt horror as he entered my bedroom and noticed on the dresser opposite my bed the yellow Smurf-filled rotating chamber from Gift Expressions, which was right next to a newer, much larger custom-made wooden display case, the latter of which contained row after row of Smurf figurines, some three hundred in total. The sight literally stopped Kit dead in his tracks. His face was expressionless as he stood there and stared at the army of Smurfs before him. He must've felt his knees buckle, because he braced himself on the dresser before slowly taking a seat at the foot of the bed, his eyes still focused on the collection.

"I need a minute," he mumbled.

"Are you OK?" I asked, chuckling nervously because I couldn't tell if he was being serious or doing another bit.

"Let me please just have a minute in here alone," he reiterated, more forcefully this time. "Close the door on your way out."

"OK . . ." I said, my nervous giggling masking my underlying confusion and concern. As I started to pull the door closed, I saw Kit retrieve his point-and-shoot from his pocket. It was as if he needed his camera to help him comprehend the incomprehensible.

I then proceeded to hang out in the living room waiting for Kit to work through whatever it was he was working through in my bedroom. I was nervous, but I was mostly just perplexed that out of all my issues it was the *Smurfs* that freaked him out the most.

As I sat on the mangy sofa that had belonged to my late uncle Frank and looked at my comparatively sad hodgepodge of an apartment, it became noticeably clearer to me how different Kit and I really were, aesthetically speaking. Kit's personal living space looked like it had been ripped out of the pages of *Architectural Digest*. Mine looked like it had been ripped out of *Yard Sale Weekly*.

After about ten minutes, Kit emerged from my bedroom, looking considerably less stressed out than when I left him.

"I'm OK," he assured me, before acknowledging, "That was a *lot* to take in."

What I *didn't* tell him right then and there was that the five hundred Smurfs on display represented just a fraction of my overall collection, the rest of which was in storage bins under my bed. Baby steps.

"I like your Regis and Kathie Lee poster," Kit said, nodding to the personally autographed promotional portrait of the *Live* cohosts hanging on the wall over my full-sized bed (right next to the framed poster of Cyndi Lauper's 1988 big-screen acting debut, *Vibes*). I didn't have the heart to tell him that I wasn't making an ironic, cheeky statement. It was a souvenir that I'd proudly procured at the Garden State Arts Center leg of their ten-city, circa 1990s variety show tour that I'd attended with my grandmother. Again, baby steps.

With the dust from the Smurf drama settling, we decided to rest our heads under Cyndi, Regis, and Kathie Lee, with an eye toward a possible midday nap. There was more turmoil in our immediate future, though, as Kit suddenly started rubbing *my* cuticles.

"I'm sorry," he sighed. "You're making my cuticles itch."

Not a single word in that sentence made any sense to me, but I could tell Kit was in the throes of some kind of panic attack so I just remained silent as he dug into my fingernails.

"I'm scared," he whispered as he stared straight up at the ceiling.

"Of what?" I asked nervously.

"Of screwing this up."

"Is this about the Smurfs?" I inquired.

"No. I've been having a lot of anxiety lately. About us. About this. I don't know if I can do this."

OK, I'm officially scared. I did not know where this was going, but the word "breakup" seemed like a reasonable guess.

Fucking Smurfs!

"I don't understand where this is coming from," I said, my worry transitioning into terror. "Everything was fine this morning."

"I don't know," he sighed, his fingers digging into my cuticles. My attempt to curl up to him was instantly rebuffed. "I'm sorry. Touching makes the anxiety worse."

I kept my trap shut and remained on my side of the bed. It was an exercise in major restraint because all I wanted to do was talk more and touch more, all in an effort to get past this hurdle and be reassured that all would be OK. But Kit clearly wanted silence and space. So we just lay there, side by side—him anxious and scared, me confused and scared—and eventually drifted off to sleep.

We awoke an hour or so later, and much to my relief, Kit informed me that his anxiety cloud had lifted. "I still olive juice," he sweetly reassured me, before adding, (hopefully) tongue-in-cheek, "Don't be surprised if some of these Smurfs suddenly go missing, though."

I still had lingering concerns about his freak-out—namely, was it a symptom of some larger doubts he was having about the relationship?—but I didn't press. I was happy to just write it off as an isolated hiccup. Another Morning Tourette's, if you will.

As we got deeper into December, and as holiday mania kicked into high gear, Kit and I saw slightly less of each other. But the time we did spend together remained exemplary. Kit didn't share my intense enthusiasm for Christmas—he harbored a much more cynical attitude toward the season, partly due to the resentment he felt from having his birthday fall on December 23. But I think some of my childlike zeal for Santa Claus was rubbing off on him. To wit, it was his idea to fork over $5 for a cheeseball photo with a sidewalk St. Nick while strolling through Little Italy one mid-December night. The photo op led us to share our favorite Christmas memories. Mine occurred in 1983 when I rushed downstairs to find that every present in my designated section under the tree was adorned with Smurf wrapping paper. Even better, all the gifts themselves were Smurf-related. Kit cited the early-eighties Christmas when he received a Pee-wee Herman doll, but quickly noted that his most *memorable* December 25 was the one wherein he got up at 5 a.m., snuck downstairs, and opened all his presents while his parents slept—a stunt that landed him in the doghouse (that was also, coincidentally, his mom's worst Christmas memory). And to make matters worse, the gift he was hoping to find—the magic set he had long been coveting—wasn't even among the loot.

The idea of spending Christmas with Kit filled my head with dancing sugarplums, even if it wasn't in the cards this year. We each had out-of-town family commitments—him at home in Millersburg with his parents, me down the Jersey Shore at my brother Pete's (with sister-in-law Theresa, nephew Peter Jr., and niece Lauren). It was also a little soon to be spending the holidays together. But just having a boyfriend in New York around the holidays added an extra layer of magic.

On Tuesday, the week before Christmas, Kit emailed me at work asking to meet up that evening. We hadn't planned on seeing each other until Thursday, so his request caught me off guard.

"Is everything OK?" I wrote him back.

"Yep," he responded. "I just want to see you. And talk."

And *talk*. Fuck. That did not sound good. My mind immediately flashed back to our tense, decidedly *un*-Smurfy heart-to-heart a few weeks earlier in my apartment, and my breakup fears were resurrected anew. *There's no way he would dump me one week before Christmas*, I assured myself. Maybe he couldn't wait to give me my Christmas gift? Maybe he was just *really* missing me since we last saw each other Sunday morning?

By the time he rang my office line to let me know he was waiting outside the building, I had laid out in my mind every possible reason for his impromptu visit.

As I exited the building, I glimpsed Kit pacing around the open-air plaza in front of *TV Guide*'s headquarters on New York's Avenue of the Americas. He spotted me and his face immediately lit up. I walked up to him and could sense that something was off. He seemed troubled. We took a seat on a nearby bench and I cut right to the chase.

"Your email scared me a little," I confessed, as tears began to form in his eyes. This was the first time I had seen Kit cry, and it crushed me. It also confirmed what I feared: I was getting the heave-ho.

"I need to tell you something," he wept. "I fooled around with another guy."

This seems like a good time to point out that I was not new to the adultery rodeo.

I was a junior in high school when the scourge of infidelity first touched my life. My co–best friend and glorified beard Ada Tricoche summoned me to her house one school night under the guise of hanging out. But I would quickly discover that I was walking into a trap.

As I made my way down to her cozy, finished basement, I found my *other* co–best friend and secret crush, Jason Lualhati, sitting on the couch. Jason and Ada were tangential acquaintances at best, meaning it was only through their individual relationships with me that their paths ever crossed.

"Jason—what are *you* doing here?" I inquired.

Jason just sat there, silently and forebodingly, as Ada assumed the role of official spokesperson for the ensuing shit show.

"Mike, there's something we need to tell you," she said, as she planted herself next to Jason on the couch. "Jason and I started dating a few weeks ago. We didn't want you to find out from someone else."

Um, whatchoo talkin' 'bout, Fake Girlfriend? is what I *wanted* to say. Instead, I just stood there in silence, processing the nightmare unfolding before my eyes. I was shocked. I was angry. I was hurt. But more than anything, I was embarrassed. I felt like a fool.

I tried to figure a way I could walk out of Ada's house salvaging the one thing that meant the most to me—my relationship with Jason. At the end of the day, I could live without Ada's companionship, and the subsequent re-escalation of the gay rumors. But Jason I *needed*.

You see, I was in love with Jason. And I had been since the ninth grade, when the two of us bonded over our mutual obsession with *Days of Our Lives*. How obsessive were the two of us about NBC's top-rated soap? We not only attended a *Days* fan event featuring super-couple Patch and Kayla (Stephen Nichols and Mary Beth Evans) in Parsippany, New Jersey, but we rented a limousine to get there.

Unlike me, Jason was straight. And into sports. And popular. And *brilliant*. And he wanted to be *my* friend. Jason's acceptance of and fondness for me helped me get through an otherwise hellacious high school experience. He was the reason I struggled to leave Ada's basement that night. So I just stood there. Awkwardly. Silently. Humiliatingly.

For two hours.

It was only when my bladder threatened to burst that I realized it was time to call it a night.

"I hope the two of you are happy," I said, seething, fighting back tears, as I marched up the stairs and stormed out of Ada's house. I walked home, crying the entire way, my heart breaking into a million pieces.

It felt like I was heading for a repeat of that fateful evening in 1988 as Kit attempted to get the next words out of his mouth.

"It happened in the steam room at the gym," Kit continued. "There wasn't any actual sex, but there was touching. I immediately regretted it. It happened last week and it's been eating at me ever since. I was scared to tell you."

"We had unsafe sex on Saturday," I reminded him pointedly.

"I know," he sighed. "I swear, there was no sex. But that doesn't make it OK."

It sure as fuck didn't. As I sat there watching the tears stream down Kit's face, I felt anger and sadness and fear. But I also, oddly enough, felt relief and empathy. The former because Kit was not, as I'd feared, there to dump me. And the latter because he was clearly in pain over what had happened, which told me that he genuinely cared about us. And me.

I was also a little scared because this was yet another side of Kit I knew nothing about. A side that went into steam rooms not to detoxify his body but to rub one out with a stranger. It also played into my fears that I wasn't good enough.

"Say something, please," Kit pleaded.

"I'm glad you told me," I admitted. "I'm not happy it happened." I hesitated before asking the requisite follow-up, fearing what his answer would be. "Is there anything else you want to get off your chest?"

"No," Kit replied, his tears drying up. "That's it . . . Are we OK?"

I hesitated before replying. The simple answer was, yeah, we were probably going to be OK. I was too invested in this relationship to walk away over a little horseplay at the gym. But if I brushed his indiscretion off too quickly, it might send him a message that I had a high tolerance for this sort of thing.

So I issued him a chilly, somewhat ambivalent "I think we're going to be OK." I also turned down his request to escort me to Port Authority.

Before we parted ways, Kit fearfully asked, "Are we still on for Thursday?"

"Yes," I confirmed of our "Christmas" dinner plans (it was the last time we'd see each other before the holiday).

We stood up from the bench and Kit leaned in and hugged me tighter than I hugged him back.

As I replayed the events of the past ten minutes in my head on the way to the Port Authority, I questioned whether I should be more freaked out about Kit's extracurricular activity. I was concerned about it, to be sure, but this wasn't grounds for a breakup.

Kit and I didn't communicate with each other until the next afternoon, when, while at work, he emailed me asking if he could meet me at Port Authority that evening to say hi before I caught my bus home (Cosi's headquarters were right down the block on 37th Street). Even though he was still in the doghouse, I instantly typed "sure" and hit reply. Selfishly, I wanted to see him.

At around 6:30 p.m., we met up outside the Au Bon Pain in the main plaza area and gave each other a hug. I pulled away from him quickly, as the sight of him triggered a sudden wave of anger.

"My bus is at 6:45, so why don't you walk me to my gate," I suggested, coldly.

"Sounds good," he said.

As we boarded the escalator up to the second floor, small talk about our respective Wednesdays gave way to a postmortem on steam room–gate.

"I know you said we were OK, but I feel the need to check in again," he said.

"We're OK, Kit," I replied, curtly. "But I'm still processing the whole thing."

"I understand," he said. "I'm just afraid that I fucked everything up."

Kit joined me on the line at my gate. We stood there awkwardly for the next ten minutes. There was a tension in the air. I was processing this anger I was feeling, and he was picking up on it. As the bus pulled into the terminal and the boarding process began, we confirmed our Thursday dinner plans.

"I'll see you tomorrow, Mike," he said.

"See you tomorrow, Kit," I said.

"Thanks for letting me see you tonight," he said.

I boarded, took my seat, and looked out the window—there was Kit, stationed inside the terminal, peering at me through the glass like a puppy with his tail between his legs. My heart melted. I smiled and waved at him. He waved back, before mouthing the words "Olive juice."

As the bus filled up with passengers, Kit maintained his position, flashing me a cute smile every thirty seconds. I shook my head, as if to say, *You don't have to wait!* But wait he did. For another ten minutes, before the doors finally closed and the bus pulled away. We exchanged another smile and wave and "olive juice" before he disappeared from my view. Within seconds, I was already missing him. The anger I'd felt earlier upon seeing him was gone, replaced with heart-tugging joy.

In the wake of steam room–gate, a new Kit emerged, one who was contrite, vulnerable.

By the time I got home an hour later, there was an email waiting for me in my in-box. It was from Kit, and the subject line read, "Peaks, Valleys, and Unexpected Turbulence." I clicked it and began reading.

> I'm so glad you saw me.
> I got to see you.
> Hold and hug you.
> Hear you say that you're O.K.
> That we're O.K.
> You've seemed so far away since last night.
> Or maybe it was the idea of us that seemed like it was fading.
> I couldn't help but feel today's bus was a metaphor for that.
> Making me strain to make you out behind its smoked glass.
> Making me rely on my idea of you.
> Causing me to think what I would do if you weren't there.
> Weren't here. Weren't in my life.

Staring through my reflection I looked at myself and
wondered who you saw.
Then I asked myself where are you going?
Wondered if our tickets are for the same destination.
On the same flight.
Perhaps though, our journey is the destination.
Then tickets are not required and to that I'd say, now boarding.
Have your tray table up and your seat belt securely fastened.
There may be unexpected turbulence.
If I'm scared, I'll know you're in the seat next to me.
Holding my hand.
Talking me down.
Telling me WE'RE going to be O.K.
When everything settles down there will be a quiet ding
and we'll be free to walk about the cabin.
Together.

9

Michael Ausiello
March 27, 2014 · 🌐

Kit completed his first three-day chemo cycle yesterday and will now recuperate at home for three weeks before Cycle 2 starts in late April. He's doing fairly well on the side-effect front so far—there's some light nausea, malaise and sleepiness but nothing too major. Kit's background as a world-class napper has already come in VERY handy.

In an effort to keep Kit nourished and avoid any substantial chemo-related weight loss, I was plying my huzzzzzband with homemade, high-fat shakes, courtesy of the Magic Bullet blender my Maryland-based brother, David, and sister-in-law Pam had shipped to us as a wedding/get-well present.

My secret recipe included one eight-ounce bottle of vanilla-flavored Ensure, one cup of vanilla ice cream, a tablespoon of Skippy creamy peanut butter, a scoop of whey protein powder, and a drizzle of constipation-alleviating castor oil. All told about six hundred calories. Kit had been averaging two of these nutrient-rich shakes a day, followed by a dinner that consisted of whatever food he happened to be craving at that moment, usually ordered via New York's foremost takeout app Seamless. (Depending on my mood or hunger level, I'd either piggyback on his order or grab a vegan cheeseburger from the health-food shop down the block.)

As Kit took a shower one morning, I whipped up Shake No. 1 of the day. I should mention that this was no ordinary day. For the first time since Kit started chemo more than two weeks ago, I was leaving him home alone for an extended period, to attend to some classified *TVLine* business: a special, intimate screening of HBO's Ryan Murphy-shepherded TV adaptation of Larry Kramer's AIDS opus *The Normal Heart*. I was scheduled to interview Murphy about his passion project the next week, and this viewing (slated to begin at noon at HBO's midtown offices) would be my final opportunity to see the film before doing so. It was a big, buzzy piece of television with an all-star cast that included Julia Roberts, Mark Ruffalo, Matt Bomer, and Jim Parsons, and while I could have reassigned the screening/story to another member of my team, I'd been looking forward to covering this project from the moment it was announced. And, selfishly, I didn't want The Lurker to rob me of the opportunity.

Plus, I'd been carrying roughly 25 percent of my typical *TVLine* workload—all from the comfort of my living room couch—since embarking on this cancer journey with Kit some six weeks ago, and maintaining ownership on a big story like this would go a long way toward making me feel like I hadn't completely abandoned the site I'd launched three years ago.

Of course, the closer it got to show time, the more it started to hit me that I'd be spending my rare two-hour caregiver respite watching young gay men succumb to a debilitating terminal illness as their lovers helplessly looked on.

What in sadomasochistic hell had I been *thinking*?

As I began to consider the possibility of sending Matt Mitovich to the screening in my stead, I heard the shower shut off, followed almost immediately by a thump that sounded like Kit's six-three body hitting the bed.

I stole away from the Magic Blender to peer into the bedroom, and sure enough, there was Kit lying facedown on the bed with his head in a pillow. His body was trembling. And he was panting.

"Kit, what's happening?" I worriedly asked as I darted to his side.

"I'm having pain," he told me in between labored breaths.

"Where?" I asked.

"Grab me a towel," he pleaded.

I ran into the bathroom, fetched his towel, returned to the bed, and placed it over his naked, soaking-wet body. He was in so much pain he wasn't even able to dry himself off.

I resisted the temptation to touch him because, based on experience, Kit in distress was not a Kit who liked to be handled.

After about three minutes, his breathing started to stabilize. He moved the towel off his back and slowly started drying himself. He then cautiously shifted onto his side.

"Where is the pain?" I whispered.

"My ass," he said. "I was just standing in the shower and all of a sudden I felt a sharp burning sensation. My knees practically buckled."

"How is it now?"

"Better," he sighed. "I think it's passed."

I attempted to put on a strong, non-panicked face for Kit, but inside I was freaking the fuck out. That was the most pronounced display of physical suffering from Kit I'd witnessed so far, and the fact that I had no idea what had caused it made it all the more terrifying. Was it a side effect of the chemo? Was it the chemo attacking The Lurker? Was it, God forbid, The Lurker *growing*—which would mean the chemo wasn't working and Kit might not even be able to hit Dr. Davis's one-year survival prediction?

In the meantime, I was already mentally preparing to break the news to Mitovich that I was blowing up his afternoon to send him to the *Normal Heart* screening.

"I made you a shake," I informed Kit, my first attempt at trying to get our otherwise "normal" morning back on track.

"I'll take it outside," he said, referring to the private deck that was becoming something of a sanctuary for him these past few weeks as winter gave way to spring.

The "secret" terrace perched outside our bathroom window had been one of the apartment's big draws when I signed my one-year lease back in August. It was a quirky, imperfect space, to be sure: To access it you had to climb through our bathroom window. And the deck itself sloped slightly downward, which made sitting in our outdoor chairs, while not untenable, slightly awkward. And at a modest six-by-six, the quasi-terrace could accommodate a maximum of four people comfortably.

On the bright side, it was an outdoor space. In the West Village. And one that provided us a *Rear Window*–esque peek into the living rooms and bedrooms and backyards of our tony neighbors' multimillion-dollar brownstones. We also got to hear birds chirping and watch squirrels scurrying and see the freakin' sky. These are precious commodities in Manhattan.

The deck afforded the frequently weak and tired and nauseous Kit the chance to get out of the house without having to actually *leave* the house—and just as the weather was starting to improve. It was ideal for smoking weed, entertaining the occasional guest (Missi, Nina, and Rose had all dropped by in the past week), and, as on this morning, drinking a protein shake while coming down from an alarmingly severe pain episode.

Sadly, the fact that the space was relatively unsecured save for three horizontal steel railings that framed the perimeter meant that Kit's partner in crime and photographic muse—Mister Scooch—couldn't join him unless he was leashed. And Scooch did *not* like to be leashed.

Last week, Kit decided to live dangerously by inviting our skittish-yet-curious feline progeny into the great outdoors for the first time since we adopted him a decade ago (so afraid of going outside was Scooch that we had to find a vet who made house calls).

After some initial hesitation, Scooch rather enjoyed this mystical new alfresco realm. In fact, he loved it. We watched in wonder as every gentle breeze and falling leaf and flying fly left his little Scooch face mesmerized. But our overwhelming fear that at a moment's notice he could give chase right over the ledge and down three stories to his death outweighed whatever parental pride we were feeling. So Kit shooed Scooch back into the house just as he was adapting to his new environment.

As Kit got settled into his now signature sideways position on this late, mild morning, I could see a disappointed Scooch peering through the bathroom window as if saying, *Come on, dads, I wanna come out and play, too. I'll be good. Promise!*

I saw Kit flinch as he rested on his side, and I immediately panicked. "More pain?"

"Just the normal amount," he said. "Not the head-spinning pain from the shower. Maybe it's related to the constipation."

Ah, yes, the constipation. Bowel movements had not gotten easier yet, another worrisome sign. Kit had been spending hours at a time on the toilet just to yield a few little pebbles. It had been four days since he'd produced anything but gas.

"You're still going to your screening," Kit announced to me, as if he were inside my head.

"Like hell I am," I shot back.

"I'm OK, Bodge," he insisted. "I feel like a bowel movement might be coming on. That'll keep me busy for the next couple of hours."

"I can see if Missi can take a few hours off of work to . . ."

"I'm *fine*," he protested. "I'm not a vegetable. Not yet, anyway."

I looked at him and could tell by his stern, resolute expression that he'd made up his mind about this.

"You text me the *second* you—"

"I will," he interrupted. "I promise. Enjoy your movie."

I floated the idea of picking up a late lunch for the two of us afterward. He shook his head, looked at me, and pointed to his lips. "What goes in, must come out," he quietly hummed. "Makin' poops starts with the mouth."

I leaned in and rewarded his adorably impromptu poetry reading with a kiss. And then I reminded him, "You can't stop eating, though."

"Lemme see how this bowel movement goes and then we can discuss lunch," he said. "What I *will* take now is a coffee from Starbucks. The caffeine should help speed up the process."

"You got it," I told him before grabbing his now empty shake glass and dropping it off in the kitchen sink on my way out the door. Once I hit the sidewalk, I immediately called Dr. Davis's office and left a message about Kit's troubling pain spell. I needed her to rule out the worst-case scenario running through my head (that the tumor was growing).

I returned home five minutes later, handed Kit his coffee, and confirmed for the tenth time that he was cool with my leaving him unchaperoned and that he'd text me in a heartbeat if he needed anything. And for the tenth time, he issued me a blanket confirmation. Then I headed out.

As I cabbed it uptown to HBO's 42nd Street headquarters, I stared at my phone anxiously, waiting for Dr. Davis to call. I also considered texting Kit to see how he was doing, but I held off because it had only been four minutes since I left him. I then once again second-guessed my decision to go to the screening, since all I'd be thinking and worrying about the entire time was Kit, so what was even the point? But I knew I couldn't bail. I got the sense that he needed me to maintain some semblance of a normal life, just as I imagined I would have needed him to do if our situations were reversed. It was only a couple of hours.

Fifteen minutes later, I was sitting in HBO's posh screening room waiting for *The Normal Heart* to start, my eyes still glued to my phone for a text from Kit or a call from Davis. I then decided to kill more time by checking my email and was startled when a new one from Kit appeared with the subject line "Holy Shit!" I took a deep breath and opened it.

The first thing I saw was a close-up image of the inside of our toilet bowl accompanied by the following caption:

"Normals at the bottom. Guinness record on top!!!! Thanks for the coffee!!! I feel great!"

I let out a spontaneous, happy sigh of relief so loud I almost felt the need to apologize to the folks sitting around me for disturbing the preshow peace. I'd never been so happy to see a literal pile of shit in my life. I quickly wrote him back, "Amazing! Thank you so much for sending that. Show's about to begin. I love you!!!"

Michael Ausiello
April 13, 2014 · 🌐

Just when we were beginning to think we dodged the hair-loss bullet—
it's been nearly three weeks since he began chemo, after all—Kit awoke
Wednesday morning to a pillowcase covered in brown strands. Upon making
the discovery, he summoned me from the kitchen with an alarmed, "Michael!
It has begun!" A few tears were shed, but the sadness quickly gave way to
curiosity and astonishment. Cut to Kit spending the next three days gleefully
grabbing fistfuls of hair out of his head SIMPLY BECAUSE HE COULD (and
also because he knew it unsettled me). And then on Saturday, he decided
to accelerate the process with a thorough and complete head shaving in our
bathroom. Playing the role of barber was yours truly and, despite some major
reservations on Kit's part, I'm proud to say not a drop of blood was spilled.
News flash: Bald Kit looks just as sexy as Hirsute Kit.

It was a little less than a week into Chemo Part 2, and Kit was
slowly coming out of what he had dubbed a "chemo coma." Unlike the
first cycle, which had had minimal side effects save for the hair loss,
nausea, and fatigue, this round was taking a real toll. When he wasn't
sleeping he was vomiting, and when he wasn't vomiting he was thinking about vomiting.

On top of that, the sharp pain he'd experienced in his ass while
showering a week ago was not, as we had hoped, an aberration. He
was now unable to walk, let alone stand or even switch positions in
the bed, without triggering a major pain event. Dr. Davis and her team
remained at a loss to explain exactly what was causing this, but given
the high success rate this specific chemo regimen had on this specific tumor, they remained optimistic that the pain spells were a by-
product of the drugs chipping away at The Lurker. But they were also
not ruling out that they could have been the tumor expanding to the
point where it was brushing up against nerve endings in the rectum.

The fact that bowel movements remained a massive undertaking
seemed to support the latter theory. "Imagine trying to push a mix of
broken glass and barbed wire out of your ass" was how Kit had recently

described the four-hour ordeal that was him trying to go. That's right—*four hours*. The first hour he was in bed or on the couch emotionally working up to the act of pooping, then the next two hours he spent on the toilet *doing* it while clasping a rolled-up magazine, and then the fourth and final hour he was recovering from it. The pot gods and, to a lesser extent, the constipation-causing morphine mitigated the pain, but only a fraction of it.

In the meantime, we took the bad days one hour at a time and prayed that the Universe would soon throw us a good one, like it seemed to have done today. Since waking up this morning, Kit had scarfed down a cheese Danish and iced chai latte from Starbucks, relocated from the bed to the couch while only hitting a 4 on the pain scale, and there was even talk of us going for a walk around the block.

For the time being, I was just happy to see him out on the couch next to me watching *AbFab* reruns while I attempted to crank out my first "Ask Ausiello" column in nearly a month. I was even considering hitting the gym for an hour of cardio.

Our chill, pain-tolerant morning was violently interrupted by the deafening sound of the downstairs doorbell. Did I mention that the particular brownstone in which we lived featured intercoms in the three units but not actually door-opening buzzers?

I pushed my laptop aside, hopped down the stairs, opened the door, and was greeted by the UPS man.

"Package for Christopher Cowan," he announced.

"That's us," I confirmed, as I looked past him and saw what appeared to be two giant rolls of wire fencing alongside a large Home Depot box. What the hell was my husband up to?

I signed for the packages, and then Mr. UPS Man helped me drag the loot into the vestibule before taking off. I sized up the deliveries and quickly determined that there was no way I'd be able to carry them up the stairs all at once. Instead, I grabbed one of the rolls of fencing—or hardware cloth, as they were labeled—and headed toward the third floor.

Before I was even in our living room, Kit—clearly hearing the bulky item bang up against the wall and the stairwell during my climb—excitedly screamed, "Is it my fence?!" I walked into the dining room and dropped the roll on the floor. Kit looked at it and let out an enthusiastic "Yes!"

"Is this what I think it is?"

"Mister Scoooooch," he bellowed. "I've got good news."

"Who's going to install this?" I asked him, genuinely curious.

"I am," he insisted.

"You're going to fence in our deck all by yourself," I pressed him, now becoming annoyed because I had a bad feeling I was going to get roped into assisting him, and if there was one thing I detested more than terminal cancer it was manual labor.

"I'm going to try," he said. "If I can't do it, I'll wait and have my parents help me when they come visit." He then added, "Don't worry, you won't have to get your hands dirty." He knew me too well. "Just do me a favor and bring it out onto the deck."

"There's another roll downstairs. And there's a big box," I informed him, just so the record was clear that I'd already expended a lot of energy on this project.

"Those are the mats," he said, proudly, missing the point of my passive-aggressive jab. "Now we don't have to sit on the hard wood."

I rolled my eyes at him before walking back down the two flights of stairs and then back up the two flights of stairs with the box of mats in one hand and the rest of the wire fencing in the other. As I trudged through the living room and passed Kit, I made a point to bang the bundles up against every inanimate object in my wake just so the record *also* showed that none of what I was doing was as easy and fun as the tail-wagging expression still plastered on his face indicated.

As I was about to climb out of the bathroom window, I could see Kit heading toward me in the bedroom. He made a pit stop on our bed to catch his breath and, presumably, let the pain die down. He was holding a pair of scissors and what looked like a box cutter. Jesus Christ, he was going to tackle this project right now.

I was concerned, but I was also happy to see him energized about something, and feeling strong enough to even consider taking on a project like this. But mostly I was relieved because, beyond having me lug this shit up two flights of stairs and out onto the deck, he was not guilting me into helping him.

With all three packages on the deck, I climbed back through the window and walked over to him.

"You were having such a good day," I sighed. "Please don't push it."

"I'm just going to inspect it, make sure the size is correct," he assured me. "If I need to stop I will stop."

"But . . ."

"*Buh, buh, buh, buh, buh, buh,*" he interrupted, adopting his signature Mike Silencing Technique. He then slyly inquired, "You were going to the gym, right?"

My irritation gave way to amusement, as I was full-on savoring the sight of Kit once again acting like Kit.

"I'll be back in an hour," I told him. "Text me if . . "

"Bye now!" he interrupted, before adding with mock sincerity, "I *luuuuuuhve* you."

I kissed him on the lips, and slipped on my gym clothes as I watched him proceed from the bed to the deck, closing the window before Scooch could sneak out.

I tied my laces, grabbed my headphones, and walked over to the bathroom window. I saw Kit positioned on his side inspecting one of the rolls of fencing, and my heart . . . I just felt so much love. I knocked on the window, waved goodbye to him, and headed off to the gym.

I returned exactly ninety minutes later with two Coco Açai Bowls purchased from the Juice Generation in the lobby of the Equinox, worried about what would await me inside. I prepared myself for the worst, which would have been Kit sitting back on the couch, depressed because cancer had prevented him from doing something else that he loved. Maybe I'd get lucky and he'd just be sound asleep.

I walked into the apartment and he wasn't in the living room. He also wasn't in the bedroom. I then noticed the bathroom window was . . . the bathroom window was wide open? But . . . the Scooch.

I stepped into the bathroom, looked out on the deck, and Kit was on his knees in the corner securing the final section of fencing.

He had fenced in the entire deck in ninety minutes, and the mesh wiring was so thin it hadn't obstructed any of our view. It was almost invisible.

And whaddaya know. Perched on the ledge was Mister fucking

Scooch, smoking a cigar and sipping a martini like he owned the joint. My jaw dropped. My heart filled. I was . . . speechless.

"I still have to fix a few areas," said my perfectionist husband. "And it's a little crooked on one side. But I can have the Scooch out with me now. It'll do for now."

"It'll do for *now*," I exclaimed as I stepped out onto the deck to grab a closer look at his incredible handiwork. "Bodge . . . this is amazing."

Kit put down the scissors and took a break on one of the two cushioned, waterproof mats now lining the floor of the deck.

"Mats!" he said with glee. "Come sit."

I joined him on the adjoining mat. I looked over at Mister Scooch sitting safely within Kit's cozy little home away from home. I turned to Kit and whispered, "I love you."

He looked at me, smiled and bragged, "What *can't* Kit do?"

Michael Ausiello
May 9, 2014 ·

We received some disappointing news this morning—a fresh MRI confirmed that the chemo cocktail Kit had been prescribed had no impact on The Lurker. In fact, the bastard grew a little bigger over the past seven weeks (which explains the increased discomfort Kit's been feeling). Also, a few suspicious nodules turned up in his pelvic region, which also blows. The encouraging news is that there are other chemo cocktails out there, and Sloan Kettering has recommended a new recipe that they hope will succeed where the last mixture failed. Kit resumes treatment next Friday—the docs needed the extra week to boost his chemo-impaired white blood cell count. If all goes according to plan, he'll be on this regimen for the next several months. We're also meeting with a radiation specialist to see what options are available on that front. All told, a little setback, but the fight continues.

Roughly twelve years ago, Kit and I—in an effort to rescue our foundering romance—decided to invite a tall, dark, handsome stranger into our relationship. There were a handful of unspoken ground rules: There would be no kissing. No oral. No penetration. No sex of *any* kind. Talking was allowed—and the topics could even veer into lewd territory—but nudity was forbidden. And we had to always meet on his turf.

The invisible fine print in said contract allowed for some wiggle room on that last one in the event one of us were to be felled by terminal cancer and rendered immobile. And so, earlier this week, Kit and I took advantage of that loophole and extended a formal invitation to our longtime therapist, Tony Frankenberg, to come to our home for what would be our first session since Kit's cancer diagnosis nearly two months ago.

Needless to say, after twelve years of meeting Tony in his cozy office just off of Madison Square Park, the prospect of seeing him not only out in the wild but inside our home had us feeling nervous and vulnerable on this late spring afternoon. Well, it had *me* feeling nervous and vulnerable. Kit's hands were currently pretty full mentally and physically preparing to embark on the arduous journey that was getting out of bed and walking to the couch in the living room for our 1 p.m. appointment.

While Kit waited for his morphine pill to kick in before beginning his move, I was furiously vacuuming the remaining cat hair off of the red IKEA chair that Mister Scooch slept in and that today would serve as Tony's perch. The one and only concern Tony had expressed to me about making this rare out-call visit was that our little Mister Sister Scooch Monster might trigger his cat allergy. I assured him I would remove as much of our little guy's DNA from the premises as possible before his arrival.

I didn't want anything to derail today's session. This was the longest Kit and I had gone without seeing Tony since we had retained him back in 2002 in the wake of Kit's second infidelity lapse, which occurred several months after the infamous steam-room incident (and this one included more than just touching). I was hoping we'd be able to resume our biweekly routine once the chemo started relieving Kit's symptoms. But the chemo had been a bust, and while we were hopeful that the radiation would succeed where the liquid poison had thus far failed, my brain and my heart were preparing for the worst. And we—*I*—could use a little of Tony's wisdom and counsel right about now.

I was also curious where Kit's head was at. We focused so much of our time on symptom management and not nearly enough talking about his possibly imminent death because it was all so scary.

Kit made his way onto the couch just as our pants-shitting doorbell blared. I headed downstairs, opened the door, and—yep—totally fucking weird seeing Tony Frankenberg standing on our stoop. Wearing a spring jacket. And jeans versus his customary khakis. He looked like a real person as opposed to the psychiatry god I was used to seeing.

Shrinks—they're just like us.

"Hi, Tony," I said to greet him, solemnly.

"Hi, Mike," he responded, warmly.

I welcomed him in, and the second he hit the vestibule, we did something we'd never done before: We hugged each other. And I immediately started crying.

"Thank you so much for coming," I whimpered.

"Of course."

I pulled out of the embrace and was jarred by the sight of what appeared to be tears forming in his eyes. Another first. Tony was supposed to be our rock. The calm amid the storm. I felt the impulse to comfort *him.*

I led him up the stairs to the third floor and into our apartment. Kit was sitting on the couch sideways, his back to us. He turned around and smiled at the sight of Tony.

"Tony!"

"Hi, Kit!"

I gave Tony a mini-tour of our home. He raved about its "incredible character and charm." I then showed him to his chair, assuring him that it'd been thoroughly de-pussied. I took my place next to Kit on the couch as Tony put his bag on our floor and took out his notebook.

The entire scene remained incredibly disorienting. Tony Frankenberg was in our apartment. The man who had helped us navigate every possible relationship land mine thrown our way, from Kit's infidelity to my boner-killing body dysmorphia, to Kit's scary compartmentalization skills, to my unhealthy obsession with my job, to Kit's short fuse, to my Smurf collection, to our mutual superiority complexes (him with technology, common sense, and sex toys, me with pop culture, financial planning, and Smurf collecting), to our habitual codependency. The man who had been our cheerleader and champion. The man who had never stopped believing in us even when we were ready to throw in the towel. He was now sitting across from us in our living room as we faced the biggest crisis of our relationship.

And then it hit me like a fist in the face: Tony couldn't fix this problem. Our relationship was ending and, for the first time, he wouldn't be able to save it. I took Kit's hand and started sobbing.

"Michael, make a lot of room for those feelings," Tony said, signaling the start of the session.

"Seeing you here," I wept. "It's just . . . very emotional."

"Kit, what is it like for *you* to have me here?"

"It's actually less weird than I expected," he said, matter-of-factly.

"Well, you have the advantage of being slightly high," I said, ribbing him.

"This is true," Kit confirmed with a smile, triggering a chuckle in Tony. "I honestly don't know how people get through something like this without pot. I feel very lucky in that respect."

"Michael filled me in when we spoke on the phone about the chemo not working," Tony continued. "How are you both handling that?"

"We're drawing short straws," Kit acknowledged. "But being sick has put a lot of things in perspective for me, in terms of what matters and what doesn't. I'm partially relieved. I don't have to stress about neglecting my 401(k). I don't have to worry about who's going to take care of me when I'm seventy."

"That was gonna be *me*," I huffed as I turned to look at Kit. "I was going to take care of you. We were going to take care of *each other*."

Kit looked at me, sadness filling his eyes. He squeezed my hand.

"Mike, stay with those feelings," Tony implored me.

"You mean *anger*?"

"*Are* you angry?"

"Yes, I'm fucking angry," I snapped, tears running down my face at a steadier clip. "It's so completely unfair."

"It's heartbreaking." Tony exhaled, as sadness radiated from his eyes.

His simple acknowledgment of our tragic predicament ratcheted up my feeling of despair and I began to bawl. Kit grabbed my hand, prompting me to look over at him just as the words "I love you, Mike" left his mouth.

"I love you, Kit," I whimpered in return.

"I want to make sure you take care of yourself—not just me," Kit added.

"What *are* you doing to take care of yourself, Mike?" Tony asked.

"I go to the gym occasionally," I replied. "And I do a little *TVLine* work here and there."

"I tell him he should get out more," Kit chimed in. "Go to dinner with friends. Go into the office every once in a while. Just get a break from all of this. And give me a break, too—no offense."

"Easier said than done. I know it would be good for me. But it's hard to leave this apartment. I need to be here. I *want* to be here."

"Kit, can you understand why it would be tough for Mike to leave?" Tony asked.

"I do," Kit replied, before looking at me and genuinely adding, "I would be fucked without you."

That felt good to hear. And I acknowledged as much by squeezing *his* hand.

As the session continued, we brought Tony up to speed on the next steps in Kit's treatment (mainly the radiation). We also talked him through some of our frustrations with Sloan Kettering, and how dark humor had been one of our most reliable coping mechanisms. Tony laughed when I told him how the rarity of Kit's rectal cancer had prompted him to declare to every nurse or doctor he encountered, "I have a famous anus!" He was also amused when Kit casually slipped into conversation our intentionally counterintuitive cancer rallying cry: "We make lemons out of lemonade."

And before I knew it, our sixty minutes was nearly up.

"Tony . . ." Kit said as the session drew to a close. "I need to know you are going to be here for Michael after I'm gone. That you're going to see him individually."

More tears. The thought of showing up to Tony's office every week without Kit by my side was just too much.

Tony hesitated, his eyes welling up. "Of course I will," he assured Kit.

He then continued, "I want you guys to know how incredibly moved and inspired I have been by your love. I feel honored to be a witness to it. Your relationship has had a big impact on me, personally and professionally. It changed my life. I love you guys."

Tony was now full-on crying. And it was breaking my heart. And apparently Kit's, too, because for the first time in the session he was also weeping.

"We love you, too, Tony," Kit responded, sinking me deeper into an emotional abyss. I nodded in agreement because I was too far gone to speak.

Just as Tony was closing his notebook, Kit's mood did a 180 as he yelled "Butterfly!" and pointed to—yep—a big, bright butterfly that had invaded our living room via our screen-less window. It was swirling overhead. It was so stunning I found myself searching its wings for a Pixar watermark.

I looked back at Kit, whose eyes remained utterly and completely charmed by our winged visitor. He looked downright happy. And tickled. And touched. And just so fucking *present*.

I glanced back at the butterfly, which was now gliding through our kitchen. I then shifted my gaze over to Tony, who was also wonderstruck, only his eyes weren't fixed on the butterfly. They were locked on Kit.

He saw it, too.

10.

Michael Ausiello
June 29, 2014 · 🌐

On Friday, Kit completed his fourth week of radiation (that's 20 sessions, one a day with weekends off). He has five sessions left, and then he rests/recovers for a few weeks before his doctors determine what's next—a decision that will hinge on the results of his next scan at the end of July.

The very promising news: During the second week of radiation, Kit began experiencing a sharp decrease in symptoms. By the third week, the excruciating pain that was making it difficult for him to stand, let alone walk more than three steps, had largely vanished. He was still having discomfort, but for the first time in months it was manageable. Clearly, the radiation is decreasing the size of The Lurker, but, again, we won't know how much the bastard has shrunk until scan-time.

Oh, and his hair is growing back. It's approaching buzz-cut length, which is making for some VERY satisfying (for me, at least) head rubs.

Kit was officially on the rebound.

After enduring a demoralizing couple of months filled with intensifying pain and crushing setbacks, Kit—with twenty of twenty-five radiation treatments under his belt—had experienced a dramatic turnaround. The radiation oncologist overseeing his case expressed genuine surprise at how quickly he'd begun to feel relief in the rectal region (after just one week/five sessions).

Clearly, the radiation had succeeded where the chemo had failed, improving Kit's quality of life in the process. The sharp, debilitating pain that had rendered him immobile had all but vanished. He was able to sit down like a normal human being again, albeit not for long periods and with the aid of a donut cushion. His appetite had returned, although he still remained somewhat skittish about eating constipation-causing foods like red meat and french fries because, frustratingly, bowel movements continued to be a challenge. (In a major can't-win-for-losing type situation, the radiation had diminished the tumor, but it had left in its wake significant irritation.) All told, though, Kit was in a much better spot physically than he had been a month ago. We'd finally drawn a long straw!

Regrettably, none of this had officially changed the overall prognosis. Although Dr. Davis had not explicitly weighed in on this topic, my gut (and covert online research) told me that Davis had factored into her dire one-year forecast an initial positive response to treatment. As we'd been warned at the outset, one of the myriad difficulties with high-grade neuroendocrine cancer of the rectum was that these tumors were relentless fuckers; they tended to grow back quickly.

Kit's upbeat attitude suggested that his focus was on winning this battle without worrying too much about its effect on the war at large, although he had heartbreakingly remarked to me yesterday while we were leaving radiation session No. 20, "Maybe I'll get another five years out of this life." Yep, the best-case scenario floating around in Kit's head had him dead before he turned forty-six—and I couldn't help but think even *that* outlook seemed extremely optimistic.

In the meantime, I felt a tremendous responsibility to make the most of this window of relief Kit found himself in before it closed, possibly for good. So I channeled my inner travel agent and started brainstorming ideas for a getaway that both incorporated another of Kit's true loves (the ocean) while also taking into account some of his ongoing challenges (pooping and sitting down for prolonged periods).

Kit was not the least bit interested in assisting me with this travel project. I'd traditionally been the vacation planner in our relationship and—despite the decidedly higher stakes surrounding this excursion—he was in no rush to fix what wasn't broken. And while I loved the trust he put in me to oversee such an important task, his seeming indifference only compounded my stress. If the final vacation of Kit's life proved to be a bust, there would be no one to blame but me. On the bright side, if there was one thing I'd learned from my many years in the breaking TV news biz, it was that I worked well under pressure.

I suggested to Kit that we invite his parents along and he signed off on that proposal without hesitation. Bob and Marilyn had visited us over two long weekends since the beginning of Kit's treatment, loading their SUV up with a variety of Kit's rural Pennsylvania favorites (blueberry custard pie from the food auction, his mom's homemade— I can't even type this without wincing—stuffed pig's stomach) in the hopes of jump-starting his then feeble appetite. They'd been crashing at the Jane Hotel, which was literally right up the street from our apartment. (Were a longer stay to be in their future—which seemed like an inevitability—Kit had already decided that he would give them the keys to his Brooklyn man cave, which had gone largely unused as of late; of course, first we would need to delicately explain to them *why* their now married son had felt the need to get his own apartment in a different borough, and then he—or I—would need to make a trip across the East River to safely stash Kit's suitcase of sex toys.) I was sure they would have preferred to visit more often and stick around longer, but they'd been extremely respectful of Kit's need for space, and his strong desire that they not have orchestra seats to his suffering.

To help mitigate their feeling of isolation, I'd been providing them daily briefings by phone. And if Kit was feeling strong enough to participate, I'd conduct the daily call via speakerphone. They always put up a strong front over the phone, but I could only imagine the hell they were going through. Now that his condition was improving, there was an opportunity for them to get some real quality time with their only child.

Needless to say, they were beyond grateful for the invitation. And ever since we'd told them that we were eyeing the weekend before the Fourth of July, a very eager Marilyn had been proactively emailing me Airbnb listings for super-cozy houses available for rent along the Hudson River in Upstate New York.

My heart, however, was set on finding something near—or along—the ocean. Preferably in the Hamptons, which ranked near the top of Kit's list of happy places (right behind the riverfront in Millersburg and the backwoods Pennsylvania theme park time forgot, Knoebels). Wyeth had an outpost in the tony Southampton village of Sagaponack, and two summers ago, Kit and his work wife, Missi, had happily volunteered to work full-time in that location. (I spent a good chunk of every summer on the West Coast for business, including San Diego Comic-Con, so Kit's extended Hamptons retreat worked out well with our schedules.)

It was, by Kit's own account, the best summer of his life. When we'd catch up by phone or email or text, he'd regale me with stories of morning swims in the ocean, followed by seven-hour shifts at the store, then an *evening* swim in the ocean, and, lastly, dinner at his boss John's nearby rental cabin. And unlike at home, where Kit's pot consumption was fiercely judged and monitored by yours truly, I imagined the wacky tobacky restraints were off. Kit never outright confirmed this to me, but considering Missi was a fellow pot aficionado, it wasn't a huge leap to take.

So dear to his heart was the summer of 2012—and so grateful was he to John for making it all possible—that for Christmas that year he sifted through the thousands of photos he'd taken during those three months, selected his fifty favorites, and after a diligent months-long retouching process, converted them into a professionally bound book. Gifts make John super-uncomfortable, so instead of handing it to him in person, Kit simply left it on the seat of his Range Rover.

The problem with the Hamptons, however, was that by June the summer housing rental stock was largely depleted. I called a few ocean-front resorts, like the ultra-swank Gurney's in Montauk, but they were similarly booked up. And while John would've gladly let us all crash at his house, I was pretty sure if we stayed there, Kit—who had been on leave from Wyeth since starting treatment three months ago—would willingly, perhaps happily, get sucked into helping out at the store.

It was hard for me to adequately convey just how much Kit missed going to work every day at Wyeth, but this should paint a pretty ac-curate picture: When Dr. Davis broke the devastating news to us back in May that two cycles of chemo had failed to shrink Kit's tumor, Kit fell apart in the exam room, and the first anguished words that left his mouth were "*I just want to go back to work.*"

I *so* wanted that for him, too. But as far as this getaway was con-cerned, I wanted the four of us to have our own uninterrupted time in our own private space. I was happy to share him with his parents. But that was where I drew the line.

So I shifted my search to something smack in the middle of my retro wheelhouse: the Jersey Shore. Some of my earliest vacation mem-ories were of my family (older brother Pete, younger brother David, Mom and Dad) renting a house just outside of Seaside Heights for two weeks every summer (long before the strip became stigmatized by a certain MTV reality show). More recently, Kit and I would occasionally escape the city on a Saturday or Sunday and drive to the Point Pleasant boardwalk with my maternal grandmother Ronnie and aunt Joan in tow. We'd spend a few hours playing Skee-Ball and coin-pusher (add-ing any points earned to our growing certificate of credits), followed by dinner at the nearby Shrimp Box. But Airbnb had sparse listings in both locales. And what *was* available required a minimum one-month stay, and Kit had another week of radiation to complete as well as more chemo on the horizon.

And that was when I had a childhood flashback. Or more like an epiphany. Call it a flashiphany.

The pink hotel in Ocean City, New Jersey.

I couldn't for the life of me remember the name of the place at which my family had vacationed some three decades ago, but I *for sure* remembered the color. Every inch of the ten-story structure's art deco-y exterior was bathed in pink. And as the only high-rise building along the sleepy town's coast, man, did it stand out. But it wasn't the hotel's distinctive rosy hue that triggered my brain rush. It was what was on the top floor. Actually, it *was* the top floor.

Resting atop this giant pink erection was a sprawling, three-thousand-square-foot penthouse apartment, featuring multiple bedrooms and bathrooms, a full-sized kitchen, a washer/dryer, and (the pièce de résistance) a massive wraparound terrace boasting unobstructed views of not just the Atlantic, but all of Ocean City. Did I mention the terrace also came with a private mini swimming pool? 'Cause it did.

I knew all of this because it was the penthouse where my parents had put us up in the summer of 1988. Mom and Dad's successful mortgage company PMD Abstract (Peter, Michael, David, get it?) afforded us the opportunity to go on a number of fancy-schmancy family vacations during my high school years (St. Martin, Puerto Rico, Hawaii), but nothing could've prepared me—or my brothers—for what awaited us behind that space's private, keyed elevator entrance.

It remained a mystery as to how my parents had even stumbled on the place. Or what had led them to even look in Ocean City, one of the few Jersey Shore communities we had yet to step foot in. But I was pretty sure—especially in hindsight—that their decision to splurge on the accommodations was directly tied to the fact that my mom was, at the time, in the throes of her cancer battle. And perhaps they suspected it could be the final vacation she would share with her family, and vice versa.

And, turns out, it was. Five months later my mom would succumb to throat cancer.

The parallels between my mother and Kit's cancer stories were already somewhat eerie: Both of them had seen their initial symptoms intensify during a winter trip to Atlantic City; both had been diagnosed in the month of March; and both had experienced a summertime rebound. As many boxes as this pink hotel might have checked off in terms of Kit's situation, there was something staggeringly morbid about taking him to the scene of my mom's last hurrah for what could be *his* last hurrah.

But then I visualized Kit lounging on that massive terrace listening to the waves crash in the distance, surrounded by the three most important people in his life while smoking as much pot as he wanted because there were no neighbors to bitch about the stench, and I pulled up my laptop, Googled "pink hotel" and "Ocean City NJ" and—voilà—a photo of the familiar-looking structure appeared atop the search results, alongside the name the Port-O-Call. Of course. How could I forget. The Port-O-Call.

After taking in the initial relief that the hotel was still standing thirty years later, I anxiously queued up the official Port-O-Call website and scoured the accommodations page to make sure they hadn't chopped up the big penthouse into a dozen mini-penthouses or, even more galling, turned the space into a dance club called Snooki's Lair. Luckily, they hadn't (on both counts). The penthouse still existed. In fact, according to the blurb, the floor-through mega-suite featuring "panoramic views of the Atlantic Ocean, Beach, Boardwalk and the amazing Atlantic Skyline" had recently undergone a swank new remodel (one that had sadly eliminated the private pool, but you can't have everything in life).

And get this: Despite my calling with just two weeks' notice, the penthouse happened to be vacant the weekend before the Fourth of July—which was the time frame we wanted. The sprawling space was booked pretty much the entire summer *except* the one weekend we wanted it. It was as if my mom—and, perhaps, my dad if he wasn't still peeved at me for coming out to him while he was on his deathbed—had descended from heaven and thrust a bright pink sign in my face that read, "It's a sign!"

So I reserved the penthouse for three nights, which had us returning to the city on Monday morning, just in time for Kit's final week of radiation treatments. I excitedly informed Kit—and then Marilyn and Bob after him—that I'd selected Ocean City as our destination and that we would be revisiting a bygone Ausiello family haunt. I did not, however, divulge the part about it being the site of my mom's final vacation. While it was unlikely such a disclosure would have led Kit to veto the Port-O-Call, I had zero doubt he would've spent the entire weekend proposing alternate names for the hotel, à la the Cancer Inn or the Pink Crypt or the Last Resort. And as much as I loved dark humor, I was not sure his parents would find it all that amusing. But more than that, I didn't want him to even entertain the thought that he was destined to meet the same fate as my mom. Not at a time when he was finally basking in a little ounce of hope.

So, on this warm Friday morning, Bob and Marilyn drove in from Millersburg and followed Kit and me in our rental car down the shore to the Port-O-Call Hotel. And, as we stepped off the keyed elevator, the reaction from the three of them was not unlike the one I'd had thirty years ago.

"Holy hell, look at this place," Bob effused.

"I hear waves . . ." Kit said.

I immediately led them through the living/dining room—which, despite the remodel, looked exactly as I remembered (almost spookily so)—and out onto the terrace. Yep, still breathtaking.

"Will you look at this," Marilyn marveled as she stepped up to the railing.

"It's the entire floor!" Bob added as he began walking the perimeter.

I, meanwhile, received confirmation that Kit was pleased with our home for the next three nights not with words but with—what else—his camera. He whipped out his point-and-shoot and began snapping pictures of the view, which was all Atlantic Ocean to our east, the faint outline of the Atlantic City skyline to our north, long sandy beach and accompanying boardwalk to our south and Ocean City's Victorian-drenched historic district to our west. He stopped for a second to breathe in the salty ocean air before resuming his picture-taking.

"What do you think?" I asked him, clearly fishing for a verbal confirmation that he was, indeed, pleased.

"It's perfect," he confirmed. "Thank you for this."

He then looked over at his mom and dad, who were excitedly pointing to a cruise ship out on the horizon, before turning back to me and repeating with a weighty whisper, "*Thank you.*"

It ended up being a damn near perfect weekend. Kit and I got in a little beach time on Friday afternoon (with Kit actually braving the freezing ocean waters for a quick swim). The four of us walked the boardwalk on Saturday night (we *almost* made it to the end before Kit started feeling some pain, forcing us to turn around). We had local seafood for dinner all three nights, brought into our spacious dining room by yours truly, from the venerable 16th Street Seafood Market.

But the standout moments—for me at least—were the simple, quiet hours the four of us spent just chilling out on the deck, playing Phase 10, pointing out scenic curiosities, reminiscing about vacations of yore, etc. At one point, I awoke from a nap to find Bob looking out over the balcony, bookworm Marilyn (whom I'd never seen happier and more content) with her nose in a novel, and Kit just staring at me. I whipped out my iPhone and decided to risk "cancer photo"–phobic Kit's wrath by capturing the moment with video. Much to my surprise, he didn't protest. Instead, he mouthed the words "I love you" before taking on the role of on-camera host.

"We're here in beautiful Ocean City, *New Jersey*, with the folks," he began, slowly, dramatically, cheekily extending his arm out like a *Price Is Right* model showing off a brand-new Mazda CX-5. "We have Marilyn, with her forty library books..."

"Marilyn, wave for the camera," I instructed her.

"Hi!" she beamed, while excitedly waving.

"And Bob," Kit continued, "the Grand Master of Mahjong." Bob turned away from the view long enough to crack a half smile for the camera, which, for the subdued Bob Cowan, was a lot.

Kit then reached down for the bottle of bubbles he had resting on the deck next to his lounge chair.

"Yeah, blow some bubbles to close out this beautiful video," I urged him, with a tinge of sarcasm.

His first attempt at producing a bubble fizzled out. "These bubbles are very finicky," he gently huffed, before breathing through the plastic wand's hole a second time. This time he produced a steady stream of shiny bubbles of varying sizes. The breeze carried the glossy spheres over the edge of the deck and out toward the ocean.

Then, while still focused on producing bubbles, he abruptly said, "Bye!" as if telling me, "You got your cute little cancer video. Don't push your luck."

"OK . . . *bye*," I mumbled, as if to say, *Thanks for humoring me. I'll stop the video now.*

Just as I went to hit the red button on my iPhone, Kit picked up his point-and-shoot and positioned the camera lens right up against the plastic bubble wand's hole. He pointed it toward the sun, squinted his eye, and started snapping away. I wasn't entirely sure what the point of this peculiar exercise was, but my hunch was he wanted to capture the sun through a glycerin-y filter. It was in this moment that I made the knee-jerk decision to continue recording. Oh, how I loved watching Kit's photographic mind at work, particularly out in the wild versus in a studio. Kit on an impromptu photographic mission—whether it should occur while walking around New York or in our bed on a lazy Sunday morning or in his grandmother's timeless living room—was Kit at his most Kit. And I was willing to risk having my iPhone flung over the balcony for the sake of posterity.

So I stealthily kept the video rolling and watched as Kit rotated the wand slightly to the right to get a different angle before firing off another dozen snaps. Just when I thought he had his money shot, he tilted the wand to the left and clicked off another six shots. He was so focused on the task at hand he wasn't even aware that I'd never stopped filming . . .

"*I will delete it*," he icily threatened me, without even looking up from his camera.

With a mix of fear and amusement, I instantly hit the stop button and put my iPhone down on the deck.

If I'd taken no other video that entire weekend, I'd have been happy. In that short sixty-second burst, I captured all of the quintessential Kits: There was Heartfelt Kit, who could make me feel like the most special person on the planet with just a simple look; Cunty Kit, who could simultaneously embrace and throw shade at the Jersey Shore; Oddball Artist Kit, who could bring the same level of passion to a photo project involving a plastic bubble wand and some glycerin as he would to one showcasing a $40K Eames rocking chair; and Slightly Terrifying Kit, who could send a shiver down your spine with just a few words and a minor tonal shift.

And should Kit have made good on his threat to go into my phone and destroy my video keepsake, well, the joke would have been on him because I'd already emailed a copy of it to myself!

I woke up early Monday to sneak a quick run on the boardwalk before our planned 9 a.m. departure. I scanned my iTunes library for the *Dirty Dancing* soundtrack—which was the album I distinctly recalled listening to on my Walkman during our 1988 trip here. And as I jogged past the saltwater taffy stores and the arcades and the souvenir shops, I transported myself back twenty-six years and tried to recall some of the highlights from that fateful final vacation with my mom. Aside from me and my brothers frolicking in the rooftop pool, the only image I was able to clearly remember was one of my mother sitting at the head of the dining room table, flipping through the newspaper while smoking a cigarette, in defiance of her doctor's orders. And after every fourth or fifth puff, she would let out the nastiest and phlegmiest of coughs, the unsettling sound serving as a stark reminder that the massive tumor she had lodged in her throat was likely growing back.

Perhaps if iPhones had been around twenty-six years earlier, I would have been able to access happier memories from the week we stayed at the pink hotel in Ocean City. But for now, that's all I got. And it filled me with sadness.

For the record, Kit's trip to the Port-O-Call wasn't his last hurrah after all. We squeezed in two more mini-getaways that summer, including a post–Fourth of July trip back to Millersburg, during which Kit took me on the umpteenth walking tour of his beloved hometown, and even invited me to join him in his special secret childhood refuge under the bridge trestle. The tour—which I sobbed my way through—lasted about an hour and I took dozens of photos (and some video) of Kit taking photos. And Kit never once threatened to flush my iPhone down the toilet.

That would be our last trip to Millersburg together.

And at the end of July, upon returning from San Diego Comic-Con, I took a car service from JFK directly to the Wyeth cottage in the Hamptons, where Kit greeted me with literal open arms. (Missi had confided to me via text a few days earlier that "Kit is in a funk. He is really missing you.")

We spent the next six days lying out on the beach, touring the

Wölffer Estate winery (home of our favorite rosé), scoping out our friends Ben and Allison's new Sag Harbor weekend home, going out to dinner (with Kit's boss, John, and girlfriend/business partner, Tiffany), and, of course, napping.

I didn't want to leave. I wanted to stay in the Hamptons with Kit forever. And I wanted time to stand still so his cancer couldn't progress any further. Dr. Davis helped me with my first wish, granting my request that we return to Sloan for chemo on Tuesday instead of Monday.

On that final bonus night, we waited until the sun was fully set, grabbed a blanket, a bag of pretzels, and a bottle of wine and parked ourselves on the eerily deserted beach. We cuddled. I cried. We snacked. We drank. We listened to the waves. I cried some more. And Kit—captivated by the subtle red glow bathing the otherwise pitch-black beach from a nearby campfire—took a selfie of us. He staged the photo-op so that the flames from the makeshift blaze could be seen off in the distance behind us. The image was movie-quality stunning.

On the drive back to the city the next morning, Kit confessed to me that for the past few days he'd been experiencing a slight increase in discomfort in his bum. And about an hour outside of Manhattan, he came down with a brand-new symptom—a migraine headache.

That magical week in the Hamptons would be our final vacation together.

11.

Michael Ausiello
September 3, 2014 · 🌐

After experiencing improved symptoms for much of the summer, Kit's pain level ratcheted back up in mid-August and intensified with each passing day. We had a scan done on Friday and got the disappointing results today: The primary tumor—aka The Lurker—is back to its pre-radiation size.

Not only is this an aggressive tumor, but he's a stubborn bastard as well.

We're obviously disappointed, sad and a little angry that nothing they throw at this thing seems to be working. Luckily, the docs still have a few more tricks up their sleeves—including a different form of chemo (the first dose of which Kit will receive on Friday). More radiation may also be an option further down the road. So the fight continues.

I loved Debra Messing, but I wasn't feeling this show.

As we did every year around this time, Kit and I slowly made our way through the large stack of pilot DVD screeners the major broadcast networks sent me and my fellow TV journalists ahead of the new fall TV season. And together we engaged in our own mash-up of *Mystery Science Theater* and *Siskel & Ebert*, riffing on the pros and cons of each freshman series as the episodes unspooled.

Last night we watched the pilot for the CW's *Arrow* spinoff *The Flash*, which netted a rare two enthusiastic thumbs-up from us. We were far more split on the series currently queued up, NBC's *The Mysteries of Laura*, which cast Messing as a harried single mom juggling young twin boys and a demanding job as a New York City homicide detective. Kit seemed to be falling for its simple, throwback charms, even likening Messing's nontraditional sleuth to a sort of modern-day Jessica Fletcher. I, however, was on the fence. Messing was fully committing to the material. But the material was just meh. And in this era of Peak TV, the material needed to be about six rungs up from "just meh" if it wanted to shoehorn its way onto my already overcrowded DVR.

Of course, I was only 10 percent engaged in what was happening on-screen. The other 90 percent was focused on the brain scan Kit had undergone earlier this evening, the results of which we were currently waiting on from Dr. Davis. She'd promised to ring us tonight before 11 p.m. or first thing in the morning with the lowdown, and my eyes kept vacillating between our TV and the kitchen counter, where my iPhone was currently charging away.

As the clock on our Time Warner Cable box ticked past 10:30 p.m., it seemed more and more likely that the evening would end on a cliffhanger. And that suited me just fine. I'd rather go to sleep tonight thinking there was a chance Kit might still be able to beat this thing instead of knowing he would be dead by Christmas.

I saw the writing on the wall, though, and it was telling me that the persistent, worsening migraines plaguing Kit over the past few weeks were a result of the cancer having spread to his brain. Davis's team repeatedly dismissed this new symptom as a residual side effect of the chemo. And in my desperate desire to believe that to be true, I did not question the diagnosis with Davis directly. I wanted to trust that her underlings had conveyed the new development to their boss and that she agreed with their shoulder-shrug assessment. Sadly (but not unexpectedly, given the pervasive level of incertitude surrounding Kit's care) that pipe dream of mine had been shattered earlier today, when, while Kit and I were on the phone with her discussing the pros and cons of surgically excising Kit's massive rectal tumor as a palliative (not curative) measure, I casually mentioned the headaches. It was the first she was hearing of them. And she did not brush them off; she ordered an emergency MRI "just to be safe."

What Davis *didn't* tell us, but which I—and I was sure Kit—surmised was that if the scan confirmed that the cancer had metastasized to the brain, it was game over. Kit was already facing dispiriting odds with the disease located in "just" the rectum, liver, and lungs. You didn't have to be a you-know-what surgeon to know that if you added the brain to the equation you were basically fucked six ways till Sunday. Any hope of Kit's beating the disease or prolonging his life span by a few years would vanish. So, yeah, I was cool with Davis taking her sweet ol' time.

What I was *not* cool with was the temperament of Messing's insufferable prepubescent twins, who, like most TV juveniles these days, deserved to be spun off directly into a Dumpster in New Jersey. I was in the middle of venting my frustrations about Laura's demon spawn to Kit when my iPhone rang. My heart rate quadrupled as I sprang up from the sofa and bounded over to the kitchen counter. I immediately recognized the number.

"It's Davis," I announced to Kit, who promptly shut off the TV. I unhooked the phone from the charger and carried it over to Kit on the couch. I sat down, took a deep breath, and clicked on the speakerphone.

"Hi, Dr. Davis," I said cheerily, hoping my upbeat tone would somehow influence the results she was about to deliver. "Kit's here next to me."

"Hi, Doctor," Kit chimed in, adopting a similarly optimistic timbre. I tried to read him for any sign of fear or angst, but all I saw was the coolest, handsomest of cucumbers.

I hurriedly banged out a drive-by prayer in my head, asking God to please let Davis's voice have an air of lightness to it. She had delivered a lot of shitty news to us over the past seven months, so I was now able to glean from the very first syllable out of her mouth if she was about to ruin our day, our week, or our entire lives.

"Hi, guys . . ."

Fuck. She was in full-tilt Grim Reaper mode. I grabbed Kit's hand and held on tight.

"The news isn't good, I'm afraid," she continued. "We found a number of nodules on the brain. Several of them located near the brain stem, which is most likely what's been causing your headaches."

My heart sank. I squeezed Kit's hand and looked into his eyes. I saw the disappointment register on his face.

"How big are they, Doctor?" I asked, trying desperately to fight back the tears that were already streaming down my cheeks.

"They're fairly tiny, but there are a lot of them," she explained. "I'm so sorry."

Dr. Davis wasn't saying the words "It's curtains," but we both knew it was. I was full-on bawling now. Kit, meanwhile, remained stoic.

"So what happens now?" he asked.

"Well, we'll treat the brain with radiation," she said. "I've already sent a note to your radiologist, Dr. Halstead. We'll want to start right away. I'm also going to prescribe some steroids to help with the headaches, which you will take in conjunction with the Excedrin."

"Does this mean surgery is now off the table?" Kit asked.

Dr. Davis hesitated before confirming, reluctantly, "It does."

Typically when Davis lowered the boom on us, I instantly fired off a half-dozen follow-up questions in my desperate search for a silver lining, something—anything—for us to hang our Hope Hats on. But for the first time, I had nothing. Kit replaced me as chief interrogator, although he was taking a horrifyingly more direct approach with his line of questioning.

"What are we looking at here, Doctor?" Kit asked, sending a shiver down my spine. "Six weeks? Six months?"

"More than six weeks," she replied, solemnly. "Six months . . . ? Probably not."

"OK," Kit said, as he hung his nodding head down.

Davis wrapped up the call by telling us that someone from Halstead's office would be in touch tomorrow morning about getting the brain radiation ball rolling. I clicked off the speakerphone and immediately embraced Kit on the couch.

"I'm so sorry, Kit," I cried.

"It's OK," he said soberly. "We gave it our best shot."

"It's not fair. It's not fucking fair."

"I'm actually relieved," he told me resolutely, as I pulled out of our hug. "I know where I stand now. I know where this is headed. It's weirdly comforting."

I knew what he meant. I felt a little of it, too, the relief. So much of my mental and physical energy the past seven months had been expended on trying to avoid the dire outcome Davis had predicted. But now it was undeniable: Kit was going to die. And soon.

But mostly I was sad and angry and terrified at the prospect of having to say goodbye to the most wonderful person to ever step foot in my life.

"Hey, I have some new pot I've been anxious to try out," Kit said. "How about you grab yourself a glass of wine and we head out on the deck?"

My husband's remarkable resilience was once again rearing its beautifully bald head at the darkest of times. Instead of a pity party, he was organizing an *actual* party.

"That sounds nice," I replied, as I took a tissue and blew my gross, snotty nose. Kit clicked his fancy new morphine pump to get a bolus dose in his system before embarking on the excruciating process that was standing and walking, while I retrieved a bottle of Wölffer Estate Rosé from the fridge and a glass from the kitchen cabinet. Kit, wincing in pain, then led the way through the bedroom and into the bathroom. He snatched the round blue Tupperware container that housed his pot accessories next to the toilet, unlatched the window, and we both slinked out onto the deck, with Mister Scooch pulling up the rear as usual.

I plopped myself down on the concrete ledge, not far from Scooch's regular parking spot in the corner. Kit, meanwhile, assumed his signature position, sprawled out sideways on one of the two parallel white mats. I looked up at the star-filled sky and soaked up the crystal-clear, seasonably mild night.

As I poured my first glass of vino, I decided to ask Kit a question I'd been dreading.

"Are you afraid to die?"

He lit up his one-hitter, sucked in the cannabis, and slowly exhaled, the smoke billowing out of his mouth, over the fence, and into the neighboring courtyards. I could see him ruminating over the question.

"I'm not," he responded sincerely. "I had a great life . . . I'm scared of what the end looks like. But I'm not afraid of dying."

He then added, "Promise me you won't let me die in a hospital."

I took a beat to allow my heart to finish shattering into a million pieces before responding steadfastly, "I promise."

"And please look after my parents," he continued. "I'm worried about them."

On this request, I hesitated. The last thing I wanted to do was make a promise to my dying husband that I wouldn't be able to keep. The question of what my relationship with Kit's parents would look like without Kit had quietly been weighing on me for months. The fact was, I just didn't know the answer, mostly because I just didn't know how all of our lives and priorities would shift when the person tying us all together was no longer here to tie us together. Would Marilyn and Bob want anything to do with me, or would my presence be an aching reminder that their only child had been snatched away from them? And would similar feelings of anguish and resentment be triggered in me when I saw *them*? What if I just wanted to hole myself up at home and block out everyone and anyone who wasn't Kit?

Also, what exactly did Kit mean by "look after"? Would I relocate to Millersburg when their health started to decline? Would I carry on our beloved annual Christmas tradition solo, complete with Phase 10 card games and gift exchanges and lottery scratch-off marathons? What if they needed more of me than I was capable of giving?

Rather than subject my interrogation-phobic spouse to my litany of neurotic follow-ups, I swallowed another sip of wine and reassured him with utmost confidence. "Your parents will always be in my life. I will be here for them. I promise."

As hard as it was to have this discussion, I felt a sense of relief that we were finally broaching the subject of what my life would look like without Kit in it—something I'd been reticent to do prior to Davis's call this evening. I then decided to take it a step further and share something that could have a direct impact on my proximity to Kit's parents.

"I was thinking . . . I might move to Los Angeles," I told him, trepidatiously.

"I figured you would," he said, unfazed, as he lit up his one-hitter before taking another puff.

"How would you feel about that?"

"I think you should do it," he said, triggering a deluge of relief inside me that, in turn, triggered another cry spell. I'd known I would have to have his blessing on this, but I hadn't been aware just how important it was until right now. I needed to know he'd be OK with the idea of me packing up and moving so far away from his parents. I needed to know he would be OK with me putting *me* first.

"That means a lot," I told him. "Thank you."

"I want you to be happy. And that includes someday meeting someone else and—"

"Stop right there," I interrupted him, as teardrops dotted my wine. "I appreciate you saying that. But I can't go there."

A silence fell over the deck as Kit looked up at the stars and I tried to enjoy being in the company of my two favorite guys on this beautiful fall night. A light breeze whipped across the deck, causing Mister Scooch's adorable little cat nose to twitch.

"Is there anything you want to get off your chest?" I asked him, cementing the discussion's no-holds-barred theme. "Now's the time to unburden yourself."

Kit emitted another puff of smoke, contemplating the question at hand before responding, "I can't think of anything," He then turned the tables on me: "Anything else you want to ask me?"

Aside from the death thing, there was really only one other unresolved issue I wanted to put to bed once and for all—for my sake and perhaps for Kit's, too. This would not be the first time I posed this particular question to him. More like the third or fourth. And in each instance his answer had always been an unequivocal no. But this would be my first time asking Cancer-Era Kit.

I took a deep breath, which was followed by a sip of wine and a second deep breath.

"Did you have sex with Todd?"

Almost before I could finish asking the question, Kit said, "Yes."

And, for the first time tonight, *he* started crying.

"I'm so sorry I lied to you," he yelped.

A year ago, I would've reacted to this admission by vengefully taking a match to his beloved font collection. But tonight, I was grateful we had the opportunity to partake in this air-clearing moment together. I felt zero anger or resentment.

"Kit, it's OK," I assured him. "It's *OK*. I forgive you."

I could see the relief instantly wash over him. "*Thank you*," he bawled. "You have no idea what an enormous gift you just gave me. Thank you, Mike." Kit wiped his tears before continuing: "He's a good guy, Mike. And he's got a great eye for design. You should lean on him if you ever need apartment tips or advice. We share a lot of the same sensibilities."

"And don't worry about heaven," he added. "I'll get it ready for us."

As I imagined my fastidious husband teaching God's grounds keepers how to paint the Pearly Gates without leaving unsightly brushstrokes, I took another sip of wine and asked Kit if there was anything else he'd like to tell me.

"Please don't fix your teeth," he said, referring to the crooked, crowded bottom row that had long wreaked havoc with my smile, not to mention my confidence, but which Kit had long cherished. "I love your imperfect smile."

I demurred. "Sorry, no can do. My first stop after your funeral is the orthodontist."

"*Please*," Kit begged playfully.

"It's not up for discussion," I maintained with mock-seriousness before changing the topic entirely. "I think I'm ready to try some of this pot you've spoken so highly of."

"Really?" he said, genuinely surprised because I'd been teasing him with this prospect for the past six months, ever since Dr.

Voight informed me that he was concerned about Christopher. But for whatever reason—maybe out of fear of liking it too much and thereby adding another vice to my cache of emotional crutches that already included wine, fountain Diet Coke, and pretzel rolls—I kept putting it off. But as I sat on that deck, the prospect of my never getting the chance to learn the dope ropes from the marijuana master himself felt wrong on so many levels. It was a regret I couldn't afford to have.

"Yep," I told him. "It's time."

"Get over here," he said, and I placed my wineglass down and relocated to the adjoining white mat next to Kit. He handed me the one-hitter as well as a small plastic contraption with two parallel chambers, which he informed me was called a dugout.

"One of these compartments is for the one-hitter, the other has the weed," Kit explained, as he began to mime the following steps: "Take the one-hitter out of one compartment, and lightly grind it into the other compartment two or three times."

He handed me the accouterments and I carefully mashed the slender pipe into the pot chute.

"Good," Kit said. "Now put the empty end in your mouth and light the other end with the lighter, and then inhale slowly. Don't exhale right away, though. Let it sit in your lungs for a few seconds."

I got tripped up on the pesky lighter, which didn't seem to want to catch. I handed it to Kit and asked him to roll the spark wheel for me, an instinct I'd developed over the course of our relationship because what was the point of struggling to do something when you were tethered to a person whose tagline was "What *can't* Kit do?"

"No," he protested, shooing the lighter back toward me. "Try it again. Take your time."

I let out a little sigh before giving it another go.

Nada.

I tried again.

Bupkis.

And once more.

Houston, we have a spark!

I quickly sucked on the pipe before I lost the flame, as Kit looked on with rapt attention. After about two seconds I switched off the lighter, pulled the device out of my mouth, and exhaled. Graceful, it was not.

"That wasn't a very long hit," Kit noted. "You might not feel anything."

Au contraire. I felt like I'd just swallowed a flaming piece of coal.

"My throat is burning," I alerted Kit.

"Just relax," he said, calmly. "It's OK."

"It's still burning," I exclaimed, approaching freak-out mode as I considered the very real possibility that I'd inflicted permanent damage on my windpipe. "I think I took too much."

"Hey," Kit said, gently. "You didn't take too much. Take a sip of water."

He motioned to the glass of water he had off to the side. I picked it up and took a swig. And then another. After the third sip, my throat began to cool off. As did I.

"Better?" Kit asked.

I nodded with relief, prompting Kit to lean in and plant a kiss on my lips.

"Welcome to the stoner club," he purred, like a proud teacher.

"I don't feel high yet," I informed him, slightly disappointed. I *did*, however, feel safe and loved and . . . kinda fucking cool.

"Take another hit," he instructed me. "And hold it in a little longer this time."

The lighter failed to catch on the first try, but the second time proved the charm. I inhaled, and with my confidence increasing, I held the fumes in a few seconds longer before exhaling. Kit had not taken his eyes off of me the entire time.

"Any burning?"

I shook my head.

"Feeling anything else?"

Again, I shook my head, slightly disappointed.

"Give it a few minutes," he said.

As I sat there waiting for the buzz to kick in, I felt an enormous sense of relief that I was able to set aside all of the pot baggage I'd accumulated in order to finally enjoy this long overdue moment with Kit. I liked to think I would've gotten here without a nudge from The Lurker, but I wasn't certain. And . . . *Holy fucking shit, it's kicking in.*

I could sense that Kit was picking up on my energy shift as I transmitted a message to him that went something like this: "I'm sailing. I'm *sailing. I'm saiiiiiiling!*"

I fixed my eyes on the huge tree hugging our deck, and as I never had before, I found myself really noticing it. The bark. The branches. The leaves. It was as if I were seeing it and its colors and its texture for the first time.

"I feel it," I declared to Kit, who suggested I lie down on the mat and get comfortable, which I did. The change of position shifted my view away from the tree and toward the sky. Kit lay down next to me and took my hand.

In the corner of my left eye I could see Scooch's tail swishing around. In the corner of my right eye I could see Kit's profile. And straight ahead I saw stars, their intensity slightly dimmed by the city lights. It was as if I were seeing everything through a dreamlike filter, with a super-sharp focus added on.

And suddenly, like a geyser, my eyes became submerged in tears. Only it didn't feel like crying. It just felt like my body secreting fluid through my eyeballs, cleansing my soul in the process. I felt an overwhelming sense of peace.

"I love you, Kit," I murmured.

"I love *you*, Mike," Kit said.

I had never felt more present in a moment in my life. I wished time could stand still, trapping the three of us on this deck for eternity. Everything I needed, everything I wanted, was right here.

Our transcendent moment was shattered when, out of nowhere, I started . . . chuckling. And then the chuckling gave way to a moderate cackle. And then, with tears still streaming down my face, I just burst out laughing uncontrollably.

"What is going on?" Kit asked with a slight giggle. His simple, four-word query struck my funny bone's sweet spot, exacerbating my chortle attack.

"I don't know!" I yelled, as, suddenly, my emotions took another sharp turn and I felt a massive wave of sadness overtake me. Another batch of tears quickly followed. I was now simultaneously laughing and crying. Happy and sad. I was so overcome by the perfect storm of emotions that I was forced to sit up. Kit propped himself up on his elbow and looked at me with an air of bemused judgment as I wiped the still-overflowing tears on my sweatshirt amid my giggle fit.

I was a fucking mess. And Kit was living for it.

"Oh, honey," Kit said, sassily. "Back away from the crack pipe. You've had enough."

And, with those prettily bitter, slightly cunty words, Kit sent me over the edge, as my laughing reached such an intensity that I was barely able to breathe.

"OK, time to come inside," Kit said, as he packed up the pot and shooed me toward the bathroom window. "Let's put you down."

I fumbled toward the exit while still chortling. Kit held the shutters back as I steadied myself through the window, as if performing a high-wire act. Scooch whizzed past me, clearly not wanting any part of this unfolding disaster.

Once inside, Kit latched the window behind us and escorted me to the bed, my unrestrained laughter now filling up the apartment.

I have Nicole Kidman to thank for keeping me from Kit during our relationship's first major health-related tribulation.

It was the end of January—nearly three months since our fateful Webster Hall hookup—and, by this point, Kit's apartment was rapidly becoming my primary crash pad. Sure, I'd schlep home to New Jersey on critical TV-watching nights, like *Gilmore* Tuesdays and Must-See TV Thursdays—Kit's lack of cable and interest in TV in general necessitated this. And we would venture out to our "suburban pied-à-terre," as we came to refer to it, on the occasional weekend (especially now that Kit and the Smurfs had agreed to put aside their petty differences for the sake of the man they loved). But for all intents and purposes, 25 West 68th Street—well, one impeccably curated room within a shit hole of an apartment at 25 West 68th Street—had become our love nest.

We began cultivating couple-y routines. For instance, Kit introduced me to this crazy concept called *making dinner*. His go-to weekday dish: pasta with marinara sauce along with some kind of protein, typically MorningStar Farms faux Chik Patties (to cater to his new vegetarian-ish boyfriend). Just as appetizing as the food itself was watching Kit play the role of head cook. Even when whipping up a simple pasta-and-Chik-Patty meal, he moved about the kitchen with confidence, swagger, and just a dash of Swedish Chef–like buoyance. And I learned stuff! Like, for instance, you didn't have to heat the Prego in a separate saucepan; you could just wait until the pasta was cooked and drained and then mix in the cold sauce with the steaming hot penne and—*voilà*—dinner was ready. Also, did you know that frozen Chik Patties can be made extra-crispy by taking them out of the frying pan a little early and throwing them in a toaster for a minute? I sure didn't!

Once the cooking portion of the show was done, Kit would *nervously* distribute the pasta onto two plates under the close scrutiny of the Portion Police (I just wanted my fair share!). He would then place one Chik Patty on each dish before cutting a third patty down the middle and placing half on my plate and half on his. We'd then sneak off to the bedroom—without, ideally, running into or engaging roommate Kirby, who, despite the occasional drive-by sighting, remained something of a Maris Crane figure to me—to devour our meals and share highlights from our respective workdays, while Belle and Sebastian, Kit's favorite group, played in the background. Upon completion, we'd return to the kitchen to do the dishes—Kit washed, I dried—before retiring to the bedroom to have sex or spoon or just entertain ourselves on our respective computers.

On non-Bloomfield weekends, we'd go out to dinner at either Harry's Burritos on Columbus Ave (beef tacos and frozen margarita sans salt for him; grilled tofu burrito and Diet Coke with extra ice for me) or Big Nick's Pizza on 71st (we'd start with a mussels marinara appetizer with extra bread for dipping and then split a medium veggie pizza with whole wheat crust). This would be followed by a trip to the four-story Barnes & Noble behemoth down the street, where we would each grab a half dozen magazines—everything from *Dwell* (Kit) to *Details* (me) to *Architectural Digest* (Kit) to *Smurf Collecting Monthly* (one guess)—and then plant ourselves in the top-floor café for two hours drinking iced tea while pointing out interesting articles to each other, with Kit jotting notes in his little black "idea pad." We'd end the night by splitting a peanut butter frozen yogurt cone from the dive-y candy shop at 74th and Columbus.

In the blink of an eye, our lives had become intertwined. I loved being around Kit. Nothing else in my life brought me the kind of immeasurable joy—not my job, not my family, not my friends—as sitting across from Kit at Barnes & Noble, passing magazines back and forth to him. It was easy. Comfortable. Fun.

We'd already adopted pet names for each other. Kit was my "Poops" and I his "Doops," both of which were derivations of "Poopiedoops," a term whose origin has eluded etymologists to this day.

Kit also answered to "*Peepie*doops," a nod to the delayed trickle of urine that would lightly moisten his tighty-whities after he was done peeing. This was something he was initially embarrassed about, but after seeing how giddy it made me to watch this strapping twenty-nine-year-old man run around with dew spots on his undies, he would excitedly point to his drizzly drawers and marvel with childlike wonder, "*Peepiedoops!*" (These names would all eventually be jettisoned and replaced with the far simpler Bodge.)

For all of our differences, we were incredibly compatible—physically speaking, as well. The size and shape of our bodies created the coziest, most soul-enriching canoodle. As the smaller of the two, I backed myself up into Kit's embrace (while mimicking the dump truck–style warning beep), and he would promptly wrap himself around me like a human Venus flytrap. We were like two puzzle pieces connecting, so much so that Kit took to whispering "click" in my ear once we were fully attached. Whenever we attempted to mix it up by doing a reverse canoodle—little ol' me awkwardly spooning big ol' Kit—it would generally last about thirty seconds before Kit declared, "Let's do this right," at which point we would revert to our nature-intended positions.

We started switching up our sexual roles, too. Kit began dropping hints about wanting to bottom for me. It was already pretty firmly established that Kit—whose crowd-pleasing endowment made him catnip for the gays during his five years in Miami, or so legend (read: Kit) tells it—was the more experienced one in the bedroom. But his *appetite* for sex also far exceeded mine. Many nights I was content with some heavy petting followed by an epic canoodle session. That was not the case with Kit. The man had needs. And I was going to do everything in my power to meet those needs and avoid him seeking satisfaction elsewhere, like, you know, the steam room at the gym. (Despite my best efforts to sweep that little transgression of his under the rug, it continued to quietly feed my inadequacy fears.)

Basically, I knew that if I was going to get this job done right, I would need an unbreakable erection that lasted up to four hours. So, after years of hearing about this magic little blue pill, I ventured to my primary care physician and asked him for "some of that Viagra, please."

Less than twenty-four hours later, I—ignoring my MD's recommendation to "start with a half a dose, just to see how your body reacts"— popped an entire pill and showed up on Kit's doorstep with what felt like early-onset bubonic plague. I was nauseous, dizzy, and feverish. But I was also sporting a rock-hard pocket rocket, and no amount of pre-performance anxiety was diminishing its firmness. The stage had been set for me to satisfy my man.

"Tonight's the night," I declared, as I boldly, proudly grabbed Kit's hand and placed it on my appendage.

"Holy hell," he exclaimed, before (I think) jokingly adding, "Did you pop a Viagra before coming over?"

Oh, shit. I hadn't really thought about whether I was going to divulge to Kit the truth about my chemically induced phallus. So faced with a split-second decision, I decided not to shatter the illusion.

"No, I didn't pop a *Viagra*," I chuckled, as I held his hand over my girth-tastic groin. "This is just how much I want this . . ."

And I continued to believe there was nothing to be gained by telling him the truth, and potentially making him upset or even angry at what he might perceive as my deception, especially since, as I learned during this ongoing discovery phase of our courtship, Kit had a bit of a short fuse. And it wasn't just a nocturnal phenomenon, à la Morning Tourette's. Kit was prone to reacting emotionally, irrationally, and with a compromised internal censor during his waking hours, too, particularly in situations wherein he was faced with obscene incompetence or he felt he had been wronged.

Case in point: If a car sped up to cut him off as he was crossing the street, he would pound on the trunk as the vehicle zoomed by. If a pedestrian was walking too slowly in front of him, he would hiss so loudly it'd startle them dead in their tracks, giving Kit the sidewalk opening he needed to pass them right by. When the manager at the Galaxy Diner (aka our favorite Sunday-morning breakfast spot) stubbornly refused to heed our request to change the channel on the large-screen TV hanging on the wall near our table—which was airing a CNN special that depicted in graphic detail a patient undergoing open heart surgery—an incensed Kit engaged in a shouting match with him before insisting we leave and never return.

I began to seriously worry that one of these people would pull out a gun and shoot him. I even warned him, "Someone is going to pull out a gun and shoot you."

Luckily, he had yet to turn his venom on me, that one isolated Morning Tourette's–fueled outburst notwithstanding. But I had no interest in poking the beast within. Growing up with a father who had a legendarily violent temper taught me to avoid confrontation at all costs, lest you wanted to be smacked across the face or, worse, forced to kneel on the tiled kitchen floor for an hour with your outstretched hands weighed down by a dictionary.

So, in that sense, I was relieved that on this particular weekday morning in January—just hours before our big date with Nicole Kidman—Kit was awoken *not* by his "bull in a china shop" boyfriend, as he had begun to affectionately dub me, but by a persistent sharp pain in his abdomen. It was the most alert I had seen him before 8 a.m.

"I don't think I'm going to work today," he moaned. My offer to run out and get him some Pepto-Bismol at the corner store was summarily rebuffed. "It'll pass," he shrugged. "It's probably from the Mexican we had last night."

This was my first glimpse of "sick Kit," so it was hard to gauge if he was exaggerating, downplaying, or something in between. Regardless, it was unsettling to see him in distress. Thanks to the considerable disease-and-death baggage my parents left me, it was even a little worrisome. Thankfully, my mind only took a brief *What if it's liver cancer?* detour before comfortably parking itself at Kit's unofficial food-poisoning diagnosis.

Truthfully, I was more concerned that he might not be able to make the special industry screening of *The Others* we had on the books for that evening. I had already seen the superb Kidman-fronted thriller when it first opened over the summer, but I enjoyed it so much I wanted to experience it again with Kit. One of the perks of having a boyfriend was getting to share the things you loved with the *person* you loved. So I had tracked down a publicist over at Dimension Films, the studio behind the pic, and scored us a pair of tickets to a private screening exclusively for Oscar voters (and Kidman groupies like myself). I had been looking forward to our big *Others* outing all week and I *really* needed Kit to throw up or shit out that nasty-ass burrito before the proverbial curtain rose at 8 p.m.

"I'll check in with you later this morning," I told him before heading off to work. "Keep your phone close by. Hopefully, you'll feel better and can go to the movie tonight."

"I'm sure I'll be fine by tonight," he said confidently.

Unfortunately, his symptoms, which by mid-afternoon also included vomiting, worsened over the course of the day. Even the Pepto-B he fetched from the corner bodega was bringing no relief.

"I don't think I'm going to make the screening tonight," he regretfully informed me by phone at around 5 p.m.

"Then I'm not going either," I insisted. "I'll come bring you some soup and kisses."

"No," he snapped, his blunt, albeit medically induced, rejection stinging a bit. "No offense, but I'm not in the mood for company. Go see the movie."

It did not feel right going without him. He was the reason I'd even *gotten* the tickets in the first place. But since he didn't want me doting on him, it seemed silly to let them go to waste. So I decided to attend the screening anyway. I considered asking my BFF and former wingman Matt Eriksson to be my plus one, but a subtle strain had been placed on our friendship since Kit had arrived on the scene. I already felt guilty about pretty much abandoning him these past two months as I got swept up in all things Kit, and it didn't feel right offering him Kit's hand-me-downs. Also, being with Matt reminded me of how much I missed him and our friendship, and served to highlight one of the not-so-fun sacrifices I had made in the name of Kit. So I decided to go alone.

"But I'm coming over to check in on you after it gets out," I maintained.

Despite being somewhat preoccupied with Kit's health—*food poisoning*-preoccupied not *liver cancer*-preoccupied—I managed to once again lose myself in *The Others*, in large part due to Kidman's searing, haunting, career-best performance. All the Oscar pundits were predicting she'd get recognized for *Moulin Rouge!* when nominations were announced next month, but for my money, her work in *The Others* was far superior (and I loved *Moulin Rouge!*).

The movie ended and I immediately powered up my phone to check in on my under-the-weather man. I noticed I had a voicemail. It was from Kit.

"Mike, it's me. I'm at Mount Sinai Hospital not far from my apartment. I think it's Tenth Avenue. I have appendicitis. I'll probably be in surgery when you get out of the movie. My phone battery is about to die, so I need you to do me a big favor and call my parents to let them know what's going on. My mom's name is Marilyn and my dad is Bob. Just tell them you're a new friend of mine." He then gave me their phone number, before concluding, "My mother is going to insist on coming into the city. Tell her *not* to. I love you."

Fuck me. Fuck Nicole Kidman. Fuck *The Others*. Kit needed me and I wasn't there for him. With my pulse quickening, I called Kit back, hoping to catch him on his cell before he got taken into surgery. It went straight to his voicemail. Fuck. I took a seat outside the screening room to catch my breath and plot my next move.

His parents. Kit asked me to call his parents. I have to call his parents. I have to call his parents who don't even know I exist, let alone that their son is gay, to tell them that their only child is undergoing emergency surgery.

Jesus. Mary. And. Joseph. Fuck. Me.

I exhaled slowly, and as I punched the number into my flip phone, I appealed to the gay gods to help me not royally fuck this up.

One ring.

Two rings.

Three rings.

Before there was a fourth ring, a gravelly-sounding man said, "Hello."

"Hi ... Is this Bob?" I asked.

"This is he."

"My name is Michael. I'm a friend of your son's. His phone battery died and he asked me to call you to tell you he's having his appendix removed. He's in surgery now."

"Hold on a moment, let me get a piece of paper to write this down," he said calmly, before plunking the phone down and returning a few seconds later. "Kit's mother Marilyn is in Allentown at a basketball game so I want to make sure I get all the information. What hospital is he at?"

"Mount Sinai," I said. "Kit also wanted me to tell you that you shouldn't come into the city."

"Oh, his mother is going to want to come in," Bob said.

"Kit assumed as much."

Crickets.

"What did you say your name was again?" he asked, suspiciously.

"Mike. Kit and I just met a few weeks ago," I replied, choosing my words *very* carefully. "I'm headed to the hospital now. I can call you back with an update when I get there."

"You better give me your number," he said. "Marilyn's going to want to talk to you when she gets home."

I relayed to him my number, after which he very slowly repeated it back to confirm its accuracy.

"Yep, that's correct," I assured him.

"OK, we'll talk to you soon, Mike," Bob said. "Thank you for calling."

I hung up and quickly conducted a postmortem of the call in my head: Had I just outed Kit to his dad? Had I gotten the message across that Kit did not want them coming into the city? Oh, and could Kit's dad have *been* any more laid back and chill? I determined that I'd done the best I could have given the improbable circumstances, and ran outside to hail a cab to Mount Sinai. With any luck, Kit would be out of surgery when I got there and ready to receive me.

On the ride uptown, my concern for Kit started to mount. What if, God forbid, they didn't remove his appendix in time? Or there was a catastrophic complication during surgery? The thought of losing him just two months after I found him sent a sizeable shiver down my spine. We hadn't even taken our first vacation together. Or met each other's family. I quickly talked myself off that particular ledge, reasoning that the Universe had already punched the maximum number of holes in my tragedy card. Kit was going to be fine.

Instead, my mind fixated on another area of concern—I might not be granted permission to see Kit because I was neither a blood relative nor his legal spouse (if such things had been legal then), a prospect that brought my blood to a low simmer. I was fully prepared to go to war with the hospital staff if necessary. The image of an unglued Shirley MacLaine in *Terms of Endearment* screaming at the nurses to "give my daughter the *shottttttttt!*" popped in my head. Come hell or high water, I was going to be at Kit's side. And if it meant delivering an Oscar-worthy breakdown scene in the lobby of New York's Mount Sinai Hospital, so be it.

"Hi, I'm here to see a patient by the name of Kit Cowan," I informed the receptionist as she typed his name into her computer.

"We don't have anyone here by that name . . ."

"Give my boyfriend the *shottttttttt!*" I interrupted, pounding my fist on the desk.

OK, that's *almost* what happened. In reality, I placed a muzzle on my inner MacLaine and looked at the receptionist all puzzled and confused-like. No one here by that name? Had Kit, in his presurgical haze, sent me to the wrong hospital?

"Are you sure?" I asked. "Are you spelling Kit K-I-T?"

"We have a *Christopher* Cowan," she said.

"Yes, *Christopher*," I replied with enormous relief. "Kit is his nickname. I'm sorry. It's *Christopher* Cowan." It was the first time I had ever heard anyone refer to him as Christopher. It sounded super-formal and weird.

"He's out of surgery and in recovery," she advised me.

"I would like to see him," I informed her sternly.

"He can't have visitors just yet," she replied. "Go ahead and have a seat. It shouldn't be too long."

Huh. MacLaine wasn't needed after all.

"So, he made it through surgery OK?" I inquired.

"Yes, it seems so."

"Thank you," I said. "I'll just take a seat over here."

Before I had even plopped myself down in one of the waiting room chairs, my cell rang. It was a 704 number. It was likely Kit's mom. *Deep breath.*

"Hello?" I said.

"Hi," a honeyed-yet-stern woman's voice replied. "This is Kit's mother, Marilyn."

Through those six simple words, I was able to glean the following: Unlike Kit's slightly scattershot, cool-as-a-cucumber dad, his mom was Not. Fucking. Around. Her boy was in trouble and her maternal instincts were firing on all cylinders. And that meant dispensing with any and all pleasantries.

"Hi, Marilyn, I was just about to call—"

"Is he still in surgery?" she interrupted.

"No, he just got out and he's in recovery," I explained. "He's not allowed any visitors so I'm—"

"And which hospital did you say he was at?" she asked, sending me a clear signal at this point that she wanted less chitchat and more information.

"It's Mount Sinai," I informed her. "I think the cross street is 59th. If you give me a second, I can find the number—"

"That's OK, I can find it," she said. "They said he's doing OK?"

"Yes, they assure me the surgery was a success . . . Kit was going to call you himself, but his battery was about to die on his phone."

[Crickets]

"Kit never mentioned a Mike to us before," she added, suspiciously.

Oh, boy, here we go.

"We only recently became friends," I explained, shit threatening to pour out of my ass faster than an aged-out soft-serve machine at Dairy Queen. "We met through a mutual friend . . ."

"Let us know if anything changes, please, Mike," she interjected, clearly preparing to wrap up the call, much to my relief.

"I absolutely will," I assured her. I resisted the urge to remind her of

Kit's wishes for her *not* to come into the city, on account of the fact that she was scaring the shit out of me. Also, prolonging the conversation meant risking her grilling me further about who I was and how exactly I knew her son.

"Thank you," she concluded. "Bye now."

I hung up, took a deep breath, then raced off to the bathroom to relieve my extremely irritable and terrified bowel. Was she that chilly toward me because she suspected—feared—that I was more than just Kit's friend? Or maybe she just didn't have the warmest telephone demeanor? Regardless, I couldn't help but feel like my relationship with Marilyn Cowan had gotten off on a decidedly sour note.

I ran across the street to the deli to calm my nerves with some caffeine via an ice-cold Diet Coke (when your body tells you what it wants, believe it), then parked myself in a chair near the main reception area to wait for the all clear. I listened to Kit's voicemail again to make sure I hadn't missed any important details the first time around. I was struck by how calm and lucid he sounded.

I was also able, now that the immediate crisis had passed, to really take in the fact that we had only known each other for two months and yet I was already, for all intents and purposes, his primary emergency contact.

I also didn't take for granted that he had ended the message with an "I love you."

It had been a month and change since Kit and I formally graduated from olive juice to I love you. It happened on that Thursday night before Christmas—twenty-four hours after I checked my email on the bus back to New Jersey and added "accomplished poet" to the long list of Kit's enviable talents.

I arrived at Kit's apartment after work brandishing a large wrapped present and a Cheshire grin. To say I was excited to give him this gift would be an understatement. The fact that Kit professed to being something of a Grinch around the holidays only ratcheted up my excitement. If anyone could show him the true magic of Christmas, it was I. And the look of cautious anticipation on his face when he saw the gift in my hands suggested my conversion therapy was already taking hold.

"Can I guess what it is?" he asked, playfully, as he reached for the gift.

"No," I protested, shooing his hand away, slightly horrified at the prospect of him spoiling his own surprise—even though I was fairly certain he would never in a million years guess what was hidden beneath the simple Santa-adorned wrapping paper. I placed the gift down on the bed and positioned myself on one side while Kit plopped down on the other.

After he complimented my choice of wrapping paper, I gave him permission to open it. Given his high anticipation level, I assumed he would violently tear the paper off. I assumed wrong. He instead grasped the gift in his hand and lifted it up, taking in the weight of it. I could see the wheels turning.

"You're determined to ruin this surprise, aren't you?" I harrumphed with a mix of annoyance and, truth be told, glee. Kit was clearly having fun. And so was I.

He proceeded to shake the mysterious bounty ever so gently as I warned him to "Be careful . . ." He then put his ear up to the surface, as if snooping for an auditory clue. He continued this enjoyable reconnaissance mission for a few more minutes before he began to gently, slowly, methodically peel back the corners of the wrapping paper, declaring, "This can be reused!"

As he started to remove a larger swath of the paper, my eagerness intensified, my eyes glued to his; I did not want to miss his reaction. I could hear what sounded like a faint drum roll in the distance as his retina made first contact with the present—a slightly weathered red-and-blue vintage box emblazoned with the words "Sneaky Pete's Magic Set."

Suddenly, the atmosphere in the room became heavy, and Kit's giddy expression turned decidedly solemn. His general vibe morphed from the giddy "Ooh, I got a gift!" to "*Oh . . . I got a gift.*" He folded the wrapping paper, set it aside, and proceeded to just stare at the toy that had eluded him throughout his childhood. I was on the edge of my seat, waiting for him to say something. But he just sat there, silently, his jaw slightly ajar, his eyes tearing up. He then sprang up from the bed, retrieved his point-and-shoot, and snapped a dozen or so pictures of his new toy from various vantage points. He then put the camera down, sat on the bed beside me, looked me straight in the eyes, and said, "I love you."

"Good," I replied, fighting back my own tears now. "Because I love you, too."

And we kissed. He then hugged me tightly and said, "Thank you. That was really special."

And with that, my first Christmas gift to Kit was an unqualified, smashing success. And he hadn't even looked under the hood yet!

"Look what's inside!" I said enthusiastically, as Kit excitedly pulled open the fifty-some-odd-year-old box to discover talking dice, miniature magic flower pots, card tricks, a cut-the-lady-in-half figurine, and, of course, a magic wand. He promised to put on a show, but only after he presented me with my gift.

"It's not as good as yours," he warned me ahead of time.

"I mean, how *could* it," I razzed him.

"OK, stand up," he instructed me, "and close your eyes."

"Uh-oh," I replied as I rose to my feet, closed my eyes, and grabbed his hand. He led me a few paces past the bed, and I could hear him slide the curtain back on his makeshift wardrobe/closet. "Am I going back into the closet?!"

"OK, open them," he said.

I raised my eyelids and looked straight ahead inside Kit's closet. Only something was very different—one quarter of it had been emptied, and right above this newly bare section was a tiny label maker–made nametag. It simply read "Doops."

The amazing, thoughtful, homemade gift needed no further explanation, but Kit excitedly provided one. "You now have your own space for clothes," he exclaimed, as he raced over to the temporary closet I had haphazardly created on the far corner of his desk, grabbed one of my button-down shirts, threw it on a hanger, and popped it on the garment rod. He was basically demonstrating to me how a closet works. And it amused me to no end.

"Hey," I said, as I pulled him aside. "I love it. It's perfect. Thank you."

"There's even a spot for your shoes!" Kit continued, as he grabbed my sneakers and placed them in a separate compartment near the bottom of the wardrobe. "See?!"

I didn't think anything could edge out the Smurf-filled 1983 holiday season atop my list of favorite Christmases of all time, but even before Kit whipped out his magic wand and did his best David Copperfield impression, 2001 had taken its rightful place at No. 1.

The blare of the hospital intercom snapped me out of reminisce mode, and I noticed it was now well past midnight. I approached the reception desk to inquire about Kit's, er, Christopher's status.

"You can head up to Recovery," the receptionist informed me.

Relieved, I walked briskly to the elevator, headed up to Recovery, and checked in at the nurses' station.

"Follow me," the nurse said, as she led me past five beds before we reached Kit. "Please keep it short. He needs his rest."

There he was. Incapacitated. Hooked up to machines. It was a jarring, unsettling sight. I imagined for a brief, chilling moment what it would feel like if he was in the hospital for something more serious than an appendectomy, and my heart skipped a beat. I then quickly banished said thought from my head.

As I approached the bed, he turned his head and locked eyes with me. He managed to eke out a smile. I leaned in and gave him the softest of kisses on his lips.

"I still think you could've made the movie," I whispered, to which he smiled again, before promptly falling right back to sleep. With the clock approaching 1 a.m., I decided, under the nurse's recommendation, to head home. I didn't feel comfortable crashing at Kit's place without Kit being there (who would protect me from Kirby?!), so I hopped a bus to NJ with an eye toward hightailing it back into the city first thing in the morning. And I do mean *first thing* in the morning.

Less than six hours later—at 6:30 a.m. to be exact—I was back on a bus heading for the city. Assuming I got to the hospital by 7:30, that would give me at least an hour with Kit before I had to get to work.

I once again didn't need Shirley MacLaine's assistance in getting past security; I was allowed to head right up and into Kit's now regular room. I walked in and found him considerably more alert than I had left him six hours earlier. His face lit up when he saw me.

"Could you *be* any more dramatic?" I zinged him, as I planted a more forceful kiss on his lips.

"How was the movie?" he deadpanned.

"How are you feeling?" I inquired, ignoring his dig.

"I'm sore. But I feel better than I did before the surgery."

Kit went on to recount his night from hell, which essentially entailed his toughing it out at home as the symptoms grew increasingly more debilitating, before finally declaring "Uncle" and staggering out to the street to hail a cab to the emergency room.

"You think that's bad," I countered, "I had to talk to your parents."

"I'm sorry you had to do that," he said. "It's just, God forbid something happened to me during the surgery . . ."

"It was fine," I assured him. "Although I'm pretty sure your mother already hates me."

"She's on her way into the city," he said.

"What?!" I bellowed. "I swear I told her not to come." And that was, well, kinda-sorta true. I had told his *dad* to tell her not to come. I had been too scared to deliver the message to his mom myself.

"It's fine," he sighed. "I knew she wouldn't listen. Now I have to worry about where she's going to sleep and what she's going to eat. And soon. I may be getting out of here this afternoon."

"I brought you a little get-well present," I said, before reaching into my backpack and pulling out a Doctor Smurf figurine. I placed it on his nightstand. "I'm heading to work, but this guy is going to be my eyes and ears while I'm away."

Kit reacted with a bemused grin—which was a big step up from the look of terror on his face last month when he encountered my collection in the bedroom of my apartment. "Get over here, you," he cooed, signaling he wanted a kiss. I happily obliged.

"I was planning to come back when you're discharged and help you home," I informed him. "But I'm guessing your mom will be here by then . . ." I wanted to both give him an out to tell me not to come while also making it clear that, mother or no mother, my preference was to be at his side when he was discharged.

"I know," he sighed. "The two of you were going to meet eventually."

"Who are you going to tell her I am?"

"I don't know. I haven't figured that out yet," he said, a little agitation setting in. "It may be time for me and my mother to have a little chat."

"You mean *the* chat?" I asked, genuinely surprised—and a little concerned—that my existence was leading him to take such a monumental step.

"OK, no more questions," he barked. "Off to work with you."

"But . . ." I responded, playfully.

"*Buh, buh, buh, buh, buh . . .*" he said. "Keep it up and I won't show you my scars."

I planted another kiss on his lips and then headed off to work. Everything felt like it was moving so fast. What if his mom flipped out? How was I not going to blame myself?

At work, as I typed up my morning news roundup, I was preoccupied with thoughts of Kit's mom. Had she arrived yet? Was Kit going to tell her at the hospital? Was she going to crash at Kit's place tonight and, therefore, force me to sleep in New Jersey and away from Kit on his first night home?

Luckily, I wasn't kept in suspense for long. Around 2 p.m., Kit phoned to let me know he was being discharged around 4.

"Is your mom with you now?" I asked, tentatively.

"She's down in the cafeteria getting something to eat," Kit said. "Before you ask, I haven't told her yet."

"Did she have questions . . . ?"

"She asked where the Smurf on my nightstand came from. I told her you had given it to me. And that was the end of that."

"Uh-oh . . ." I said. "Are you sure you still want me there?"

"Yes," he said, without delay. "But you need to act like a friend, so no kissing or calling me 'Poops.'"

The little gay activist in me was appalled at all of the words that had just come out of Kit's mouth. I wanted to get confirmation that he was still planning to have The Talk with her, so at least I knew my trip back into the closet would be short-lived. But I didn't want to apply any further pressure to him. And I also didn't want to lose my hospital visitation privileges. The mere fact that Kit was inviting me to be in the same room as his mother—and a hospital room, no less—was an enormously brave step.

"Also," Kit added, "she's staying with me tonight."

"I figured as much," I sighed.

"I'm sorry, Doops," he said. "She's just going to be here for one night."

"It's fine . . . I would've liked to have been the one taking care of you on your first night home, but I get it. Let me wrap up here at work and head over."

"Actually, I have a small favor to ask . . ." he said, the inflection in his voice suggesting said favor might be a size or two up from small. "I need you to stop by my apartment and, um, clean it up before my mom's arrival."

"You mean hide stuff?" I clarified.

"Pretty much," he said. "I don't remember what's out in the open, but . . ."

"I don't have a key," I interrupted.

"Kirby will be home," Kit noted, clearly having thought this through. "Just knock on the door and he'll let you in. Explain that I'm in the hospital and you're picking up a few things for me."

"OK . . ." I replied, barely hiding my concern about the prospect of being alone with the allegedly unpredictable, unpleasant Kirby. I'd never witnessed his volatile behavior firsthand. And the few times we had crossed paths in the apartment, he had been perfectly civil to me. But Kit had built him up to be something of a monster, a characterization he was now backpedaling on.

"Don't worry," Kit said. "He's not going to murder you. And if he *does*, you had a good life."

"Well, if he *does* murder me, you're going to have a tough time explaining to your mother what that crusty washcloth on your nightstand is for," I shot back.

"Good point," he said. "Well, you better protect yourself then. You're an athlete after all."

"This conversation is endlessly amusing, but I have a sex dungeon to sterilize, so I better be off."

"I *love* yoooou," Kit keened playfully.

"*Mmhmm*," I harrumphed with a mix of faux annoyance and *real* annoyance. "See you in about an hour. Maybe."

I hung up the phone, shut down my computer, and hopped a cab from *TV Guide*'s midtown office to 68th and Central Park West. During the ride, I managed to calm my jitters about Kirby and just focus on the task at hand. It was time to man the fuck up.

I breezed by the doorman—they pretty much all knew me by now—headed up to the third floor, and gently knocked on the door once. There was no answer. I knocked on the door again, this time with a little more power behind it. Still no answer. Shit. Of all the scenarios I had played out in my head, Kirby being MIA had *not* been one of them. I decided to give it one last shot, and loudly pounded three consecutive times—the force of which pushed the door slightly ajar. And, just like that, I was faced with another improbable scenario—breaking and entering the apartment with Kirby *inside*.

I nudged the door open and tiptoed into the hallway. I immediately heard the blare of the television coming from the living room, dashing any and all hope that Kirby might not be home. As I took another step toward Kit's bedroom door, the floor creaked beneath me and suddenly I found myself at the fore of a chase scene right out of *Jurassic Park*. What started as a quiet rumble in the distance quickly escalated into a series of thunderous booms that became progressively louder. They were the footsteps of a beast. And it was heading straight for me. Paralyzed with fear, I just froze in the hallway, prepared to accept my tragic fate. As Kit had so eloquently reminded me, I had indeed had a good life.

Suddenly, I was face-to-face with Kirby. Although we'd whizzed by each other a half-dozen or so times, this was the first opportunity I'd had to actually see him up close. He was short, stout, and . . . harmless-looking. He stood before me brandishing a half-eaten piece of fried chicken in one hand and a remote control in the other.

"Oh, you're Kit's friend," he said, annoyed but also relieved that a rapist wasn't descending upon him. "Kit's not here. He doesn't get home from work until around seven."

"I know, he's in the hospital," I explained. "I'm picking up a few things for him."

As I waited for him to ask me *what* Kit was doing in the hospital, he instead said, "Do me a favor, next time you come over without Kit, knock."

"Actually, I did—"

Before I could finish my sentence, Kirby did an abrupt about-face and retreated back to the living room, leaving a trail of chicken crumbs in his wake. On the bright side, at least our exchange had been quick and bloodless.

I entered Kit's room and securely closed the door behind me. I dropped my backpack on the bed, rolled up my sleeves, and got busy de-gaying the space. As if equipped with a Terminator-like motion analysis detector, I scanned the room looking for vulnerabilities. I noticed among Kit's little village of curiosities the statue of a small green man, smiling, with a disproportionately large, erect penis. I grabbed it. I combed over his bookshelf and spotted two VHS gay porn tapes sandwiched between the *Sex and the City* and *AbFab* box sets. I then raced into the bathroom and snatched the Peter Meter and the fornicating dinosaurs from the medicine cabinet. I surveyed the room one last time, looking for anything I might've missed. I pulled the curtain back on Kit's wardrobe and looked around. As I was about to declare that space all clear, my eye caught the "Doops" tag atop my side of the closet. I stared at it for a second, before reluctantly pulling it down and adding it to the pile.

I grabbed one of Kit's numerous empty shoeboxes, loaded all of the items into it, and kneeled down to stash it beneath the bed. While clearing out a space, I came upon Kit's mini-hoard of sex toys. They, too, were in a shoebox, only the lid was off and the contents exposed. I had known the cache existed. But I'd never actually taken a close-up look at his collection, partly to be respectful of his personal space and partly because the gay sex shame ingrained in me as a child was still renting out space in my psyche. Also, I sensed—feared—that there were aspects of Kit's sexuality he was protecting me from. Or perhaps I was protecting *myself* from.

It was time I found out just how kinky my new boyfriend was, so I pulled the stockpile of personal pleasure objects out from under the bed and rested it between my legs. And I started rifling.

I didn't recognize half of these freaky items, or the person they belonged to. I imagined his mother finding them, and having all of her base fears about gay people being sex-obsessed deviants confirmed. That is, if she had such fears. Maybe I was projecting my own mortification on her? And on Kit? No matter, I didn't like how the treasure trove of erotica was making me feel, so I grabbed the lid, secured it tightly, and tucked the shoebox so far under the bed a cockroach would have trouble finding it.

Next, I grabbed the new shoebox filled with Kit's comparatively more PG-13-rated novelties and jammed it under the bed as well. Then I stood up to eyeball his room one last time. It all looked perfectly sterile and safe and inoffensive. Like a sitcom bedroom. My work was done.

I zoomed out of the apartment—shouting a super-quick "Goodbye, Kirby!" as I went—and hailed a cab to the hospital. It was time to meet Marilyn.

Before entering Kit's room, I paused in the hallway to make the mental shift from Kit's lovey-dovey, super-shmoopie boyfriend to Kit's buddy. Pal. Friend. I was just there to help a homeboy get his ass home from the hospital. No biggie.

As I turned the corner into the hospital room, the first thing I saw was a fully dressed Kit sitting up in his bed with a shopping bag beside him. There was a pleasantly attired, bespectacled, raven-haired woman—in the fifty-five- to sixty-year-old range—flitting about the room with purpose. She looked like someone's mother. She looked like someone's mother named Marilyn.

"Mom, stop creating problems just to solve them," Kit sighed as I approached the bed.

"It's cold outside and that jacket is not going to keep you warm," she insisted, as she took a blanket out of one of the closets and draped it over Kit, seemingly unaware that I had breached the perimeter.

"I'm not walking onto the streets of New York wearing a stolen hospital blanket," Kit retorted, overplaying his agitation for comedic effect upon seeing me. "You trying to get me arrested, woman?

"Mom, this is Mike," Kit said, nonchalantly switching gears. "Mike, this is my mother. She's in rare form, so watch out."

Marilyn paused her aggressively protective mama bear routine, looked me in the eye, and reached out her hand. "Hi. It's nice to meet you," she said, all professional and businesslike.

"Hi," I replied, cordially but not *too* cordially because, you know, I was just one of Kit's bruhs from the basketball court. "It's nice to meet you, too."

Meanwhile, my head started spinning from the epically surreal nature of what was transpiring. I was standing in a hospital room with the man I loved and my future mother-in-law and I was trying like hell to pretend like this wasn't a moment I would remember for the rest of my life.

"We're waiting for the nurse to come with the wheelchair and then we're outta here," Kit informed me.

"How are you feeling?"

"Sore, but the Vicodin is tasty," Kit said, before adding with surprising sassiness—considering he wasn't out to his mom yet—"I told the nurse I want total sensory deprivation and backup drugs." (I would come to find out years later during a weekend-long *AbFab* marathon that this sassy retort, like so many of his sauciest zingers, was appropriated from the cult comedy. Every 15 minutes I'd hear one of the series' two boozy leads—Eddy or Patsy—utter a strikingly familiar crack. And every time my jaw would hit the floor, after which I'd turn my head and, with a mix of disillusionment and reverence, shoot a gleefully sheepish Kit a look like, *Are you kidding me*?!)

Marilyn continued to keep herself plenty busy organizing and tidying, and actually I wasn't sure what the hell she was doing, but man, she was *busy*.

"Marilyn, did you drive in?" I asked, a preventative measure to avoid what I sensed was a fast-approaching awkward silence. Kit let out a guffaw, as if the mere suggestion that his mother would operate a vehicle on the rough-and-tumble streets of Manhattan was preposterous.

"No, I caught an early bus from Kutztown," she explained, assuming I knew what the hell Kutztown was.

"Ah, *Kutztown*," I deadpanned. "I hear they have some of the world's finest bus stations."

My joke landed with a thud. Kit just looked at me and shook his head.

OK, then, well . . . small talk it was!

"Did you hit much traffic?"

"No," Marilyn replied, as she lifted her suitcase onto one of the empty chairs, in preparation for our exit but mostly just to stay in motion. She was behaving like the bus in *Speed*. If she dipped below 50 mph she'd explode.

"That's good," I opined. "Things tend to be quiet in January after the holidays. All the tourists are gone."

[Crickets]

"Bob stayed behind?" I inquired before immediately wondering/worrying if it was too soon to be addressing Kit's father as "Bob." What else would I call him? Mr. Cowan?

Kit jumped in. "My dad hates the city with a fiery passion."

"Yeah, Bob wasn't cut out for city life," Marilyn agreed.

At this point, it was clear that I was going to be doing *all* of the heavy lifting over the next some-odd hours that the three of us were together. Kit's eyes were fixed on the doorway, waiting for his ride to arrive. Marilyn was otherwise occupied reconstituting the hospital room. All of my questions were proving to be conversation-enders, not -starters. And no one was laughing at my jokes.

Marilyn, were you aware that I'm fucking your son? I informed her, giddily. *Well, actually, he's fucking me most of the time. I occasionally fuck him. The important thing to know is that we are fucking. A lot.*

Yeah, so I didn't actually say that. But the awkwardness in the room was such that I needed to create some form of entertainment, even if it was only in my head.

"Ah, here she is!" a relieved Kit exclaimed as the nurse entered pushing a wheelchair. "I'm getting sprung!"

"You're chariot awaits, sir," the nurse retorted, matching Kit's playfulness.

Kit scooched to the edge of the bed, but was stopped by what appeared to be a sharp pain in his stitched-up abdomen. Marilyn and I both instinctually lunged toward him and let out near-simultaneous variations on "be careful" and "slow down" and "Jesus Christ are you OK?!"

"I'm *fine*," Kit announced, shooing us both away.

I quickly retreated, as any platonic friend would do. Marilyn, how-ever, charged in.

"Kit, you need help getting up," she said dotingly, grabbing his arm.

"*Mom, I got it*," he barked, determined to get himself in the wheel-chair on his own. "I was up walking around earlier. I just need a min-ute."

Kit worked through the pain, stood, and relocated to the wheel-chair. Upon landing in the seat, he sighed, "There we go. That wasn't so bad."

He then ordered me to help his mom with the bags, which came as a huge relief because it meant I finally had something to do besides standing around pretending not to be his boyfriend.

I approached Marilyn, who was clumsily juggling her own suitcase and a mysterious secondary duffel bag, as well as the shopping tote from the bed holding what I presumed were Kit's belongings.

"Marilyn, let me take—"

"*I got it*," she cut me off, clearly not willing to let me share *any* of the burden.

"Are you sure?" I asked. "My hands are empty."

"Nope, I'm good," she maintained.

I looked at Kit, hoping he'd intervene and knock some sense into his mother, but he was already halfway to the elevator with his new medical chauffeur/BFF. By the time we hit the street, Kit was so busy chatting up the nurse that he didn't realize the ridiculous scene unfold-ing just a few paces behind his wheelchair. Marilyn, balancing what seemed suddenly like sixteen suitcases as if her life depended on it, was stumbling down the walkway toward the curb while I awkwardly, silently walked alongside her with my hands completely effen *empty*. Strangers were scowling at me left and right, like, "How dare you make that old woman carry all those bags by herself!"

As I wondered what I was even doing there, my anger toward Kit began to build. It was as if he had thrown Marilyn and me together and then shrugged, "Eh, you guys work it out among yourselves." That little fucker.

"*I* will go find a cab," I declared loudly and boldly before anyone (read: Marilyn) beat me to the punch. I raced over to the far busier

Tenth Avenue in the hopes of flagging down and directing a driver to our position on 59th Street. But with rush hour upon us, nearly all of the cabs passing by were occupied. I began to worry that I was going to fuck up my one and only job, thus making me feel even more useless. I wanted Marilyn to see that I could take care of her son if need be.

Just as I reminded myself that none of this was actually about a *taxi*, guess what pulled up? A taxi. I pointed the driver to 59th Street as I raced over to meet him.

"It's coming around," I informed everyone, proudly.

"Took you long enough," Kit sassed. "Where did you find it, New Jersey?"

Of course *this* would elicit a laugh out of stoic Marilyn. The nurse chuckled, too. They were all ganging up against me! I shot Kit a chilly look for throwing me under the cab like that, then assisted the driver in loading the luggage into the trunk, which freed Marilyn up to get yelled at by her son for trying to help him get into the cab.

As Kit and his mom got situated in the backseat, I checked to see if there was room in the front for me. It was filled with the driver's crap, so I took a deep breath and jammed myself in next to Marilyn, who then straddled the center hump. I instinctively started to relay the address to the cabbie.

"We're going to—"

"Sixty-eighth and Central Park West," Kit pointedly interjected, as if to sternly remind me, *My mom doesn't know you practically live there, too!*

Fuck. Now Kit was pissed at me. Marilyn's suspicions that something was rotten in Denmark had no doubt been further raised. And I felt further marginalized and third wheel-y.

The good news: Thank God we didn't have far to go.

I felt an overwhelming urge to say something. Anything. But I resisted. It was time to let someone else fill the dead air. Instead, I started emotionally preparing myself to say goodbye to Kit. Although he hadn't explicitly told me that my presence would not be required once I got him and his mom settled at his apartment, I knew I wouldn't be sticking around. Kit needed space to have The Talk with his mom. And I wasn't going to get in the way of that. Also, on a self-preservation level, there was only so much of this "I'm not madly, deeply in love with Kit" act I could take.

At the same time, I began to feel anticipatory resentment toward Marilyn for preventing me from being with Kit on his first night home from the hospital. I wanted to be the one to take care of him.

We arrived at Kit's apartment, and I charged out of the car and made a beeline for the trunk. I was going to assist bringing those bags upstairs whether Marilyn liked it or not. As a show of good faith, I left the heaviest, bulkiest, most cumbersome one behind so she didn't feel left out. The three of us, led by a glacially paced Kit, made our way up to the third floor and into his apartment. It immediately became clear that Kirby was MIA—*phew*. We got into Kit's room and I could see him looking around to make sure I had confiscated all of his unmentionables. He didn't throw any blankets over anything, so I assumed my search-and-shroud mission had been a success. He gently rested on the bed.

I dropped the bags on the floor and decided not to prolong the inevitable.

"Do you need anything before I head off?"

"No, I think we're good," Kit said.

"I'm happy to run to the pharmacy and pick up your prescriptions..."

"They're not going to be ready for another hour or so," Kit noted.

"I can get them for you," Marilyn interjected, while feverishly unpacking her suitcase, as if marking her territory.

"Everyone settle down about the meds," Kit sighed. "I just walked through the door."

"It was nice to meet you, Marilyn," I said.

"Same here," she replied, pausing her unpacking. "Thank you for your help today."

Instead of reminding her that *I actually didn't help at all because you refused to let me help at all*, I took the high road (which I've been known to do on rare occasions!) and offered a simple "You're welcome" instead.

With Marilyn's back turned, Kit mouthed "I love you" to me, melting my heart. I wanted so desperately to kiss him. Snuggle him. Wait on him. Care for him. Instead, I mouthed "I love you" back before walking out, feeling sad for myself. And a little scared for Kit, knowing he was about to tackle one of the toughest conversations of his life. Unless he got cold feet.

He did not get cold feet.

The following morning, after his mom left for Pennsylvania, Kit phoned me to confirm that the deed had been done. Per his relatively brief account, Marilyn cried and blamed herself, before ultimately hugging him and professing her unconditional love for her son. It was clear she would be a work in progress. But a crucial first step had been taken.

"Did my name come up?" I inquired, sheepishly.

"You came up," he assured me. "She knows who you are."

With Marilyn back home, I was able to assume what I felt was my rightful place as Kit's post-surgery caretaker. I left work early that evening and dropped by Barnes & Noble to procure a selection of Kit's favorite magazines, before popping over to Harry's Burritos to fetch our dinner and quickly running up to the 74th Street candy shop to pick up two medium cups of peanut butter frozen yogurt. I then showed up at Kit's doorstep bearing get-well gifts galore. Ready to take care of my No. 1 guy.

12.

Michael Ausiello
October 10, 2014 · 🌐

Some exciting news in the world of Kit Cowan.

Earlier today, Kit underwent successful colostomy surgery at Memorial Sloan Kettering Hospital. You did not misread that—the arrival of a colostomy bag is cause for celebration. Due to the location of the primary colorectal tumor, bowel movements have been—and continue to be—a torturous exercise for Kit. They've been the root of more than 50 percent of his pain. So eliminating them from his daily regimen should drastically improve his quality of life.

He'll remain in the hospital through the weekend to recuperate from the procedure and also to learn about the care and upkeep of his new friend Mr. Stoma.

With the cancer now in his head (although brain radiation from September had succeeded in slowing the tumors' growth there), and the end of his one-year life expectancy rapidly closing in, one afternoon in early November, during a weeklong in-patient stint at Sloan Kettering, Kit began preparations for what would inevitably be his final Christmas. He had been admitted because his medical team, led by Dr. Davis, wanted to see if an epidural catheter would help ease the crippling pain he was experiencing—pain that was delaying the start of a new round of radiation on the primary rectal tumor. (Regular pain meds, including the in-home opioid pump, were barely helping at this point.) The epidural immediately brought relief, and he began undergoing the first of five daily radiation treatments. (Frustrating fact: Sloan policy prohibits the use of an epidural catheter at home, which is why he had to be hospitalized.)

With his pain level reduced from a 10 to a zero, Kit's morale enjoyed a measurable boost. I decided to compound his happiness by having him upgraded to a private room (which was basically the same as a regular room, just eliminating the second patient and forking over $500 a night out of pocket). So upbeat was Kit that he urged me to start packing his schedule with visitors, some of whom he'd been putting off seeing because he just wasn't in the right head space. It was during his second of five days in the hospital that he dropped the C-card.

"What are we doing for a Christmas tree this year?" he asked me.

If BuzzFeed were to create a list of Mike and Kit's 20 Most Heated Arguments Ever, about a quarter of them would involve a Christmas tree.

Even though I managed to slowly thaw Kit's iciness toward the holidays over the course of our relationship, there was one Christmas-themed tradition that never failed to activate his inner Abominable Snowman: tree trimming.

Our first experience staging a Christmas tree together occurred in early December 2002, not long after we celebrated our one-year anniversary. Kit had recently completed overseeing the renovation of my first New York City apartment—a 250-square-foot studio in Hell's

Kitchen that he unofficially shared with me while still maintaining his Upper West Side pad—and I was excited to introduce a real, live Christmas tree into the space. I was also pumped to share the full holiday experience with Kit; as wonderful as our maiden Christmas had been—Sneaky Pete's Magic Set and all—it hadn't featured any of the Yuletide trappings, namely a tree.

Well, guess what? Christmas tree decorating cast an even brighter spotlight on our polar-opposite aesthetic sensibilities. You see, I was keen on re-creating my childhood tree—classic Douglas fir, with miniature multicolored blinking lights and hundreds of sentimental ornaments procured and preserved from family vacations, my mom's early eighties crafting phase, and, of course, Gift Expressions' legendary Smurf section. Kit, meanwhile, was looking to make an artistic statement. His vision included unearthing out of storage the vintage midcentury modern aluminum tree he had discovered at a flea market in Miami in the late nineties, adding clear non-blinking lights, and—here was the kicker—hanging on its branches six dozen identical *jet-black* baubles that he had excitedly rescued from the deeply discounted clearance bin at IKEA last year because no one in their right mind would ever buy *jet-black Christmas balls*.

Realizing, ultimately, that he was fighting an uphill battle with Father Christmas himself, Kit offered to step back and let me take the lead on our inaugural tree trim. And then shortly thereafter he proceeded to back his ass up and take a giant, steamin' dump on what I had long considered to be one of the most joyous parts of the most wonderful time of the year.

"Why are you stringing lights on the back of the tree where no one will see them?" he sneered.

"You can still see them through the branches," I respectfully countered.

"Why are you hanging *ornaments* on the back of the tree where no one can see them?" he jeered.

"For the same reason I'm hanging the lights there," I explained, before reminding him, "I'm not in the business of decorating half a Christmas tree, my love."

"You're hanging the tinsel like a drunk hooker," he barked as I strategically draped the thick, silver garland around the tree with an eye toward maximum dip consistency.

"This is how my dad always did it," I insisted.

"Was your father a drunk hooker?" Kit asked, earnestly.

I demurred, my agitation growing. "No. As far as I know, my father was not a drunk hooker."

"'Cause only a drunk hooker would hang garland on a tree like that. Look at the size of your dips. You'll run out before you get to the bottom section."

I did not speak another word to Kit that evening, and *not* because he was right about my coming up short on the garland. I was livid— almost to the point of tears—that he didn't realize how much his blunt critiques were hurting me. And if I hadn't been so angry, and if the silent treatment hadn't been my default mode of retaliation, I would've explained to him that I missed my parents and I was trying to recapture some of that childhood Christmas magic with the new guy in my life by my side.

He knew he had fucked up, though. And as he would often do after acting insensitively, he eventually apologized for being a prick, as well as for calling my late father a sauced-up prostitute.

Tree debacle aside, the rest of our second Christmas—which also happened to be my first joining him in quaint, homespun Millersburg with his nervous but welcoming mom and dad—was pretty damn perfect. And over the next decade, each successive Christmas seemed to illuminate Kit's dormant elf a little more, a fact underscored by the enthusiasm, resourcefulness, and creativity that he brought to his present-giving. There was the year he gave me the elusive "Surprise Bag" Smurf. The year he gifted me with an in-home carbonation maker so that I could whip up my own fountain diet soda versus having to schlep to Chipotle ten times a day (it broke my heart when I had to tell him that the generic diet cola mix was not up to my high standards, rendering his gift an unqualified bust). The year he created a sumptuously bound, three-volume dictionary of "Poopisms"— aka hundreds of words and expressions that were known only to us, grouped by such categories as "Anger Management," "Snack Time," "Sleeping," and "Hot Guys."

"Our love has grown and changed over the last few years," he wrote on the accompanying card. "And it's also created something: our own language. Here are some of our most memorable and favorite phrases. Enjoy and Merry Doopmas."

Tree trimming, however, remained our Vietnam. In the wake of our second tumultuous collaboration in 2003—which ended with my ordering Kit out of the apartment when, during a burst of anger, he referred to my assemblage of Smurf- and Muppet-themed ornaments as "something Chris Hansen would seize as evidence during one of his *To Catch a Predator* ambushes"—we decided to alternate years. The results were surprising, to say the least.

For his first solo turn, Kit did, indeed, make use of his dusty old-school aluminum tree. But instead of chilly jet-black balls, he used warm, Smurf-colored blue ones. And then he embedded a dozen of my miniature Smurf plush dolls deep inside the branches, punctuating the blue, white, and silver slice of holiday heaven with clear lights. And parked alongside the whole thing was a certain four-foot-tall vintage, extremely rare Smurf statue he'd snapped up from an old German shopkeeper on eBay (the same statue that would later accompany me to my *TVLine* office). The whole display was the most spectacularly Smurfy thing I had ever seen in my life. Most shocking of all, it was *tasteful*. And *artful*. I'd slapped a lot of adjectives onto my Smurf displays over the years, but tasteful and artful were not among them.

And it was in that moment that I showered my miracle-worker boyfriend with his first "What *can't* Kit do?"

Despite his runaway success, Kit immediately opted out of the tree decorating rotation, much to my shock and (yes) disappointment.

"Tree decorating is a lot of work!" he playfully whined one night as we lay on the couch enjoying the Smurfy fruits of his labor. "And, I . . ."

" . . . What?"

"I . . ." he continued, hesitantly, as if fearing he'd someday regret the words about to come out of his mouth. "I kinda miss your tree. There, I said it! Happy?!"

As I looked at him, a big pile of puppy-dog sweetness and vulnerability, I was, indeed, happy. He missed my cheesy, tacky, cornball tree.

He loved my cheesy, tacky, cornball tree. Translation: He loved and accepted and appreciated and was charmed by *me*, in all my cheesy, tacky, cornball glory.

"What are we doing for a Christmas tree?" Kit repeated, as I struggled to form an answer.

It was a good question, since last year we'd decided that our days of having high-maintenance real trees, what with their daily water requirements and frustrating needle shedding, were over. It was time to make the switch to artificial.

But with everything going on, hunting for a fake tree was not high on my to-do list. Christmas, in general, was not at the forefront of my mind. It was in the back of it, actually. I was dreading it. The happiest time of the year was arriving during the worst time of my life, and I was ready to stick my hand out of my car window and instruct St. Nick and his eight reindeer to go by.

It didn't help that we were coming off of our most magical Christmas since Year 1's seminal magic set triumph. Living on the top floor of a quaint West Village brownstone had its perks, one of which—as we'd discovered last year—was that the space was a Norman Rockwell painting just waiting to be brought to life. Turned out, the only thing my classic Christmas tree was missing was a fireplace, a cozy low-hung ceiling, and three six-over-six sash windows, each of which Kit adorned with big, classic, colorful C9 Christmas light sets, all precisely measured out so each window was perfectly symmetrical. Those storybook windows looked as stunningly magical from the inside as they did from the outside, and I knew this because we spent many a night slowly walking down the block toward our apartment marveling at the burst of Christmas cheer emanating from the top floor of 6 Jane Street. "That's our apartment!" I would brag to Joe and Jane Passerby while pointing to the windows, to Kit's slight embarrassment.

Christmas 2013 was already going to be a tough act to follow *before* Kit got sick. There was also a part of me that feared Kit might die before Christmas or on Christmas or, worse yet, two days after Christmas like my mother. So anytime I glanced at my mental calendar and noticed December 25 creeping toward me, I ran in the opposite direction.

But then Kit asked me what we were doing this year for a Christmas tree, and my happy state of avoidance was shattered.

"I haven't thought about it, to be honest," I replied.

"I'll take care of it," he said, resolutely.

"Are you sure?"

"Yep. It'll give me a project while I'm lying here in the hospital. I need a project. Christmas will be my project."

Three hours of Internet shopping on his iPad later, Kit shared with me a list of his top six artificial Christmas tree picks, all of them in the fir category and all of them from a company called Balsam Hill, which, per the website, billed itself as the "leading provider of high-quality, realistic artificial Christmas trees." Or as Kit observed enthusiastically, "This is where Ellen gets her tree from!"

I reviewed the options, shared with him my top two faves, which were pretty much in line with his top two faves, and we ultimately settled on the seven-and-a-half-foot Fraser Fir. For the next couple of days, while he lay in the hospital enjoying the tremendous relief brought on by the lower body–numbing epidural, he began every text to me with "Did the tree arrive?!" It was to the point where he didn't want me to visit him at the hospital, out of fear UPS would show up and find no one home. When the tree at long last was delivered, three days later, I tipped the UPS man $20 to help me get it up the two flights of stairs, because apparently Kit had ordered the *largest and heaviest and most grandiose artificial tree in the Northern Hemisphere.* (That'd teach me to ignore the fine print.) The box actually couldn't fit into our entryway, so I had to leave it on the top landing outside our door.

The next day, UPS returned with more (albeit smaller) packages, all of 'em addressed to Kit Cowan.

"Three more boxes came for you today," I texted him before heading to the hospital.

"Don't open them," he immediately typed back. "They're Christmas presents. Put them in my closet."

The following day three *more* boxes arrived. By the time Kit was discharged at week's end, the bottom of his closet was packed with deliveries. When he arrived home, he immediately sorted through them to make sure nothing was missing. I, meanwhile, started to ponder an insanely surreal, gut-wrenching question: What did *I* get Kit for his last Christmas?

I should point out, my run of awesome Christmas gifts for Kit continued well after my 2001 Sneaky Pete's Magic Set triumph. The one I was most proud of came a few years later, when I wrapped up the official vendor floor/schematic plan from New York's National Stationery Show at the Jacob Javits Convention Center, with one table circled in red—the one I had reserved for him. I was tired of hearing him talk about all these cool ideas he had for a greeting card line. It was time for him to make his dream of launching his own company a reality. He was between jobs at the time, so there was a window of opportunity. Five months later, Pretty Bitter—"Stationery That Pushes the Envelope"— was born.

It all seemed well on its way to becoming a moot point when, just days after returning home from the hospital, Kit—no longer enjoying the relief provided by the epidural, and Sloan Kettering still refusing to even consider administering it at home because it was "against policy"— experienced a dramatic pain uptick. And the opioid pump was barely helping. Concurrently, he started to become confused and disoriented.

His mental spiral began in earnest a week before Thanksgiving when, after I offhandedly mentioned that the tablet version of the *New York Post* was no longer compatible with my old, out-of-date iPad, he insisted on going online to order me the latest one for Christmas. I was both surprised and thrilled, as it was the most enthusiastic and alert I had seen him in days. He grabbed his iPad and began browsing his go-to tech sites in search of my new iPad. He asked me what color I preferred (black), how much memory I needed (I deferred to him on that), and how quickly I wanted it shipped (no rush).

"OK, all set," he declared. "Grab my wallet, please."

I ran into the kitchen, fetched his wallet off the counter, returned to the bedroom, and handed it to him. He whipped out his Chase bank card, and I looked on in confusion as he placed the card's metallic strip against the iPad screen, as if it had a built-in credit card reader or something. He held it there for a few seconds—perhaps waiting for a beep or something?—before pulling it away and trying again. I couldn't believe my eyes.

"Hey," I said. "What are you doing?"

"I'm trying to pay for it," he replied with frustration, as he pressed the card harder against the screen.

"I don't think it works like that," I told him, choosing my words carefully so as not to spook him.

"What do you mean?" He looked at me, confused.

"I mean . . ." I hedged, quickly thinking on my feet, "I think your credit card strip is worn down."

"Let's try your card," he suggested.

"No, it's OK," I insisted, as I grabbed his iPad and set it on the floor. "We can order it later."

I downplayed the episode as an opioid-induced anomaly. But the super-sized brain lapses persisted.

A day later, Kit woke up in the middle of the night, panicked and screaming, "What room is this? Where are we?" He later heard a noise on the roof and freaked out. "We have to hide under the bed—they're coming to get us."

The real gut punch came the next morning as I was plying him with an Ensure drink.

"What are you still doing here?" he asked me, nonchalantly.

"Where else would I be, silly?"

"In Tampa. Where you live."

My heart sank. I prayed Kit was punking me.

"Tampa?" I chuckled, nervously. "Why would I be in Tampa?"

Kit proceeded to stare at me with a mix of bemusement and agitation, as if hoping *I* was punking *him*.

"That's a dumb question," he snapped.

Suddenly, it was clear to me that he was not joking. I could see it in his eyes. He was not looking at me like Kit looked at Mike. And it was chilling.

"Kit, who do you *think* I am?" I reluctantly pressed, because I couldn't think of a more horrifying question to be asking the person you had spent pretty much every single day with for the past thirteen-plus years.

"That's enough," he shot back. "You're not funny."

"Kit," I said calmly as I grabbed his hand. "I'm Michael. Your *husband*. I'm your Bodge. I think you're a little confused from the drugs."

Kit yanked his hand out of my grasp and just glared at me, angrily, as I saw the wheels frantically turning in his head. It was not unlike the look of someone running around a multilevel parking garage trying desperately to remember where they parked their Volvo, before starting to worry that perhaps it had been stolen.

"Please stop," he begged me.

"Kit, who do you think I am?" I asked him again, against my better judgment.

"You're Bill," he said, referring to his longtime college friend and the husband of his BFF Jen, both of whom had recently visited from Tampa.

I just sat there quietly as my body absorbed the shock that Kit no longer knew who I was.

Kit had forgotten me.

Kit had forgotten *us*.

Thirteen years of memories—including our magical midnight swim in Puerto Rico's Bioluminescent Bay, the all-nighter we pulled at the Jacob Javits Convention Center getting the Pretty Bitter booth ready in time for the start of the National Stationery Show, our white-knuckle helicopter ride through the Grand Canyon, the time we watched *Saturday Night Live* lampoon *Oprah's Favorite Things* and both laughed so hard we literally rolled off the couch clutching our chests, the time I gaslit him into thinking that on three separate occasions in a single day he just *happened* to find $6 lying on the ground while we walked around New York City (after I giddily informed him that it was me and not the Universe leaving him the gifts, he seethed, "I hope you get a hangnail")—gone in the blink of an eye. And it nearly delivered a knockout blow to my heart.

I scrambled to come up with a way out, all while hoping he'd snap out of it and regain his memory of us. Short of assuring him that, yes, I was fucking around and *of course* I was Bill—something I simply couldn't bring myself to do—no good could come out of continuing this conversation. This was not an argument either of us was going to win.

So I did the next worst thing: I abandoned him.

"I'll be right back," I said, as I stood up and walked out of the bedroom. I took a seat at our dining room table and I stared out the window at the leafless tree, stoically. And I started counting the branches. And when I ran out of branches to count, I picked up my phone, called my brother David, and confided in him through tears what had just happened.

The good news: One hour later, Kit was back to knowing who I was. But his general delirium persisted. The visiting nurse increased his opioid dose to help with the pain, which added to his haziness. He slept his way through much of Thanksgiving—barely touching the take-out turkey dinner his mom and dad picked up from the diner across the street. All the excitement he'd had toward Christmas had vanished. I wasn't even sure he remembered that he had bought a $500 Christmas tree that was sitting in a box in the hallway. Regardless, the next day, while he was asleep in bed, I decided to assemble the thing in the usual spot next to the fireplace. As I was stringing the lights on, I looked into the bedroom and noticed Kit moving around in bed. He turned his head toward the living room and saw the tree.

"Pretty," he mumbled.

"I'm saving the ornaments for you," I told him. "Think you're up for coming out here and helping me?"

He nodded his head.

Thirty minutes later, Kit was sitting on the couch next to the giant ornament box, pointing out the "huge area in the middle of the tree" where I had failed to string any lights. Some things never changed. I then asked him to start passing me ornaments from the box, with instructions for him to add a hook if one was missing.

The first one he handed me was a trolley car, a memento from our amazing weekend in San Francisco. As I hung it on the tree, I started crying. God, we had taken some great trips together. And we were great travel companions. We rarely fought when we were on the road. It was as if all of our problems were temporarily put on hold when we crossed the New York state line.

Soon after, he handed me the porcelain ball that I had picked up at the souvenir shop after our terrifying, mesmerizing helicopter tour of the Grand Canyon. There was the ceramic coquí from our weeklong trip to Puerto Rico. But it was the miniature wooden lean-to from our extraordinary stay at The Point resort in the Adirondacks that sent me reaching for the tissues.

"*That* was a vacation," I cried to Kit, who continued to remain mostly silent—albeit present—during the process. He nodded and smiled. It seemed like he remembered. I was afraid to ask if he remembered.

An hour later, Kit was scraping the bottom of the ornament box. I sat next to him on the couch and we took in our handiwork.

"I think it looks pretty damn good," I gushed.

"It's beautiful," he said.

After admiring the tree for another ten minutes, Kit alerted me that he was uncomfortable and wanted to lie back down. He gave himself a shot of opioids and I slowly helped him up off the couch. The movement immediately triggered an inevitable pain spike, so time was of the essence. As I was guiding him across the living room, he held his hand out as he passed the tree and copped a feel of the nearest limb, the soft green needles grazing his skin as they quickly slipped through his fingers.

Michael Ausiello
December 2, 2014 ·

Kit Cowan update (warning: it stinks):

The decision was made today by Kit's primary oncologist not to continue with treatment. His disease is just too widespread and aggressive at this point—it would be cruel to subject him to more torturous chemo or radiation when the likelihood of success is so slim. And I agreed. In-home hospice care will start tomorrow.

This comes as Kit's condition has dramatically worsened over the past 48 hours. He's barely able to stay awake, he's not eating and, most unsettling, he's becoming increasingly confused and disoriented. The stuff that makes Kit

KIT is evaporating, and it's excruciating to watch. Also, I think nine months of fighting like a champ is finally taking a toll on him.

The focus now—my primary goal—is to make sure he is as comfortable as possible. And for him to know that he is loved.

It would mean a lot to me if you could pray for not only Kit, but also for his parents Bob and Marilyn, whose courage and strength throughout this whole ordeal has been nothing short of inspiring.

What is that extra morphine pill even doing?

It was a question I asked myself as I began the daily ritual that was gathering Kit's morning meds. Three weeks ago, one of Sloan's pain doctors—in consultation with Dr. Davis—had prescribed a once-a-day 30 mg morphine pill to supplement the as-needed intravenous opioid juice coming in through the pump. It dawned on me that Kit's metamorphosis into full-blown zombie had occurred around the same time. What if it was that one morphine pill, and not the brain metastases, as Team Sloan K believed, that was causing his extreme fatigue and low-grade dementia? Kit's pain level when in motion was roughly unchanged from before he started taking the additional dose of morphine.

So I made the executive decision to leave that one pill out of his daily drug cocktail. Just to see what would happen.

You know the sound a motorcycle or an ATV gives off when it makes an abrupt, 180-degree turn? That *Vroom Skreeyeeyeeyeeyeek!* noise? Well, that pretty much describes the sudden turnaround Kit experienced over the next seventy-two hours. Not only did his energy level spike, he regained his mental faculties and his appetite. His pain level, meanwhile, was status quo despite the absence of the morphine pill.

So profound was Kit's rebound that I called Dr. Davis's office to question whether we played the hospice card too soon. (And also to brag about how it was my call to hold back the daily dose of morphine that had clearly triggered the rebound, and to subsequently suggest that maybe Sloan Kettering should consider paying me a consulting fee.) Davis's crew, and then Davis herself in a follow-up call, tempered my enthusiasm by schooling me in the phenomenon known as the pre-death surge, wherein a patient appears to stage an eleventh-hour rally before the Grim Reaper snatches them away. I was familiar with the concept. I watched *Grey's Anatomy.* I saw how Eric Dane's McSteamy dramatically, miraculously bounced back from certain death following that plane crash only to flatline hours later.

"But I thought those surges are generally short-lived," I challenged Davis. "Kit has been like this for *three days* now."

"It's great news that he's doing better, but I . . . wouldn't read too much into it, Mike," Davis advised, choosing her words carefully. "If it continues, we can discuss having him come in for an MRI to get a better look at what might be happening."

Cut to forty-eight hours later and Kit was lying in bed scarfing down one of his longtime guilty pleasures—a Krispy Kreme donut that Jen had special-delivered to him from Florida. It was in this moment that I decided to stop obsessing over the big picture and just live in the moment. I had thought Kit was gone for good. And now he was back. And I was grateful.

I was also no longer worried about Kit dying on or around Christmas. In fact, I offered to drag out of his closet all of the loot he had ordered the previous month while in the hospital and help wrap it all for him—an offer he accepted. (This obviously meant I'd get a sneak peek at some of my own presents, but I didn't care and neither did he.) At the same time, I decided to put into motion a gift idea for him I'd been tossing around in my noggin ever since the surge began. It involved giving Kit a preview of his own memorial service.

Ever since the cancer had spread to Kit's brain in September, I'd thought about what his memorial service might look like. There was a handful of certainties. I knew there would be a New York City component, in addition to some type of service in his hometown, which was where Kit long ago had confided he wanted his ashes scattered. I would deliver the eulogy, even if it killed me. And, last and perhaps most importantly, there would be some kind of video retrospective, produced by me and, hopefully if he was available, edited by my longtime video guy Jason Averett. I was also fairly certain that the video would end up being so powerful that someone—whether it was a friend of Kit's or one of his aunts or a Wyeth colleague—would come up to me after watching it and, through tears, say, "That was beautiful. It's a damn shame that Kit wasn't here to see that."

Well, Kit was going to be alive to see it, I vowed to myself. But I had to act fast and take advantage of this window of lucidity before it closed, possibly for good.

So, over the next five days, I covertly sifted through thirteen years of video and photos stored on my laptop, while also wrangling assets out of Kit's Florida-based BFFs Jen and Beeba and his work wife, Missi. Kit's cousin, Raelean, helped me secure a selection of childhood images since Bob and Marilyn were now living in Kit's Brooklyn man cave full-time, coming over every day around 10 a.m. and then staying until *Wheel of Fortune* ended at 8 in the evening. I also asked our No. 1 gay friend Nick to catalog the hundreds of hours of video Kit had shot on the camcorder I got him for Christmas a few years back, and send me a list of highlights I could review.

On Day 5, I took stock of all the assets, sketched out a rough storyboard, complete with musical cues and time codes, and then met Jason at the Barnes & Noble in Union Square to do the handoff. I could see the heaviness in his eyes as he approached me at the front of the store, near the new releases section. It wasn't the look of someone getting ready to edit together my umpteenth Lauren Graham interview, or another of my rollicking Q&As with the cast of *Community*. We hugged, we cried, and then we got down to business.

"How quickly do you need it?" he asked me, soberly.

"Pretty quickly," I replied, before adding with a darkly satiric wink, "Don't make me tell you that it's a matter of life or death. *Because I will.*"

Jason, whose obsessive quality control rivaled Kit's, assured me he would work as fast as possible. I could tell he was nervous, though. But I wasn't. I had every confidence that Jason would knock it out of the park.

I then went to Urban Outfitters to pick up a few stocking stuffers for Kit, including a long-sleeved T-shirt with the retro Polaroid logo emblazoned on the front. It was nice to be outside. It was nice that Kit was doing well enough that I could *be* outside without having to worry that he might die at any moment. His parents knew to text me if there was an emergency.

The next day, as Kit and his dad playfully uttered the *Vroom Skreeyeeyeeyeeyeek!* noise that had come to symbolize his turnaround, I headed to the gym for the first time since October. And there was a surprise waiting for me there. I stepped on the scale and was shocked at the number staring back at me: 168 pounds—14 pounds less than a month ago. I knew my jeans were feeling looser, but I had no idea that my body was shrinking at such a rapid clip. The next thought that entered my mind was *Man, there are a lot of calories in sauvignon blanc.*

It had been a month since I'd had a sip of wine—or any alcohol, for that matter. My nightly wine routine was interrupted in early November when Kit spent that week in the hospital. The first night in his private room I decided to hang out with him until past midnight so we could watch *The Daily Show* together, as we had often done pre-cancer. By the time I got home at around 1 a.m., I opened the fridge, looked at the half-empty bottle of vino on the door, and for the first time in as long as I could remember, I reached for a Diet Snapple instead. I had no interest in consuming a glass of wine at 1 a.m. I was exhausted.

The next night, Kit and I watched TV again together, right through Jon Stewart. And once again I returned home at 1 a.m. and reached for a Diet Snapple instead of a glass of wine. And I made the same choice every subsequent night Kit was in the hospital. And by the time he was released at week's end, wine had lost its grip on me. And, more importantly, I had started to feel more present with Kit. And then it became about *Lemme see how long I can keep this up!*

Well, it had now been a month and change. And although it seemed grossly vain to be basking in something so trivial as weight loss at a time like this, I was indeed happy that my wine fast had had this unintended consequence.

The next day, Jason sent me over a first cut of Kit's video retrospective. And forty-eight hours later, after a couple of minor tweaks, I was sitting on the bed with Kit watching him watch his entire life flash before his eyes in just eleven minutes. Perhaps it was the opioids or the brain meds or a mix of both, but I struggled to read his reaction. He was quiet, still, stoic throughout, the only discernible reaction coming during the *AbFab* clips that bookended the piece. During those, he cracked the sweetest of smiles. And at the video's conclusion, as I reached for the laptop and began to close it, he offered a brief, ambiguous review: "That was . . . a lot."

13.

Michael Ausiello
December 23, 2014 · 🌐

A few years ago Kit snapped up on eBay a vintage version of those "Now Serving" signs you'd see at your local bakery or delicatessen. Last December, on the occasion of his 41st birthday, he adjusted the dial to reflect his new age. This counter took on a whole new meaning nine months ago when he was diagnosed with cancer. It now represented something of a challenge, one that Kit was determined to conquer. I'm happy to report that earlier this morning, my indefatigable husband sprang out of bed, marched over to the counter, and pulled that fucking string like the champ that he is. Happy Birthday indeed.

Michael Ausiello
January 18, 2015 ·

As if Kit didn't have enough to deal with, last Wednesday he began exhibiting a new flurry of symptoms—fever, restlessness, and delirium. He may have to be transferred from our home to Bellevue Hospital's in-patient hospice wing if things don't improve. I'm really hoping it doesn't come to that. Prayers and good vibes are welcome at this time.

I've had to make some tough decisions in my life.

Do I come out to my father *pre*–heart transplant and risk breaking his diseased old ticker before a match is located, or do I wait until a donor is (hopefully) found and pray his new organ is strong enough to withstand the trauma of learning one of his three sons likes penis?

Should I stay in my cushy, dream job as a columnist for *Entertainment Weekly* or flee the turbulent print biz for the emergent world of new media and launch an unknown, unproven TV website with nascent digital firebrand Jay Penske?

Should I secretly embed a Smurf figurine in the background of the *Gilmore Girls* Season 5 scene in which I'm appearing as an extra, as a fun wink to myself, and risk the series' famously detail-obsessed creator Amy Sherman-Palladino spotting it on the monitor and dragging me out back to the gazebo to be flogged, or do I leave the Smurf at home and just keep the focus on my acting?

But those agonizing quandaries were nothing compared to the doozy of a dilemma currently before me on this early January night: Did I have Kit transferred to the inpatient hospice unit at Bellevue Hospital in an effort to address an alarming new batch of symptoms (extreme restlessness, severe delirium, raging incontinence, and high fever) that had cropped up over the past seventy-two hours, and run the risk of breaking the promise I'd made to him four months ago on our deck that I would not let him die in a hospital? Or did I just keep him here at home and make do with the limited medical resources (i.e., drugs) at our disposal, knowing it would likely mean he would continue to suffer, possibly right up until he took his final breath? Further complicating the Catch-22 was the fact that we lived on the top floor of an extremely old and narrow two-hundred-year-old, three-story brownstone walk-up, and even *with* the aid of a morphine pump Kit was unable to sit up without it triggering a violent pain episode, let alone stand or walk down two flights of stairs (*three* if you counted the set outside leading to the front door).

I had tried all of the hospice staff's go-to in-home crisis remedies—namely extra drops of the anxiety-relieving lorazepam and increased doses of morphine—but nothing was working. And because the Universe just wanted to fuck with us a little more, all of Kit's symptoms were working against each other. His restlessness and agitation were causing him to harness what little strength he had to try and inexplicably claw his way out of bed. But, as a result of his mentally jumbled state, he had forgotten that he had a tumor in his ass that made even the slightest movement torturous. So, for the past twenty-four hours, I—with the help of Bob and Marilyn—had to forcibly hold him down every time his cancer-saturated brain sent him a panicked message that, given his high level of hysteria, probably went something like this: *Kit! Emergency! Michael has hacked into your computer and is furiously retouching all of your gorgeous images—get out of bed and stop him before it's too late!*

It was now approaching 10 p.m., and I was tired of seeing Kit suffer. I was also just plain tired. And I was beginning to blame the victim.

"*Where are you trying to go!*" I barked at him earlier today after returning from the dry cleaners, where I had dropped off our urine-saturated mattress cover to be professionally scrubbed because it was too big to fit in our washing machine. It was the first time I had ever lost my cool with Cancer-Era Kit. It was also the first time I had started to feel like I was failing him as a caregiver.

So, for the third night in a row, I called the hospice hotline and asked the dispatcher to send one of the on-call nurses to the apartment to once again evaluate Kit and discuss our limited options. If this had been during normal nine-to-five hours, Kit's regular hospice nurse would have dropped by (assuming he was available). But, as bad luck would have it, most of Kit's medical catastrophes seemed to occur at night, which meant having to deal with a nurse who knew nothing about his incredibly rare neuroendocrine cancer aside from what was in his limited-snapshot file. And that, in turn, meant having to engage in the infuriating ritual that was the pre-exam Q&A session, during which I spent fifteen minutes answering the same fifty questions about the progression of Kit's disease.

As tonight's nurse took a seat on Kit's vintage Haimi chair and opened her laptop, I reminded myself that she was just doing her job. It was not her fault. *Be kind, Michael.*

"Where is his cancer?" she began.

Look at your computer—it says it right there is what I *wanted* to say. Instead, I calmly responded, "It's in his rectum, lung, liver, and brain," the words now rolling off my tongue to the point that the horror of it barely registered.

"It says here it's also in his tailbone."

"*It* is wrong," I snapped. "This is the third time I have corrected that. The nurse last night promised she would update it in the system."

"It doesn't look like she did . . ."

"He has cancer in his rectum, lung, liver, and brain," I sighed. "Maybe by this time next week he'll have tailbone cancer, too. But let's not get ahead of ourselves."

"I will change it as soon as I get back to the office," she vowed.

"Thank you."

The nurse ran through the rest of the Qs with me, before she began formally checking Kit's vitals, something that was proving a bit of a challenge given his aggressive fidgeting. She nonetheless managed to perform her perfunctory blood pressure, temperature, heart, and lung tests, before sitting back down and delivering the same vague prognosis as last night's on-call nurse: "While we can't be certain what's causing these symptoms, the pervasiveness of the cancer is probably leading his body to break down."

She then echoed the earlier recommendation to have him transported to Bellevue, where the medical professionals could pump enough lorazepam into his system to basically knock him out. As I looked at Kit writhing away in the bed, I was *thisclose* to signing off on the idea. But there was still the pesky issue of how the fuck to get him there.

"The paramedics have a special chair-stretcher they can use," the nurse confidently assured me, as smoke started billowing out of my ears and into her windpipe, asphyxiating her.

"He has a tumor the size of a soccer ball in his rectum," I angrily reminded her. "He cannot *sit* in a chair. He certainly can't sit in a chair as it's being carried down two flights of stairs."

"Oh, that's right . . ." she sighed.

"Is there *any* way we could give him the lorazepam shot here at home?" I inquired.

"No, we're not allowed to travel with a dose that large; it can only be administered in a hospital," she asserted, before adding, "They also have a regular fold-up stretcher. These EMTs have been in every kind of New York apartment building. They know what they're doing. They won't hurt him."

"They won't *intentionally* hurt him," I corrected her.

"We can administer extra bolus doses of the morphine before we move him," she suggested. "It will be OK."

I wanted to believe her, but the so-called experts had misled Kit and me so many times during this journey that my faith tank was running on empty.

"Don't worry about the blood in the semen. It's probably nothing and will likely clear up on its own," insisted Kit's primary doctor back in January. (Turns out it was the first symptom of his rectal cancer.)

"The good news is this specific chemo cocktail should quickly shrink your tumor and bring about relief," said every single oncologist we saw in mid-March. (Fun fact: The tumor actually grew and his pain intensified.)

"The migraines are probably a late side effect of the chemo—take some Excedrin," Davis's assistant told us in August. (This just in: They were actually from brain metastases.)

"You'll be dead before your first wedding anniversary," Davis told Kit in so many words back in September. (Breaking News: Figures *that'd* be the one they got right.)

My gut was telling me the nurse's lack of experience with Kit's specific and unique cancer was leading her to unwittingly write checks her hindquarters couldn't cash. I knew firsthand the effort it took, and the pain it caused, when Bob and I walked Kit ten feet to the bathroom to pee. How would they get him into a stretcher and then get the stretcher through the apartment and out the door and around the first narrow stairway bend and down the first twelve steps and then around the second stairway bend and then down the next twelve steps and then out the *front* door into the freezing cold and then down the final six front steps and into the waiting ambulance?

Unless the stretcher came off the same assembly line that produced Aladdin's magic carpet, I couldn't see how it was possible.

But I also didn't see an alternative.

Resigned yet resolute, I told the nurse, "OK, let's bring him to the hospital. But he's not staying there. Once he's stabilized and we figure out what's going on, he comes back home."

"You're making the right decision," she assured me, before phoning the dispatcher and ordering the ambulance. I interrupted her before she ended the call to ensure the person with whom she was on the phone knew the particulars of Kit's condition *and* our stairwell *and* that he/she relayed that critical information to the paramedics.

"I don't want them showing up with a chair-stretcher," I harrumphed.

With my decision made, I began to wrap my head around the very real possibility that Kit might die in a hospital and not, as I had promised him, at home. God help me if there was such a thing as an afterlife, because I could already picture Kit waiting for me at the Pearly Gates, shaking his head while wearing a T-shirt emblazoned with the words "You had *one* job."

In the end, the medics—who showed up brandishing, yep, a chair-stretcher—managed to get Kit out of the house that night, but not without (a) breaking his morphine pump, (b) busting open his colostomy bag, and (c) inflicting so much mental and emotional pain on my husband that at one point—I think it was around the second landing—he stared into my eyes and screamed, "*Please help me! Make it stop!*"

As I held Kit's cold hands in the ambulance on the way to Bellevue, I looked at him—scared, confused, traumatized, and covered in his own shit—and flashed back to our special night on the deck in September, where he confided that he was worried what the end would look like. He would later express interest in fleeing to Oregon, which had a law allowing its terminally ill citizens to die on their own terms. I briefly looked into it, but quickly discovered that the Death with Dignity Act, as it was called, carried with it a number of residency requirements.

At this moment, I found myself really wishing New York State had a Death with Dignity Act. There was no dignity in what was transpiring tonight. Kit deserved a better end than he was getting.

"I'm sorry, we don't have any towels," the medic informed me from the front seat. "All we have is this."

He held out his hand and presented me with a thin roll of gauze. I just stared at it, dumbfounded, wondering how an ambulance didn't have something as basic as tissues or paper towels. I then took the gauze from him, tore off a big piece, and attempted to at least get some of the shit off of Kit's favorite comfy shirt.

"We'll get you cleaned up better at the hospital, babe," I whispered to him. "Sorry for the smell. Stinky poops, right?"

Roughly fifteen minutes later, Kit was in Bellevue's hospice wing sound asleep after being injected with a dose of liquid lorazepam. A tsunami of relief instantly washed over me. For the first time in three days, Kit was comfortable. And then suddenly, the events of the past three hours—and all the feelings of rage and despair and sadness and heartbreak that they had stirred up—hit me like a ton of bricks.

And I spontaneously burst into tears.

Kit remained unconscious.

It had been seven hours since he was admitted to Bellevue's inpatient hospice unit and promptly shot up with copious amounts of lorazepam, and I was beginning to fear that he might never wake up. And even if he *did* come to, I worried he might only have days—perhaps hours—left.

So after getting roughly two hours of nonconsecutive shut-eye in the hospital sleeper chair (a device so uncomfortable it made that metal plank Kit was carried away in last night look downright sumptuous), one of my first orders of business this morning was to email Jeff Jensen—whose now late wife, Amy, had succumbed to brain cancer over the summer —to ask him if he had any sage deathbed wisdom to impart to me, my goal being to walk away from this experience with as few regrets as possible. He replied with the following tip:

"Apologize for not loving him better. He will tell you that you could not have loved him more, which is true, but you need to tell him that anyway."

My initial reaction: Really? Apologize for not *loving* him more? When it came to my relationship with Kit, I was sorry about a lot of things—like how my lack of willpower forced him to hide any and all snacks he brought into our apartment, like the time I wore his favorite white Armani Exchange dress shirt to work without his permission after he specifically said it was the one piece of his wardrobe he did not want me co-opting, like how my raging jealousy and insecurity prevented me from telling him how fucking hot his ass looked in his favorite khakis—but apologize for not *loving him enough*? That was one of the few relationship things I felt like I had actually aced, particularly this past year.

But I trusted Jeff. And my guess was that saying those few simple if counterintuitive words would proactively ward off any potential postmortem guilt or regret I might encounter. And Lord knew I was a big fan of cutting both of those evil forces out of my life. So I filed his recommendation away in my head as I tried to catch another forty winks.

Make that *thirty* winks.

The doctor assigned to Kit's care here at Bellevue awakened me to share the surprising news that Kit was suffering from a urinary tract infection, likely brought on by his suppressed immune system. I felt a rush of relief, especially when the doc said Kit might be able to rebound from this setback with the aid of antibiotics, thus allowing us to return to the good ol' days when the only thing he had to contend with was terminal cancer.

I also experienced a jolt of rage as the doc confirmed to me that Kit's UTI could've easily and quickly been diagnosed and treated in our home by our regular hospice nurse, thereby avoiding last night's stairway horror show. The MD also informed me that the yellow guck that I'd been clearing out of Kit's mouth with foam swabs the past two weeks was not, as the hospice nurse thought, dried-up oatmeal from a recent breakfast. It was a fungal infection called thrush.

Just two more items to add to the long list of grievances.

In the meantime, the quality of Kit's care had improved exponentially since he'd been admitted, and this weary caregiver was enjoying the reprieve. For the first time in months, someone else was maintaining his colostomy bag. Someone else was applying antibiotic cream to the massive bedsore on his right hip that he had sustained from eleven months of lying on his side. Someone else was monitoring his new external condom catheter to make sure it was catching what little pee he was expending. Someone else was worrying about his medication.

As a result, I was free to get down to the business of being Kit's husband. And for the past eight or so hours that had meant simply sitting next to him and watching him sleep and giving him kisses and making sure he was being treated like the VIP that he was.

Eight more hours passed before Kit showed the first sign that he might be waking up. It came in the form of some light shifting and mild eye flickering.

By late evening, his eyes fully opened and he looked at me. He looked at me the way Kit looked at Mike. *He knows who I am.* Another major hurdle cleared. I rewarded him with a few ice chips, which he enthusiastically gobbled up.

Overnight, his agitation began to reintensify as the lorazepam continued to wear off. The doctor decided to hold off on knocking him out with another big shot of the sedative, reasoning that (a) the UTI-attacking antibiotics would hopefully be kicking in soon, and (b) putting him to sleep for another long stretch—during which he would continue to be deprived of much-needed sustenance—could do more harm than good.

At around 1 a.m., just as I was dozing off on my sleeper chair, I heard the familiar, unsettling sound of Kit aggressively fidgeting. Which was followed by the also familiar, unsettling sound of him moaning.

Fuck. I began to worry he was backsliding.

I rose out of the chair, but instead of rushing to the nurses' station, which was my impulse, I decided—just for shits and giggles—to try a new approach. I walked to the foot of the bed, slid my hands under his covers, and began gently rubbing his feet in an effort to calm him down. And, whaddaya know, it seemed to be working. I dared say he was enjoying it.

I then relocated to the head of the bed and massaged his hands and scalp. Suddenly, Kit's moans were sounding more like Mister Scooch-worthy purrs. And it was music to my ears, not to mention my heart, which was still in tatters after last night.

"Feel good?"

Kit nodded. We were now communicating. More progress.

I then decided to press my luck by opening the Orangina his parents had dropped off when they were here earlier. I stuck a straw in the bottle and moved it to his lips. He immediately took a sip. And then a second sip. I could feel my heart continue to mend.

I then went *really* crazy and tempted him with a little Ensure. He took a sip of that, too! Three minutes later he was munching on some of Bellevue's finest Jell-O followed by a few more ice chips. I looked on in amazement as he slowly drifted back off to sleep. I planted a kiss on his forehead before sitting back down in my resplendent chair bed to quietly celebrate my small victory.

Roughly fifteen minutes passed, and he began fidgeting anew. I immediately jumped out of bed and repeated the same exact steps in the same exact order.

Foot rub? Check.

Hand and scalp massage? Check and check.

Two more sips of Orangina, followed by two bites of Jell-O, one sip of Ensure, and lastly, two ice chips? Check x 7.

And just as before, Kit's restlessness subsided and he drifted back off to sleep.

"We have repeated this now four times in the past ninety minutes," I marveled to Bob and Marilyn in an overnight email update that I knew they would appreciate reading when they awoke first thing in the morning. "My goal is to have the Jell-O, Ensure, and Orangina gone by morning!"

Well, I almost reached my goal. By sunrise, the Jell-O and Orangina were gone, but there was still a quarter of the Ensure left. My heart, meanwhile, was now completely full. Even though he hadn't said a single word to me, it was one of the most intimate nights I had ever spent with Kit.

And Kit's resurgence continued into the afternoon. As his symptoms continued to abate, he was becoming more alert. He was even starting to form coherent words again. In fact, later that night, he expressed a desire to strip off the external catheter and get up to pee. And not in the commode next to the bed. He wanted to walk to the ensuite bathroom.

The understandably cautious nurses, naturally, vetoed this, citing his extremely atrophied muscles. They were rightfully concerned that even with their assistance his legs could give out. In fact, they were recommending he be fitted with an *internal* catheter, something I knew deep down was inevitable but nonetheless hoped to avoid.

But Kit insisted that he wanted to try and pee on his own. I intervened with this compromise: What if we placed the commode at the halfway point between the bed and the bathroom? If it looked like he was not going to make it all the way to the official toilet, he could hop on the commode. All sides agreed. (The week I had spent in the trenches negotiating with Katherine Heigl's camp the terms of her *Entertainment Weekly* cover story—the one detailing her acrimonious exit from *Grey's Anatomy*—paid off handsomely.)

With the *Chariots of Fire* theme playing in my head, Kit was helped out of bed by the two wonderful nurses, the flimsy hospital gown exposing his horrifically skeletal body. His legs, his arms—it was all bone and very little meat. As a result, he was too weak to stand on his own, so the nurses supported 99 percent of his body weight as they slowly guided him across the room toward the bathroom, with me nervously shadowing them. Each arduous step he took represented a huge mental victory for both of us. And when he passed that commode at the halfway point, I imagined him flipping it off, as if saying, "Later, you sad little fake plastic toilet."

Several minutes later, I breathed a sigh of relief when they managed to get him into the bathroom and lower him onto the toilet. All I could see was Kit's legs uncontrollably shaking from the stress and strain.

"Magazine, please!" he screamed to me, as I ran over to the bag of home essentials Marilyn had packed and brought the night Kit was admitted, to fetch his makeshift pain stick. I pulled it out of the bag—the thing was so tightly wound at this point that the TSA would probably ban it as a carry-on item on the grounds it could be used as a weapon—and raced back into the bathroom to hand it to Kit. He grabbed it and started squeezing. He was in agony. Why was he putting himself through this when he could've just peed in the commode right next to the bed?

He then ordered everyone—myself included—to leave him alone.

"Please get out," he cried. "Shut the door behind you."

And then it hit me: It was privacy he craved more than anything. He just wanted to pee in a bathroom by himself like a normal human being. He was fighting to hang on to what little dignity he had left. I had never been more in love or felt more empathy for another human being than I did in this moment.

Over the course of the next few days, Kit gained more mental and physical strength, as he continued rebounding from his UTI. I began to invite a few members of his inner circle to visit him at the hospital, including our beloved old midtown neighbor Rose, Kit's work wife Missi, and Atlantic City Nick.

I even extended an invitation to the Other Man himself, Todd.

This was not the first time Todd had visited Kit. During his second chemo cycle, in May, back when I merely *suspected* that the two of them had a fling, I received a text from an unfamiliar number; it was Todd asking if it'd be OK if he stopped by to see Kit. (From the outset, Kit tasked me with maintaining ownership over his "deck time" visitation schedule, thus allowing me to serve as the bad cop if the situation called for it—i.e., if there was someone he did not want to see, I could easily hold them off on the grounds that *Ooooh, so sorry, Kit's having a really bad day. Also, news flash, he never liked you.* I'd present the requests to Kit and he'd say "yea," "nay," or "maybe tomorrow." Bottom line: No one got in to see Kit without going through me first. I relished the power and the control that came with being Kit's bouncer.)

There was a part of me that had wanted to rebuff Todd's initial overture back in May on the grounds that *He picked me. He's mine. Deal with it. Oh, and you're nowhere near as hot as Tom Daley.* But there was a much bigger part of me that wanted to see Kit smile. And I knew a visit from Todd would accomplish that.

So I happily welcomed Todd into our home, not once, not twice, but three times. And on every occasion I escorted him out onto our back patio, closed the shutters behind me, and gave them the space to talk and smoke pot and sometimes eat takeout while I got caught up on *TVLine* work or cleaned the apartment or took a nap.

But this would be my first time seeing Todd since Kit confirmed to me back in September during our own private deck time that the two of them had indeed fucked around.

I felt a slight pang of resentment when he showed up at Kit's hospital room for his scheduled visit. But I also felt notably secure and empowered. I was no longer the unwitting spouse. I knew the truth. And I wanted him here anyway. I knew the sight of him would perk Kit up. And Lord knew Kit deserved every ounce of happiness I could scrounge up.

"Kit, special visitor alert," I announced. "Todd's here."

Kit looked up, saw Todd standing next to me, and let out a big smile. Todd smiled, too, but I could see the shock and concern behind his strained grin as he noticed how thin Kit had become since he last saw him over the summer. I felt empathy for him.

I was grieving for my husband's fucking mistress. What *couldn't* Kit do!

Kit acknowledged his visitor with a muted, hoarse "*Toddddd*," while also mustering a half smile. Todd kissed him on the cheek.

"I'm gonna go fetch a Diet Coke while you guys catch up," I informed them. "I'll be back in fifteen minutes."

I returned in exactly fifteen minutes, hung out with the two of them for another ten minutes, and then showed Todd out. As we walked out into the hallway together, I noticed Todd was crying. And as we neared the elevator bank, I noticed he was crying harder.

"Thank you for letting me see him," he sobbed. "I'm so sorry this is happening. Kit is an amazing person. And you're an amazing partner."

I suddenly felt a strong desire to hug my husband's mistress. And so I did. And not just a Hollywood hug. A warm, extended Northern New Jersey hug.

I pulled out of the embrace and promised to keep him posted on Kit's condition, before watching the elevator doors close behind him.

The next day, Sunday, exactly one week since Kit had been violently extracted from our bed, I hired a beautician to come by to give Kit a much-needed mani-pedi. And on Monday, prior to Kit being formally discharged, I arranged to have a surprise waiting for him at home.

One of the many heartbreaking aspects of Kit's cancer battle involved our mutual TV obsessions. There wasn't a ton of overlap when it came to our favorite shows, but there were a handful of programs we really enjoyed watching together. Examples included *House of Cards*, *The Walking Dead*, and right at the very top of that list, *RuPaul's Drag Race*.

On those Mondays when *Drag Race* was on, we would text and IM each other funny little reminders to keep that night's schedule clear for our date with Ru. We *loved* Drag Race Mondays. I mostly loved how happy—and animated—they made Kit. I got more of a kick out of watching *him* watch the show than out of the show itself, to be honest.

The timing of Season 6 proved somewhat fortuitous—many of the episodes had aired while Kit was going through chemo in the spring. It was the perfect morale booster for both of us. But there was also an added layer of sadness, knowing the probability was high that he would not be around to see a seventh season. And now, less than two months before *Drag Race*'s March 2 return, it would seem my fears had been realized.

So on Friday I reached out to my friends at Logo and asked if they could sneak me an advance copy of the Season 7 premiere. (It was one of only two times I leveraged the cancer card to gain special access to a piece of entertainment; the other one occurred last spring when *Dawn of the Planet of the Apes* director Matt Reeves—who co-created a little show called *Felicity* with J.J. Abrams—treated us to a private screening of the film in the comfort of our own living room weeks before its release because movie-theater seating had become untenable for Kit and he had *so* been looking forward to seeing this latest installment.) And today, Logo informed me that they were messengering the DVD to the apartment this morning. I texted my landlord to ensure that they'd be around to sign for it, and they confirmed that they would be.

Now we just needed to get the patient home.

As a result of the impassioned and heartfelt promise I had made to hospice director Elizabeth Miller to bring down her and her entire organization if Kit's level of in-home care didn't start to improve, a new set of EMTs was instructed to treat my husband like the fucking pope. They delicately, gingerly carried him up the stairs in a—get this—chair-stretcher. (Kit himself OK'd its use.) There were a few tense moments, an occasional yelp of discomfort, but nothing compared to the shit show from a week ago.

Kit was home. And, against all odds, he was not only still breathing, but he was in better shape than he had been in weeks—so much so that I grabbed my laptop, crawled into bed next to him, inserted the *RuPaul's Drag Race* season premiere disc, and pressed play. He instantly smiled upon seeing the show's fabulously cheesy opening title sequence. The fog of cancer and morphine dampened some of his enthusiasm as we lay there and watched the episode, but he did crack a smile here and there. He also applauded one of Ru's trademark sex puns during the runway show at the end of the episode. It was pretty damn special.

I closed the laptop, and for the first time in many months, Kit uttered the C-word.

"Wanna be canoodled?" he asked.

"Are you serious?"

"Let's try."

I backed myself into "the pocket of the poops," and Kit wrapped his arms around me, even letting out his customary "click." It was nowhere close to our usual, award-winning spoon. But it was close enough.

"I'm sorry I didn't love you better," I whispered to him, as I felt him breathing on my neck.

"What?" he asked incredulously.

"I'm sorry I didn't love you better," I repeated.

He hesitated, before responding with a somewhat indifferent "OK."

"*OK?*" I shot back, before adding tongue-in-cheek, "You're supposed to say I couldn't love you any better."

Kit paused again before letting out a sly, slightly cunty "OK."

I smiled. And we fell off to sleep.

14

Pinkberry with a side of peanut butter—that was what was on the dinner menu for Kit tonight. Actually, with the exception of the occasional bottle of Ensure, it had pretty much been the *only* thing on the menu these past few weeks, as he had slowly lost an appetite for—and, due to his weakened state, the strength to consume—pretty much everything else. The staff at the Pinkberry location on 14th Street and Sixth Avenue—a ten-minute walk from the apartment and where I was headed now—pretty much knew my order by heart: four medium-sized original-flavored yogurts—one for me, one for Kit, and two for our new houseguests, Bob and Marilyn. (As Kit started to rapidly decline last week, his parents had relocated from their son's Brooklyn man cave to our living room, where they'd been sleeping on a blow-up mattress.)

I was fairly certain I was single-handedly keeping this particular Pinkberry franchise afloat. We were in the middle of the coldest winter on record, so the frozen yogurt business wasn't exactly booming in NYC. It was no surprise that I was once again the only customer in the place tonight, as the mercury hovered in the mid-teens.

If Kit ended up eating half of his medium-sized cup I'd consider it a win; the last few nights he had barely touched the stuff. So far today he'd had a few sips of water. And that was it. And trust me, I vigilantly tracked every ounce of nourishment that entered his body. One quarter of my daily dark chocolate sea salt Kind bar? That was fifty calories right there. Half of an Outshine-brand lime-flavored ice pop? Another twenty-five calories. One Swedish Fish? Let's round it up to ten calories and hope no one notices. My goal of late had been to clear five hundred calories a day. But I'd been missing that threshold by a few hundred the past few weeks. When he had barely broken the one-hundred-calorie benchmark last Friday, I just stopped keeping count altogether. It was too depressing. It served as a painful indicator that the end was near.

Not that there wasn't already a plethora of signs, the most obvious one being his increasingly labored and congested breathing. One of the hospice nurses reluctantly informed me that the phlegmy noise that accompanied each one of his exhales actually had a name, albeit a colloquial one: the "death rattle." I thought she was kidding. Google confirmed to me that she was not. It described the terminal secretions like saliva that accumulated in a dying individual's throat and upper chest. What an ugly, horrible, insensitive, crass label to attach to something so heartbreaking. Kit would've loved it.

As I entered the apartment with dessert in hand, I heard the familiar sound of the local news blaring from the TV. Bob had begun to settle into his daily weekday ritual that started with the local Channel 7 news at 5 p.m. and ended with the climax of *Wheel of Fortune*'s bonus round puzzle at 7:59 p.m. When Kit still had had the ability to walk the nine steps from the bedroom to the living room (with me grabbing one of his arms and Bob clutching the other), the four of us would assemble to watch *Jeopardy!* and *Wheel* every single night since the start of hospice in early December. It became our thing. And I looked forward to it.

Bob had valiantly carried on the tradition solo, and I was grateful for it. Even though we were not all gathered together, the routine remained a much-needed intoxicant for me, especially now that wine and I were on a break. The familiar drone of the local news anchors' voices leading into Alex Trebek's soothing air of superiority followed immediately by *Wheel*'s cheery musical cues (not to mention Pat and

Vanna's laughably canned banter) served as a nice respite from the eerie, depressing silence that had befallen the apartment since Kit lost the ability to speak with any regularity. Those three hours of TV had become something of a soothing white noise machine.

I handed Bob his frozen yogurt, placed mine in the freezer for later, and entered the bedroom. Marilyn was in Kit's vintage green recliner by the bed, reading a book and keeping close watch on a sleeping, death-rattlin' Kit. I handed her her Pinkberry.

"Any change?" I asked, adopting my best library voice (because, as I'd found, libraries and deathbeds share many of the same unspoken auditory rules).

She shook her head.

I placed Kit's yogurt on the bed, then proceeded to optimistically inspect the urinary drainage bag that was hooked up to his catheter to see if it needed emptying. It remained at the same one-tenth level it had been at all day. I then pulled his covers back to check the colostomy bag. I noticed the tiniest stool—it was barely the size of a pencil eraser—attempting to push its way through his stoma. It was as if Kit were declaring, *Um*, hello. *News flash. A little poop is coming out. My broken-down, bruised, hole-punctured body is still doin' stuff. I'm not dead yet.*

I walked back out to the kitchen to retrieve the jar of peanut butter from the cupboard, before taking my seat next to Kit on the bed.

"Hey, babe, I have Pinkberry," I alerted him, while gently squeezing his bony hand, which, miraculously, was still adorned with his now very loose wedding ring. His eyelids slowly opened. That was my cue to scoop up a little yogurt, add a dash of peanut butter—so that the spoon was 70 percent frozen yogurt and 30 percent peanut butter, aka Kit's preferred percentage breakdown—and guide it into his mouth. The chill of the yogurt as it brushed up against his lips caused his eyes to widen. And to my delight, his mouth opened and he lapped up the creamy goodness. I shot Marilyn a look of pleasant surprise, and we both watched with rapt attention as he slowly worked the first bite around the inside of his mouth. He had barely swallowed it before the eager, excited beaver in me had another spoonful pressed up against his lips. I didn't want to squander any of the precious momentum.

My strategy of impatience worked. He devoured that one, too. I flashed another smile at Marilyn, who was digging into her own yogurt while joyously taking in the show before her. I started miming loud Cookie Monster noises every time Kit's mouth sucked in another bite. I couldn't tell if he was getting a kick out of it, but it was sure as fuck amusing me.

After he swallowed his sixth spoonful, leaving approximately half a cup remaining, I asked him for permission before serving him a seventh bite. He nodded yes. This was *incredible*. If I was still counting calories, Kit would probably be nearing 250—which was pretty much more than he'd had in the past three days *combined*. Was this the beginning of another energy surge? Whatever it was, I was grateful.

As I neared the bottom of the cup, Kit started to slow down.

"One more?" I asked. He shook his head. He'd had enough. I decided not to let the remaining three ounces go to waste, so I finished it off myself. It was what Kit would have wanted, seeing as how during the hundreds of frozen yogurt dates that had preceded this one over the course of our thirteen years together, Kit had always ended up sharing his final two or three spoonfuls with me. And that was because I tended to attack my frozen yogurt like a honey badger at a competitive eating event, while Kit preferred to take his time, savoring each and every bite. That resulted in my finishing long before Kit, which, in turn, resulted in Kit being forced to make a decision: Did he eat the rest by himself while I stared at him licking my lips, or did he push his cup to the center of the table and go halfsies with me on the rest? Lucky for me and my insatiable fro-yo appetite, he usually opted for the latter.

"Nice work," I raved. "You ate pretty much the whole thing." I gave him a kiss on the lips to formally reward him for a job well done. His eyes perked up, he opened his mouth, and much to my shock and awe, he eked out a very quiet, barely audible, but nonetheless heartfelt "Thank you."

Those would be the last two words Kit ever spoke.

Shortly after his big dinner triumph, Kit drifted back off to sleep. His breathing was becoming more labored, to the point where I phoned the on-call hospice nurse to express renewed concern.

"He is fighting for every breath," I stressed. "It seems like he's suffering."

She recommended I give him an additional two bolus doses of morphine an hour to ease any discomfort he might have been having, as well as 2 mg of liquid Ativan to help calm him down. This was in addition to the two drops of atropine I'd been placing on his tongue to aid with the "death rattle," which also seemed to be worsening. She asked me to count his number of breaths-per-minute. I informed her that it was roughly sixteen.

"That's a pretty normal rate," she assured me. "Fourteen to sixteen is normal."

I hung up with the nurse, administered Kit a new round of meds and bolus doses, and then informed Bob and Marilyn—who were in the final stages of setting up the blow-up mattress in the living room—that I was going to try and get some sleep. The key word here being *try*. I was contending not only with Kit's heavy, rattly breathing, but his awkward positioning, as well; he was basically in a diagonal line, meaning I had to somehow contort my body around him—or curl myself into a ball in one of the corners. Of course, sleeping anywhere else but by his side on what could have been his last night on Earth was simply not an option. Over the past eleven months, I'd shared this bed with him through all-night bouts of nausea and UTI-fueled restlessness and dementia-driven paranoia and leaking colostomy bags. I was not about to abandon him now because he was a noisy bed hog.

Morning arrived—I probably managed two hours of sleep total—and Kit's breathing had become louder and quicker; his output was now thirty-six breaths per minute. And with each one of those thirty-six breaths, his chest rose about two inches. Any way you sliced it, he did not seem comfortable.

I phoned the on-call hospice nurse and relayed my concerns. She suggested ordering an oxygen machine. I was initially reluctant to have any more medical equipment brought into our five-hundred-square-foot apartment that was already teeming with walkers and commodes and catheters and colostomy bags and morphine pumps and diapers and mattress protectors and backup morphine pumps. But even if there was a minuscule chance he could achieve some relief, it was worth it. So I gave the OK for an oxygen tank.

Within an hour, the hospice technician called my cell and informed me that he had arrived—at 6 *James* Street, which was some forty blocks south, in the Financial District. "We're at 6 *Jane* Street," I informed him, über-perturbed. An hour later, he showed up at the correct address, set up the contraption next to the bed, and placed the nostril piece in Kit's nose. He then turned the machine on, and much to my dismay, it gave off a loud, hospital-ish thumping noise every couple of seconds. He told us we'd get used to it. I flashed him a look of skepticism, signed his work order, and showed him to the door.

It was not as if the loud clang of the oxygen tank was going to disturb Kit. He hadn't opened his eyes since polishing off the Pinkberry last night. Meanwhile, the idea that the end could be very near entered my mind. In spite of that, I threw on my gym clothes and informed Marilyn and Bob that I was going to sneak off to Equinox for a quick workout. They knew the drill: If anything changed, all they had to do was text me and I'd be home in ninety seconds (again, the gym was *literally* around the corner). That was exactly how long it had taken me two weeks ago when Marilyn—out of an abundance of caution—texted me concerned that she had applied the wrong ointment to Kit's pancake-sized bedsore. In less than five minutes, not only was I at Kit's bedside, but I had the incorrect cream washed off and the correct cream applied.

Of course, I knew there still existed a chance—no matter how slight—that Kit could die while I was trudging away on an elliptical machine. I was reminded of something one of the hospice counselors had told us early on: "He will go when he is ready to go. And if you're not present, that means he wanted to spare you that moment." It sounded a little crackpot to me at the time. But it was proving useful now as I felt the strong compulsion to burn a few hundred calories.

My hour of exercise passed in a flash, and I returned home to find Kit's wheezing just as loud and labored as when I'd left, despite the assistance of the oxygen machine. And it seemed as if there were far fewer actual breaths—roughly ten to twelve per minute, which was a precipitous drop from earlier this morning. Alarmed, I phoned hospice and they sent a nurse over to give him a once-over. She checked his vitals before solemnly delivering her assessment to me, Marilyn, and Bob.

"He's actively passing," she said.

Oh, joy. Another oxymoronic, soul-crushing medical term I'd never heard of.

"What does that mean?" I asked.

"His body is shutting down," she explained.

Marilyn, who was standing next to Bob at the foot of the bed, started crying. I, however, was not buying any of what the nurse was selling.

"We've been in this situation before," I informed her testily. "Last month when he was in the hospital we were told he would likely be dead in a day."

"His systolic blood pressure is below seventy, his eyes are dilated . . ." she explained, compassionately yet pointedly. "These are the things we see at the end."

I grabbed Kit's hand, and for the first time, I noticed that the tips of his fingers felt . . . chilly. And they had an eerie light blue hue to them. I then stared at Kit's face, his mouth half-open and skin paler than ever. I looked back at the nurse, tears streaming down my face. And I nodded.

"How long does he have?" I asked.

"A couple of hours," she said, as Marilyn sobbed in Bob's arms. "Maybe more. Maybe less."

The nurse then echoed something we'd heard from a myriad of hospice personnel over the past two months when the topic turned to what to expect in his final hours: "He can hear you. Talk to him. Tell him you love him. Assure him that you will be OK without him."

The nurse offered to return later tonight to check on him again. I thanked her. Bob showed her out.

Marilyn took a seat on the other side of Kit, clutched his left hand, and whispered, "Kit, it's OK. We're going to be OK."

I just looked at her, marveling at her strength. Where was she mustering the courage to give her only child permission to die? I was not quite ready to go there. So I just sat there, on the other side of him, grasping his hand, fiddling with his wedding ring, keeping his lips moistened with the spongy Q-tips. Fixating on every one of his precious breaths.

The evening wore on, and Kit's breath output declined further. Marilyn continued to follow the hospice rulebook to the letter, letting Kit know he could pass on when he was ready and not to worry about us. Bob, meanwhile, toggled between the bed and the recliner, where he was now quietly crying. I noticed the coldness had now extended to Kit's toes. I was ready to have "the talk" with him.

"Can you please give us a minute alone?" I asked Marilyn. She was at first reluctant to let go of his hand. But she eventually granted me my wish, planting a kiss on Kit's forehead before informing him, "We'll be right back, sunshine." She then walked out with Bob and I closed the door behind them.

I took a deep breath. And I just stood at the bedside and looked at my beloved Kit, lying there helpless and so fucking skinny and hooked up to so much shit and *My God, he's only forty-two years old.* And then I plopped down on the bed next to him, grabbed the collar of his sweatshirt, and stared him in the face.

"You listen to me, Fuck Stick. I am going to be OK. It's going to be unbelievably hard, but I *will* be OK. You go get heaven ready for us, because, thanks to you, I have high standards. Thank you for the past thirteen years. Thank you for giving me a family. Thank you for loving me. Thank you for being my Bodge."

I kissed his lips, my cascade of tears dotting his long-sleeved, black-and-white striped cotton shirt. And I just sat there for a few more minutes, processing that after eleven months of fear and uncertainty and surgeries and doctors and appointments and Carmel trips back and forth to Sloan and final goodbyes with friends and pain episodes and intimacy and closure and colostomy bags and shotgun weddings and heart-to-hearts out on the deck . . . it would all soon be over. And for an instant I felt a fleeting sense of relief. For Kit. For Kit's parents. And for me.

I got out of the bed to let Bob and Marilyn back in, and I noticed that resting atop the door frame's ledge was The Lurker. Kit had relocated him from the living room to the bedroom a few months back when he started becoming less mobile; with the change of venue came a slightly tweaked narrative. Instead of The Lurker getting terrorized by a giant ceramic middle finger, it was now literally under attack from a little green army figurine. The soldier, down on one knee, was pointing a giant bazooka directly at The Lurker. Kit had perfectly positioned the diorama so that it was in full view of the bed where he had spent much of the past three months.

Part of me wanted to pick the soldier up, stare him in the face, and scream, *Why the fuck didn't you do your job? All you had to do was pull the trigger.* But there was another part of me that saw the installation as the defining metaphor for how Kit had confronted this entire year: with grace, courage, dark humor, and unquestionable fearlessness, right up until the end.

The truth was, The Lurker never stood a chance.

I opened the bedroom door and Kit's mom led the charge back in, reclaiming her spot next to Kit. Meanwhile, Bob—perhaps sensing there wasn't much time left—pulled a chair next to Marilyn by the bed.

"Hi, sunshine," Marilyn said, taking Kit's hand. "It's Mom and Dad. We're here. We love you."

As we surrounded Kit, tissues and tears everywhere, the most remarkable thing happened. Like *if I saw this play out on my favorite TV show I would roll my eyes and delete my season pass* remarkable. Mister Scooch strolled into the bedroom and did something he had not done in the eight months since Kit tasked me with going to Bed Bath & Beyond with a 20-percent-off coupon to buy a foam mattress cushion, only to be told I had gotten the wrong one and sent back to get the correct, far plusher—and cheaper—one: Scooch hopped on the bed. For whatever reason, the texture of the mattress pad had been like Kryptonite to his paws, leading him to avoid the bed like the plague. So I could hardly believe my eyes as I watched him gingerly, carefully make his way over the morphine pump and past the catheter tubing before plopping down right next to Kit, one side of him grazing Kit's abdomen and the other side of him brushed up against my leg. I looked at Kit's mom and dad in utter disbelief. I pulled out my iPhone and took a photo of Scooch shoehorned between his two dads because I knew I'd want proof later that in my compromised emotional state I hadn't imagined it.

The shock of Scooch's improbable eleventh-hour visitation quickly gave way to sadness as I took in the beautiful, heart-annihilating scene before me. Kit and Mister Scooch—my family. Some of the happiest memories of my life were just of Kit and me snuggled up in bed or on the couch marveling at something ridiculous Mister Scooch was doing with his mouth or his paws.

Scooch hung out for another two or three minutes, before hopping up and off the bed. It was just long enough, I supposed, for him to say goodbye.

Kit's breathing continued to slow down and time began to stand still. The air was heavy, almost oppressive. I felt like I was in some kind of alternative reality as I watched the most important person in my life near the end of his. Each dramatic breath was now becoming an event unto itself, the three of us hanging on to each gasp of air, hoping, praying, another one was coming right behind it.

For a split second, as I waited for him to inhale, I imagined Kit opening his eyes, looking over at me, and urgently saying, as he had so many hundreds of times before, *I'm hungry. What are we doing for dinner? Benny's?*

He began to take his next breath, and, somehow, the sheer force of the inhale told me that this was it.

"Goodbye, Bodge," I cried. As the final traces of air escaped his lungs, his mouth opened slightly wider, and the upper right corner of his lip curled upward. And it froze. I waited for another breath, but I knew one was not coming.

Kit was gone.

An overwhelming sense of loss spread throughout every ounce of my five-foot-ten frame. Like a vacuum was sucking all the energy out of me. Like a chunk of me had broken off and attached itself to Kit as he drifted away. The emptiness, and the finality that the emptiness represented, overwhelmed me.

And, then, suddenly, I was startled by the . . . silence. The deafening, ear-splitting silence. It was the sound of the most important person in

my life no longer making a sound. The oxygen machine was still clank-
ing, and Marilyn and Bob were wailing, but all my ears could register
was the noise I *wasn't* hearing. I hadn't realized how deeply tethered
my soul had been to his breathing. Until, at 10:30 p.m., it stopped.

I could really use a fountain Diet Coke right about now was an honest-
to-God thought that popped into my head as I sat on the bed staring
at the body of my freshly deceased husband. Widowerhood had left me
parched.

With a weeping Marilyn clutching Kit's hand and Bob perched beside her, I stood up, ambled into the kitchen, opened the fridge, and
reached for a Diet Half 'n Half Snapple (lemonade and iced tea), which
was not far from a half-empty bottle of sauvignon blanc. Three months
earlier I would've pushed the Snapple aside and seized the vino. But
now that I'd been off the sauce for three months—and learned that
I was capable of dealing with life's greatest challenges head-on and
without the aid of an intoxicant—I had no interest in drowning my
sorrows in anything other than aspartame. I undid the cap and took a
nice long swig. It wasn't fountain Diet Coke, but it'd do.

I took my phone from my pants pocket to check the time—it was
10:42 p.m. On February 5. Nearly eleven months to the day since his
diagnosis. Roughly six weeks shy of our one-year wedding anniversary.

I leaned up against the kitchen counter not far from the wooden
Lazy Susan that had become ground zero for Kit's pharmaceutical care.
I slowly spun the tray, eyeballing bottles of Betadine, lorazepam, senna,
atropine, nystatin, methadone, Calmoseptine. A year ago I'd had no
idea these drugs even existed, let alone how to pronounce them, what
symptoms they relieved (or, in Kit's case, *didn't*), and how many pills
constituted a normal dose.

One of the little disposable soufflé cups I had swiped from the con-
diment station at Sloan Kettering's cafeteria was resting on its side
near the edge of the circular stand. The day I had upgraded Kit's pill
delivery method from clammy human palm to miniature paper soufflé
cup had been a proud one for this fledgling caregiver. And it had not

gone unnoticed by the patient, who greeted his new drug-transport device with an "*Oooh*, fancy."

I took another long sip of my Snapple and then started in on the initial postmortem calls. I got the business stuff out of the way first, phoning the twenty-four-hour hospice hotline (the operator confirmed that the on-call nurse who had been here earlier was already en route for her pre-planned evening visit) and then the Chelsea-based Redden's Funeral Home (co-director David Duffy, whom I had met with last month, notified me that he was dispatching a team to retrieve Kit's body and transfer it to the crematorium, although he warned me—given the late hour—that it'd be a few hours).

Now it was time to notify the core people: my brothers, Dave and Pete; Kit's BFF Jen and work wife Missi; and, lastly, our therapist, Tony. I also reached out via text to my local, on-call support team that consisted of our best German friend and wedding photographer Nina and our former midtown neighbor Rose, both of whom were en route.

"Can I bring you anything?" Rose asked.

"Yes," I replied, instantly. "Can you please stop at the diner and pick me up two large fountain Diet Cokes with extra ice."

I walked back into the bedroom, and although I'd only been away for five or so minutes, the sight of Corpse Kit sent a disorienting, dizzying shock wave through my body. There were no words to describe how unreal a sight it was. I found myself struggling to see past his half-open right eyelid. Truth be told, it was actually creeping me out. It was like he was watching me from beyond the grave, making sure I didn't do something stupid like slit my wrists or, worse yet, rearrange the accent tables in the living room.

I approached the bed, reached my hand out, and attempted to force his eyelid closed as Marilyn—still crying and clutching his hand—looked on. No dice. The pesky ptosis that Kit had inherited from his father and that had bugged him for most of his adult life—so much so that he had undergone two semi-successful surgeries to have it corrected—appeared determined to terrorize *me* now.

I walked around to the other side of the bed and placed my hand on Marilyn's back and rubbed it gently, as we both looked at what was left of Kit.

"He fought so hard," I whispered through tears.

"That he did," she said. "My God, did he fight."

The doorbell buzzed, signaling that the nurse had arrived.

"I'll get it," Bob bellowed from the other room.

"It's the hospice nurse," I whispered to Marilyn, who reluctantly, slowly got up from the bed, releasing her grip on Kit's hand. With us standing side by side, I pulled her into an embrace. And we both sobbed.

I'm sorry it was Kit and not me was what I *wanted* to say to her, partly to give voice to the survivor's guilt that was already kicking in, and partly because I truly meant it. I would've done anything to spare Kit this fate. Including taking his place.

"Kit was so lucky to have such amazing, brave parents by his side through this" was what I ultimately told her.

"We were the lucky ones," she cried.

We hung on to each other for what felt like fifteen seconds, shattering the previous Mike-Marilyn hug-hold record of eleven seconds, before the nurse's arrival prompted us to unclasp. The nurse immediately offered her heartfelt and surprisingly unrehearsed-sounding condolences (I imagined this wasn't her first time at the rodeo). I asked for her assistance in helping me to get Kit cleaned up. And dressed.

"I'm putting a nice outfit on him," I announced to the room. "He's going to look sharp when they take him away. He's going to look like *Kit*."

"Of course," the nurse replied. "Whatever you need."

Marilyn walked over and planted a kiss on Kit's forehead, then left the bedroom with Bob in tow. I closed the door and took a deep breath as I mentally prepared myself for the task at hand. I had no idea where to begin, so I turned to the nurse for guidance.

She offered to begin unhooking his morphine pump and urine catheter, and suggested I handle the removal of his colostomy bag. I signed off on that plan of attack, got a washcloth and a trash bag from the bathroom, and began removing his white-and-black striped cotton pullover, a super-cozy number.

As I attempted to maneuver his long-ass arm—which was now eerily cold and somewhat stiff—out of the first sleeve, I found myself handling his body as cautiously and carefully as if he were still alive, my natural instinct ignoring the fact that he was dead and therefore couldn't feel any pain. I no longer had to worry that Kit was suffering—that was going to take some getting used to, so much so that at one point I actually uttered the words "I'm sorry, babe" when I accidentally elbowed him in the chin while pulling the shirt over his head.

Once it was completely off, my heart sank as I looked at his shockingly emaciated upper body. I'd obviously glimpsed what the ravages of cancer had done to his once-strapping six-foot-three frame, but it had always been in short bursts and when my attention was diverted (e.g., during a crisis or a quick-change or while replacing his colostomy bag). There was nothing to distract me from his skeletal, battle scar-ridden body now. Jesus Christ, he had gone through hell.

The medical port that had been surgically inserted into his chest last spring to allow for the safe and easy delivery of his chemo regimen as well as withdrawal of blood—and that used to be barely visible—was now protruding through his skin like some kind of Xenomorph Chestburster from *Alien*. The area was rife with puncture wounds from the hundreds of needles that had been used to access the port over the past seven months.

The routine surgery to have the device implanted had taken place last May, but it felt like a lifetime ago. Shortly after Kit awoke in the recovery room, I ominously informed him that while he was under the knife I had discovered blood in my urine while peeing in the hospital bathroom. To which Kit—who could smell my low-grade hypochondria a mile away—rolled his still-groggy eyes and reminded me, "You had beets for lunch, dummy."

Before starting in on the colostomy bag, I took his right arm and peeled off the bandage covering a wrist left bruised and bloodied from weeks of persistent scratching. (I had read online that when the cancer spread to the liver, as it had with Kit, one of the symptoms was itchy skin.) Despite my best efforts to make the dressing impenetrable, Kit—even in his compromised state—had always found a way in. Just three days ago I'd walked in to find blood cascading off his arm and onto the bedsheets as Kit was digging his fingernails into his wound. He was just lucid enough to tell by the disapproving, irritated look on my face that he had done a bad, bad thing.

"What did I tell you I would do if you tore into that bandage again?" I asked him, pointedly.

Without missing a beat, he looked up at me and sheepishly replied, "You'd throw me out of the bedroom window?"

"That's right," I faux-fumed, before alerting Bob, "I'm going to need some help in here picking your son up and tossing him out of the bedroom window."

I removed the bandage for the last time and cleared away some of the dried blood with the washcloth. I moved south to the colostomy bag, a contraption I had been more than happy to let Kit be in charge of when it entered our lives back in September.

But as Kit's condition worsened and he lost the mental and physical strength to oversee the bag's maintenance, I took over as CEO of his colostomy care. And after overcoming a few messy speed bumps, I became c-bag-changing champ. Like, no one was better at it than me. I would gladly engage in a bag-off with any member of Sloan Kettering's colorectal nursing staff. At my peak, I could have the old bag removed, the surface cleaned and disinfected, and a new bag attached in under two minutes, leaving barely enough time for Kit to push a fart through his stoma, let alone a stool.

I peeled off the pouch and quickly tossed it into a trash bag I then sealed before the smell could permeate the apartment, and Bob and Marilyn's grief-stricken nostrils. As I cleaned the stoma, I felt the impulse kick in to hurriedly attach the adhesive skin barrier, followed by the floating flange, and then the new pouch itself, before finally securing the whole thing with the special skin-friendly surgical tape. Instead I went against my natural instinct and left the stoma unguarded. Kit wouldn't be making any more poops today.

The nurse, meanwhile, had Kit's morphine pump detached and was now working on the urine catheter. She asked for my help in removing his sweatpants. We started at the waist, and as we drew them down, his pink Uniqlo briefs came into view, shattering the emotional detachment I'd been harnessing in an effort to get through this hauntingly surreal task. Oh, how he loved his comfy-cozy pink Uniqlo briefs, especially during the past year when the pain level in and around his ass made wearing tight-fitting clothes untenable. For our two-month wedding anniversary last May, I had gifted him with the last three pairs in all of New York (or at least in the SoHo store).

With his drawers and underwear off, and Kit's lower body as exposed as his upper body, the nurse glided the catheter tube out of the tip of his penis. The act caused my body to instinctually clench up, just as it had done the half-dozen or so times the tube was inserted and removed over the past month (ever since he lost the ability to get out of bed and urinate on his own). I looked up at Kit's face, half-expecting to see him wince in pain.

With the catheter removed, I felt the impulse to place the underwear back over his groin, to shield him from any embarrassment. But then I reminded myself that this was Kit we were talking about. He had shame about many things, but his penis was not one of them. On the contrary, he was quite proud of his enviable endowment, as evidenced by his considerable, and considerably artsy, dick pic collection. And the private *Puppetry of the Penis*–inspired shows he staged for me rivaled anything performed by the professionals in the official Off-Broadway show.

I walked over to Kit's closet and started searching for an outfit to put on him. I spotted the collared shirt that he wore on our wedding day last March. He wanted so badly to make it to our first anniversary. I pulled the shirt out of the closet, along with his favorite tan khakis and, of course, a clean pair of his beloved pink undies. I lay them on the bed and, together, the nurse and I got to work. First we slid on his briefs, then his pants, before tackling the trickiest part—his shirt. Even as a shell of his former self, Kit was still big. And early rigor mortis was only making his maneuverability more challenging.

"Sorry, babe," I muttered to Kit as I forced his left arm through the shirt's sleeve, all the while thinking, *This dress-up idea seemed like a good idea in theory.* I could sense Kit harrumphing from beyond the grave, *You do realize they're just going to slip me into a body bag, right?*

Finally, we got the shirt on and tucked in (well, the front part was tucked in; I cheated on the back). I decided to forgo trying to wrestle the blue blazer on him, and instead proceeded to the closet to fetch his beloved beige Camper sneakers. Those also for some reason proved to be a bitch to get on. At this point, I stopped apologizing for treating his body like a rag doll and just forced his feet inside the shoes.

I stepped back from the bed, wiped the sweat off my brow, and evaluated my handiwork. Kit would probably have been horrified at my sloppy styling job, but it was a vast improvement from how he had looked just twenty minutes ago. I thought his parents would appreciate it. *Someone* had better appreciate it, because it was exhausting and where the fuck was Rose with my Diet Cokes and *Oh, my fucking God, I can't believe Kit is gone.*

Just then there was a knock at the bedroom door—it was Rose, brandishing one of my Diet Cokes.

"I put the other one in the fridge," she quickly informed me. I took the cup and then went in for a hug (priorities!), as the nurse retreated to the living room.

"He's gone, Rose," I cried, as I snuck my first sip of Diet Coke behind her back.

"Michael, I'm so sorry," she said, before heading over to Kit's side.

"Kitlet," she cooed, deploying her go-to nickname for him. "You have all the answers now. You have all the answers."

Kit loved Rose like a sister. In our decade of knowing her, he never shaded her once, at least not that I witnessed. And for Kit, that really said something. He was never *not* excited to see her. My heart simultaneously filled up and shattered as I watched her straighten his collar and button his sleeves. Basically, she was finishing what I had started.

"How did I do with my styling?" I boldly asked one of Broadway's most in-demand dressers.

"Michael, he looks great," she assured me, presumably grading on a curve, given my emotionally fragile state. "You did *great.*"

"I had a rough time with his shirt," I confessed. "And his shoes. I think maybe the cancer made his feet bigger."

Rose got up, walked to the foot of the bed, and bent over to get a closer look at his feet. She did what looked like a double take before breaking out in a spontaneous fit of laughter. She put her hand over her mouth in an effort to contain the seemingly ill-timed outburst. I didn't know what was triggering her giggle attack, but I welcomed the sudden burst of lightness with open arms.

"Michael, I don't mean to laugh."

"What is it?" I asked, legit curious.

She looked up at me with the most intense, penetrating expression and said, "You put the shoes on the wrong feet."

"Are you kidding me?" I shrieked, before inspecting the crime scene myself. She was, of course, right. I was going to send Kit out of the apartment for the last time with his shoes on the wrong feet. Rose and I just stared at each other and smiled.

"You know he's cursing you somewhere right now," Rose laughed, as she began swapping the shoes.

I looked at Kit with a mix of embarrassment and amusement. I imagined him shaking his head in mock-disgust, before leaning in and planting a slightly condescending kiss on my lips. He'd then pull away and backhandedly reassure me, "You're very handsome."

Michael Ausiello

February 6, 2015 •

It's with a heavy, broken heart that I tell you that Kit passed away late last night. He died much the way he lived through this grueling 11-month ordeal— on his own terms: He went peacefully at home (per his wishes), with me and his parents (and Mister Scooch) by his side. And he fought like a champ until he took his final breath.

It's true what they say about grief coming in waves. I'm alternating between sadness, shock, numbness, relief. But I also feel a deep sense of gratitude, to a universe that put me in the right place at the right time 13 years ago, and to a support system that helped get us through these past 11 months. I never took the love for granted, and neither did Kit.

15.

The day I'd been dreading had arrived. No, I wasn't in Millersburg to scatter Kit's ashes in the Susquehanna River, per his wishes. That particular task had been delayed until the warmer weather arrived. No, on this Saturday morning, nearly five weeks to the day since Kit's death, I was sitting on the L train—one of the main subway lines connecting Manhattan and Brooklyn—en route to Williamsburg, where I would spend the next two days cleaning out Kit's man cave.

Jen and Bill—Kit's married BFFs—had graciously agreed to drive up from Tampa to assist me with the arduous undertaking that was parsing through forty-two years of Kit's boxed-up memories. Although Kit had leased the one-bedroom unit only 18 months ago, and had barely spent any time there, he had transferred the entire contents of his midtown storage unit—essentially his entire life—into the eight-hundred-square-foot space. His living room had essentially functioned as a quasi storage locker.

I would have happily put this project off for another five weeks or five months or even five years. But I was not a fan of wasting money, and every month I procrastinated I had to write the owner another $1,300 check. So the goal was to clean out as much of the apartment as possible this weekend and then deliver the unit empty by March 31.

Luckily, Kit had given me a bit of a head start. During his summer rebound, he Uber'd himself to Williamsburg on three different occasions to begin "thinning the herd" (just in case Dr. Davis's dismal one-year life expectancy prediction came true). I offered to accompany him, but he insisted on going it alone. I was relieved. I wasn't ready to face the fact that he was dying, so the thought of watching him sort through his personal treasures—and decide what to dump, donate, or bequeath—was a special corner of hell I was not anxious to visit.

Upon arriving at the brick-and-shingled, postwar two-family structure, I was reminded of its severe lack of curb appeal. It was the very definition of ordinary. This was not a house where you would ever expect to find a mailbox with the name "Kit Cowan" on it. But the place was blessed with good mojo: His close friends Caroline and Clint had previously occupied the unit. It was their decision to relocate to the suburbs that had triggered Kit's alt-home epiphany.

I said a quick hello to the delightfully no-nonsense octogenarian owner, Julie Carbone, who lived in the downstairs unit and who—fun fact—is the aunt of *View* cohost Joy Behar. The family resemblance was apparent the second she opened her refreshingly frank mouth. ("Kit got a fucking raw deal," she lamented to me.) I thanked her for letting us use the apartment as temporary housing for family and friends the past year, especially Kit's parents, who had called the pad home for all of December and January. I handed Julie a check for the March rent before reluctantly making my way up the rounded staircase to the second floor.

Before I hit the top of the landing I started to feel it. The overwhelming pain. The immeasurable loss. This was my first time climbing these stairs without Kit leading the way.

The half-dozen times I had previously accompanied Kit to his nest away from home I had always kept a bit of an emotional distance from the physical space, probably because a part of me resented it. The apartment existed, to some degree, because Kit needed to get away from *me*. I respected the retreat—and on a couple of my overnighters I was even moved by its simple charms—but I harbored a bit of a grudge all the same.

Now I just felt gutted.

I made my way into the kitsched-out kitchen, with its seventies-era bright yellow metallic wallpaper that Kit had insisted on preserving because it was so hideous it was practically artful. Imagine walking into the *Brady Bunch* kitchen while stoned (woo-hoo—I can make that reference now!). Instead of resisting the décor, he had embraced it—so much so that he had spent a week searching for the perfect carpet tiles to match the heinous hue.

On the kitchen table rested a stack of his favorite card games, including Phase 10, Mille Bornes, and UNO, all of which we had played on one of our final pre-cancer overnighters. Nearby was a ceramic coffee mug emblazoned with a Smurf and a big, bright red heart and the words "I Smurf You"—a small piece of my massive collection he had co-opted for his crash pad. The sight of the mug triggered the morning's first cry spell. The second one was waiting for me in the barren fridge, which contained two bottles of severely outdated Diet Raspberry Snapple. It was what was left from the six-pack he had purchased in advance of my first overnight; he wanted to make me feel at home.

I headed into the bathroom, which was everything the kitchen wasn't: simple, sparse, timeless, white. It wasn't unlike his first New York bathroom on the Upper West Side, right down to the contents of the mirrored medicine cabinet. I opened the door, and resting on the bottom shelf were those two horny dinosaur figurines; they were still fucking like rabbits. Unlike in the cabinet on 68th Street, though, this twosome was now a threesome: Standing a few inches away was another figurine, this one embodying the most superficial species of Smurf, Vanity (or as Kit playfully called him, "Michael Ausiello"). Vanity was too busy admiring his reflection in his handheld mirror to even notice the orgy occurring nearby. Kind of perfect.

But it wasn't the slightly tweaked homage to Kit's first Big Apple apartment that caused my next meltdown. It was the sight of Kit's grooming products—his hair pomade, his shaving cream, his toothbrush, the nail clipper. I wasn't quite sure why this pushed me over the edge. He had the same toiletries in our West Village medicine cabinet.

But it did. I sat down on the edge of the bathtub and just cried my fucking eyes out. Messily and loudly.

I collected myself and then continued my cursory inspection. Next up was the bedroom, which was basically composed of a queen-sized bed, a nightstand, and about twenty pieces of framed art leaning up against the far wall. I walked over to the closet, took a deep breath, and opened it. Hanging on the rod were the winter jackets that he had never gotten the chance to wear this season, as well as some of his fancier clothes, like his two suits. On the floor were about twelve pairs of shoes lined up. And tucked behind the shoes—far, far, far behind—was the vintage suitcase that housed his legendary sex-toy collection.

I pulled it out—it was considerably heavier than I recalled—and placed it on the bed. I had a quick flashback to thirteen years ago and the time I had sheepishly snuck a peek at his then-nascent sex trove (which was contained in a much smaller shoebox) while he was recovering in the hospital from his appendectomy. I felt a similar sense of apprehension.

I ultimately decided against opening this particular Pandora's Box, and stashed it back in the closet. Way, way, way, way back in the closet. I had enough on my plate at the moment.

I proceeded to the final and largest room, the living room, and immediately experienced my first wave of *Holy fuck, what am I gonna do with all of this stuff?* Practically every square inch of the room was covered with boxes and photo albums and exercise equipment and tools and outdated scanners and books and Pretty Bitter stock and *AbFab* box sets.

I staved off the approaching panic attack by reminding myself that Kit's parents had emailed me a list of the things they wanted. Bill and Jen would be taking a chunk (including all of Kit's photo equipment, which he had left to them and fellow college bestie/ex-girlfriend Beeba in his will). I had also invited many of his closest local friends, including the aforementioned Caroline and Clint, as well as Nina, Missi, Rose, and Nick, to drop by this afternoon and see if there was anything of sentimental value lying around that they would want. And then, of course, there would be things I wanted to hang on to.

I received a text from Jen and Bill that they had arrived and were looking for a parking spot outside, and within thirty minutes we were in full-tilt sorting mode. Bill was assigned to the bedroom to begin disassembling the furniture and taking stock of what was under the bed (I told him that the closet was strictly off limits because, officially, I wanted to go through Kit's clothes myself—and, unofficially, um, his *sex toys*). Jen and I, meanwhile, hunkered down in the living room—she was focused on Kit's vast photo library while I sifted through the two dozen unlabeled boxes, deathly afraid of what heartbreaking memento might be waiting for me inside.

There was the childhood/high school box, complete with *Star Wars* action figures (loose versus mint in box, sadly) and sticker books and report cards and Pee-wee Herman stationery. Another contained assorted novelty items, most notably a plush toy of a lascivious man with a sexual predator look in his eyes wearing nothing but a trench coat, which concealed a disproportionately large felt penis. Kit dubbed him "Mr. Jibbs" because "Jibbs" sounded like slang for naughty bits. Another contained tools. Another was packed with his many journals, all of them filled with, I imagined, doodles and inventions and therapy takeaways and pot-induced epiphanies. I didn't dare look too closely. *That* felt like a violation. I didn't dare throw them out, either. They were keepers, for sure, even if I didn't know what I'd do with them.

I reached under the diaries and there was a blank manila folder. I opened it and inside I found an eight-by-ten computer-generated sign that read, "Ask Me About My Fonts."

Grab the paddles. This one was a heart stopper.

If Kit had had a traditional burial, his tombstone would have been engraved thusly: "Kit Cowan: Ask Him About His Fonts." There were no five words in the English language that more adequately captured my husband's essence. And here's why.

When I finally resolved to ditch my Bloomfield, New Jersey, digs for the bright lights of the big city nine months into our relationship, I vowed to get rid of everything but the kitchen sink. And, of course, the Smurfs, which were safely relocated to a storage facility in Chelsea. This was partly out of necessity—I was moving into a 250-square-foot apartment in Hell's Kitchen that Kit would be frequenting often, so space was at a premium. And secondly, there was something freeing about unloading all this stuff that had little to no significant sentimental value.

I reserved a booth at the Meadowlands Flea Market, a once-a-week event in the massive parking lot surrounding Giants football stadium in East Rutherford, New Jersey, with the goal being to sell as much of my stuff as possible, all at bargain basement prices. Kit was not a fan of this plan. Kit *hated* this plan. Kit wanted to take a sledgehammer to this plan, largely because he knew I would need his help. Apparently the thought of spending an entire Saturday with me in a New Jersey parking lot baking under the hundred-degree sun while hawking Mickey Mouse statues and Miss Piggy mugs and Snoopy-themed Christmas ornaments and *Felicity* posters was a corner of hell *he* was in no rush to visit. So he offered to take the entire lot off my hands for a cool $500.

"What are you going to do with it all?" I inquired.

"That's not your concern," he hedged, before adding, "It's a win-win. You get your Saturday back *and* you make some cash."

"You're just going to throw everything in the garbage, aren't you?"

"That's none of your concern," he repeated, now with an evil mustache-twirling smile added on for good measure.

"I think I'll pass, but thank you—*thank you*—for the generous offer," I sniffed, my voice never more sarcastic.

Cut to a blazing hot summer Sunday in August 2002, and Kit and I arrived at Giants Stadium with my navy-blue Jetta packed to the brim. We located our reserved spot, set up our table, and started unloading my stuff. I was happy just laying everything on the table all loosey-goosey, but if Kit was going to be part of this horror show he was going to put his stamp on it. So he staged the items on the folding table as if he were designing a window display at Saks Fifth Avenue. There were themed sections, buckets representing various price tiers . . . He unpacked my six-foot Christmas tree and draped my tattered mittens and scarves and hats on it. It was quite a thrill watching him do his thing with my things. I didn't even get angry when he likened the project to "applying lipstick to a pig."

As I was surveying Kit's handiwork, I looked behind our table and noticed he was using the trunk of my Jetta to display some of my larger pieces, like the luggage set my maternal grandmother Ronnie had given me as a graduation present, as well as some of my holiday items, including my Macy's branded, circa 1997, limited-edition Grinch plush toy. And sitting on the green meanie's lap rested a peculiar sign that read, "Ask Me About My Fonts." I literally laughed out loud upon seeing it.

"What is that?" I asked him, my eyes bulging out of their sockets and my mouth nearing peak smile.

Playing dumb, he responded, "What's what?"

"Why is the Grinch prompting me to ask him about his fonts?" I teased.

"Oh . . . I brought along some of my font archives," he casually responded, as he hurriedly put the finishing touches on my table of goodies before the 9 a.m. opening time. "Maybe someone will be looking to buy fonts."

"How do you sell someone a . . . font?" I asked, genuinely curious.

"Buh, buh, buh, buh, buh," he shushed me. "You just worry about selling your old *Soap Opera Digests."*

I already was deeply in love with this man. But this font thing just pushed it over the edge. I wanted so badly to walk over to him in the middle of the Giants Stadium parking lot, give him the biggest kiss, and tell him how much I loved his crazy ass. But I didn't think the Meadowlands Flea Market crowd was ready for that kind of PDA. So I just smiled and delivered this edict: "Don't you dare throw away that sign when we're done here."

I spent most of the day praying someone would ask Kit about his fonts. Alas, no one did. That sign nonetheless remained my favorite part of the experience. And over the next thirteen years, I would at random moments look at Kit and snark, "Hey, I was wondering . . . could you please tell me about your fonts?" He would then flash me an "Ooooh . . . watch it, mister" look, before reminding me that I ended up banking a grand total of $350—$150 less than his initial all-or-nothing offer. The reality, of course, was that I came out way ahead that day.

So, yeah, the font sign was a keeper.

I dug deeper into the box and found another unmarked manila folder. I opened this one and . . . I couldn't believe my eyes. There were dozens, possibly hundreds, of the little lovey-dovey notes I had left for Kit over the past thirteen years, mostly as I was *quietly* leaving for work while he remained asleep. Schmoopie-ish messages written on Post-its that I'd affix to our medicine cabinet, or inside the fridge, next to the iced coffee or chai tea latte I had picked up for him at Starbucks. They ranged in length, from super short to long-ish (the latter usually incorporating some type of reminder or apology).

"Good morning, Poodle Poops! Don't forget your overnight bag! We're staying at the Bloomfield pied à terre tonight. I love you! Best, your Poodle Poops."

"My poodle love: Thanks for the delicious dinner last night. My stomach is still applauding. I'm going to do a better job of expressing my feelings and not keep stuff bottled up. I love you. P.S. Good luck at the dentist today. Sincerely, your Poodle Love."

"Poodle Doops! I borrowed $4 to save me a trip to the ATM this am. I'm good for it! Have a great day. Love, your Poodle Doops!"

"Kit. Suddenly the world seems like such a perfect place. I love you.— Mike."

I always assumed he read them and tossed them in the trash. From the thickness of the folder, it felt like he had saved every single one. It wrecked me to find them now. I'd never get the chance to tell him how much it meant to me that they meant something to him. I started bawling. I filled Jen in on my discovery and she started bawling. She crawled over to hug me. And we bawled together.

Other items that I placed in my keep pile:

* The medical ID bracelet from the liposuction surgery I underwent three years into our relationship to finally get rid of the last of my residual childhood fat that had proved frustratingly invulnerable to healthy eating and regular exercise. For the procedure Kit flew with me out to L.A. (where a friend of a friend knew of a good plastic surgeon), and then—for the next five days—he played nursemaid to my patient while we were discreetly holed up at the Courtyard Marriott in Beverly Hills (very old-school Hollywood of us). You wanna know if someone

loves you? See how they react when your pelvic region is filled with so much fluid that your balls take on the appearance of fully loaded water balloons. (Kit's reaction involved some intense giggling followed by a lot of enthusiastic photo-taking.)

* A vintage *Knight Rider* poster. Whenever I'd introduce someone to Kit and they'd confusingly respond, *"Kip?"* he would immediately clarify, "No, *Kit*. Like *Knight Rider*." And then he'd point to me and say, "Mike," before pointing at himself and going, "Kit."

* *That* special font project. Over a period of about a year, Kit would conclude his morning shower by inspecting the bar of soap to see if either one of us had left behind any pubic hairs that resembled letters of the alphabet. If one of us had, he took the entire bar of soap, placed it in a Ziploc bag, and stored it in a box for safekeeping. The box in my hands now had eleven bars of soap featuring twelve pubic hairs representing twelve letters in the alphabet. His goal was to design a font inspired by actual pubic hairs. He was halfway there.

* A copy of our relationship vision, a homework assignment that Tony assigned to us at the end of our very first session with him thirteen years ago. Kit and I parked ourselves in a booth at Big Nick's Pizza Joint on the Upper West Side, ordered a medium vegetable pizza on whole wheat crust with two bottomless cups of perfectly mixed and carbonated fountain Diet Coke, and for two hours, we hammered out what kind of relationship we wanted to be in. Then we returned to his apartment and he transferred the notes onto his computer and whipped up a suitable-for-framing one-sheet. And the following week, we shared it with Tony:

We

We trust each other completely
We can tell each other anything
We are sexually faithful
We support each other emotionally
We respect each other

We are both affectionate
We talk through problems
We make time for us

We have fun together
We have great sex
We make each other laugh
We get each other

We check in with each other
We cut past the bullshit
We can be silly with each other
We are we *and* I

We are a great complement
We are financially secure
We divide expenses
We are charitable
We expose each other to new things
We enjoy traveling together

We support each other's dreams and goals
We protect and care for each other

As it closed in on 3 p.m., Kit's friends started dropping by to check out what was up for grabs. Nick took a statue of a nude fertility god with a giant erection that Kit most recently had displayed in our Hell's

Kitchen bedroom. Missi procured a giant green midcentury ceramic table lamp that Kit had picked up at a thrift store in Harrisburg, Pennsylvania, while waiting for a train to New York. Rose took a set of midcentury-era drinking glasses Kit had found at a local flea market. Clint and Caroline grabbed a yellow stool that looked like a roll of Kodak film (perfect since Caroline was also a photographer).

And on Sunday, Jen, Bill, and I surveyed all of our piles, and quickly determined that the donation mound was by far the biggest. So we started making trips to the Salvation Army warehouse/store about twenty minutes away. And throughout the day, a huge mountain of Kit's possessions began forming near the front of the donation entrance. It was a Kit Cowan Stuff Tower. With each successive trip the pile grew. It was hard for me to see all of his treasures sitting abandoned in the scary, cold warehouse. But it helped that Kit was something of a thrift store junkie himself. Whenever we would pass a secondhand shop he would beg me to pull over so he could scour every aisle looking for a diamond in the rough, like a midcentury treasure or an eighties throwback item (see also: any 99-cent store off the beaten path, like the Atlantic City boardwalk). I felt like I was paying his thrifting obsession forward.

With just two hours left before the Salvation Army closed, we decided to divide and conquer, with Jen and Bill making trips to the donation center and me staying behind to tackle the final piece of the puzzle: the bedroom closet. I still had to figure out what to do with the sex toys. But I also had to gear myself up to go through his clothes. There was no putting either off any longer.

With the house now empty, I just ripped off the Band-Aid and started pulling stuff off hangers, one emotionally fraught, memory-laden item at a time. His favorite green Ben Sherman winter jacket. The black suit he had on the night we attended the GLAAD Awards. His beige Zara sport coat that he could pair with anything and look like the most stylish man in the room. The tuxedo he got at Century 21 but never ended up wearing. Through tears, I resolved to donate them all (except the Ben Sherman coat; that I couldn't bear to part with).

I reached farther back into the closet and my hands grazed a material that felt . . . familiar. It was a polyester-type fabric. I pulled it out and immediately noticed the jagged red pattern—almost like a healthy

EKG blip—running down the left side of the all-black, short-sleeved shirt. It was the shirt I was wearing the night we first met at the Gay Sports Ball. I remembered Kit's horrified reaction when he stumbled upon it at the Meadowlands Flea Market in my "$2 an item" pile.

"You're not selling this," he said, pointedly. "This is a part of our history."

And when we moved out of our Hell's Kitchen apartment three years ago, I once again suggested that maybe it was time to chuck it.

"No," he fumed, repeating his earlier protest. He then added, "This is our *Brokeback Mountain* shirt. When you die, I'm going to collapse in the closet while sniffing your man scent."

As I stood there inside his closet, I fought the urge to pull an Ennis Del Mar with my *own* shirt. I fought it *hard*. Even though no one else was in the bedroom or even the apartment, I felt judgmental eyes watching me, going, *You're no Heath Ledger.* But then I found myself mentally transported back to the second floor of Webster Hall, and the moment I first laid eyes on him chomping on that cocktail straw. And I thought about how much we had gone through over the subsequent thirteen and a half years. And how he was just . . . gone. And I lost it. I didn't collapse in the closet with the shirt pressed against my nose though. I just stood there, crying. And calling his name out. Begging him to come back home.

I tossed the shirt in the "Keep" pile, right on top of his Ben Sherman jacket.

Now all that remained in the closet was the dreaded suitcase of iniquity. I pulled it out and placed it on the floor where the now donated bed once stood. I unlatched it and lifted the lid. It was filled to the top with all the usual suspects. I tried to steer my head away from guilt and regret and toward embracing my husband's unapologetic sexuality. I thought I was succeeding until I heard Jen and Bill walking up the stairs, prompting me to quickly close the suitcase as if stashing cocaine during a police raid.

They walked into the bedroom, and Bill immediately looked at the suitcase resting on the floor next to me. Something about his expression told me that he knew what was inside.

"You opened it, didn't you?" I asked, calmly.

"I did," he confirmed. "I was getting overeager with my cleaning."

I looked at Jen. I couldn't tell if Bill had already filled her in on its contents. Regardless, the cat was out of the bag.

"Kit's sex toys," I quietly acknowledged to her.

She simultaneously nodded and smirked. Her blasé reaction served as a reminder that Jen had been Kit's closest friend. And Bill was not far behind. They knew he was a raging horn dog. I needed to stop hiding my shame-induced predicament from them and start troubleshooting it *with* them.

"I'm not sure what to do with them," I said and shrugged. "I'm open to suggestions."

They immediately put on their thinking caps. Bill was the first to offer a suggestion.

"We could find a Dumpster somewhere . . ." he offered.

"That idea crossed my mind, too," I responded. "But it feels wrong, like we just murdered someone and we're hiding the body."

A couple of seconds passed and Bill started to chuckle. "We could just drop them off at the Salvation Army," he proposed.

I immediately rolled my eyes, as Jen burst out laughing.

"No," I retorted. "Keep thinking."

But a funny thing happened as we stood there in the middle of Kit's empty bedroom with Kit's suitcase of pleasure and pain on the floor between us: I couldn't get Bill's crazy idea out of my head. Donating Kit's sex toys to the decidedly conservative Salvation Army was ridiculously inappropriate. But it was also hilarious.

It was so wrong it was . . . kind of fucking perfect.

Fifteen minutes later, I was sitting in the passenger seat of Jen and Bill's car, with Bill driving and Jen in the backseat, the suitcase of sex toys on my lap. We pulled up at the Salvation Army entrance, and the first thing the three of us did was unload the jackets and the shoes and toss them on the Kit Cowan Stuff Tower right at the entrance. And then I returned to the car, opened the front door, and stared at the suitcase resting on the passenger seat. I cracked open the lid, fished my hands around inside, and pulled out the vial of poppers that I'd long had a curiosity about. Someday I might want to give them a try. I stuck the tiny canister in my pocket. I then latched the suitcase, picked it up, and walked toward the entrance, Jen and Bill following a safe distance behind.

I placed it down right at the head of the Kit Cowan Stuff Tower, in front of his rolled up flokati rug and his Steve Jobs in memoriam magazines and his obsolete printer and the quirky floral art painting he found in the trash and his clothes and his glassware and his massive tea light display and his art books. I pulled a label out of my pocket, got down on my knees, and slapped it on the front of the suitcase as Jen handed me a black Sharpie. I wrote "SEX TOYS" in big letters on the label, adding an exclamation point for good measure.

I stepped away from the Tower, alongside Jen and Bill, and we took in the view, as workers and donators milled about around us. The three of us looked at each other and we just . . . smiled. Big, mischievous, Kit Cowan–inspired grins.

And then we hurriedly hopped back in the car and fled the scene, like the sex bandits we were.

16.

It was the middle of July, five months since Kit's death, and the Amtrak train was pulling into downtown Harrisburg. I was traveling light. Inside my medium-sized Manhattan Portage–branded backpack were two cans of Diet Coke, three peanut butter/dark chocolate Kind bars, a box of tissues, and a round blue Tupperware bowl containing Kit's ashes.

Although Kit and I ultimately preferred traveling to Millersburg via rental car (mostly because we loved our Target runs), during the first six years of our relationship we more often than not hoofed it to central Pennsylvania via train.

I quietly noted the ominous firsts as they got checked off: My first time making this trek without Kit. My first time climbing the long stairway connecting the train tracks to the terminal without Kit in front of or behind me. My first time walking into the station's rotunda without Kit by my side—and without his father waiting in the wings, his eyes parsing the crowd for his son and his other half while Marilyn manned the idling car.

Before Bob and Marilyn could even offer to pick me up, I'd told them I would just Uber it the thirty minutes from Harrisburg to Millersburg. Selfishly, I wanted to avoid the pain of walking into that rotunda and seeing Bob. And then looking to my right and *not* seeing Kit. I was sure I was doing Bob and Marilyn a huge favor, as well.

This wasn't, however, my first time being back in Millersburg sans Kit. That dubious milestone was hit on February 15 when Bob and Marilyn held a local memorial reception for Kit's old neighbors and classmates and friends. It took place a day after the Valentine's Day memorial I hosted in New York City, which featured remembrances from Kit's BFF Jen, cousin Raelean, Wyeth boss John, work wife Missi, and, lastly, our longtime therapist Tony. And after three days of writing and rewriting and consultations with a few of my personal writing gods (including TV über producer Greg Berlanti and my ex-boyfriend Charlie), I gave the eulogy. And I managed to get through it without breaking down, although it was a bit of a challenge delivering the introduction while his parents sat directly in front of me.

> You know, when I started thinking about what I wanted to say today, I tried to come up with a word that really captured the essence of who Kit was. And I struggled, because Kit was so many things—as everyone here can attest. So after racking my brain for days, I realized that the word that best embodies the spirit of my husband also happens to be his favorite word: cunt.
>
> He loved the word "cunt." And he loved casually slipping it into everyday conversations, whether among friends over IM, while trying to give the cat his medicine, teaching me how to sync my laptop with my iPad. It was more of a term of endearment than a cuss word though. He'd dress it up, even. Variations included: Cunt stick. Cunt lips. Dumb cunt. Cunt Dracula. The list goes on.
>
> And the reason he was so enamored with this four-letter word was because, well, there was no bigger cunt than Kit Cowan.
>
> Here are just a few examples of Kit at his cuntiest:
>
> * When we had a painting party at our apartment, Kit halted the proceedings after about fifteen minutes and

ordered everyone out because their brushstrokes weren't going in the same direction. To this day, I'm still working on repairing the damage that was done to some of those relationships.

* Kit built a stationery empire on greeting cards emblazoned with the words "Die," "Fucker," and "Asshole." His cards also helpfully warned pregnant women that during childbirth, they would likely shit themselves.

* When he was eight years old, Kit snuck downstairs early Christmas morning and opened all of his presents while his parents were sleeping, shattering his mother's heart into a million pieces. She still hasn't quite recovered from the betrayal.

* Kit didn't think twice about walking into Sloan Kettering for a chemo treatment while wearing a shirt that read "Humanity Is Overrated."

* When Kit would catch a glimpse of me getting out of the shower completely naked, he would look me up and down and say, "Eh, that's nothing to sniff at." And then he'd *sniff*.

Yes, make no mistake. The person we're honoring here today was the King of Cunts.

And we loved him for it.

We loved that he wouldn't hesitate to call us, or anyone, out on their shit. We loved the honesty. And the humor. And the humor with which he dished out his unsparing brand of honesty. And, on those occasions when his cuntiness was just plain mean, you could wait three minutes and the puppy dog in him would split away from the beast once again. He'd feel terrible. And, occasionally, he'd even apologize. Sometimes he'd get creative with said apology. Once, right after wrapping up an epic takedown of his coworker Missi, he IM'd her an image of Sigourney Weaver getting attacked by an alien, followed by the words "I'm sorry."

And there, right there, is the complicated, contradictory beauty of Kit: The magnitude of his cuntiness was matched only by the enormity of his heart. And he had a huge heart. And if you were among the lucky ones to be on the receiving end of his sweetness, you were truly blessed. His capacity for kindness and empathy was extraordinary. If he liked you, you were so, so lucky. And if he loved you, look the hell out.

I was fortunate to be one of the people that Kit loved. He loved the hell out of me the past thirteen and a half years. Yes, I was his caregiver this past eleven months, but Kit took care of *me* for the twelve years prior. He even gave me style. Well, *some* style.

You could tell a lot about the way Kit loved, too, from his relationship with our cat, Mister Scooch. When we first got him, Kit played it cool, saying he'd trade him in for a sixty-inch flat-screen TV in a heartbeat. But then you should've seen him the first time Scooch had a hairball attack. The sheer panic and agony and fear on Kit's face that something worse could be happening was profound. Scooch was fine, obviously. But Kit was traumatized.

The way Kit loved was also pretty spectacularly reflected in his gift-giving. He wasn't just good at giving presents, he was the best at it. As in, his gift-giving prowess was on another level altogether from mere mortals. He found things that proved he actually paid attention to who you were. And they were often things that couldn't be found on Amazon.

For example . . . Over the years, Kit and I adopted our own little language—words and phrases and terms of endearment that only we would understand. We called them poopisms. Four years into our relationship, he created a quasi-dictionary of our poopisms, a beautifully designed, three-volume set, grouped by categories like "Anger Management," "Snack Time," "Sleeping," and "Hot Guys," and he gave it to me for Christmas.

Another . . . On my fortieth birthday, I was awakened at 9 a.m. to the sight of a Muppety-looking puppet who was rocking a snazzy jacket and bow tie, had dark brown hair and the biggest smile, and he was holding a microphone with the *TV-Line* logo on it. It was me in puppet form. And Kit proceeded to put on a show, with my Muppet doppelgänger interviewing me about my birthday.

After my grandmother died, I shared with Kit one of my favorite memories—watching *Love Boat* with her on Saturday nights in her living room during my biweekly sleepovers. Right before we sold her home, he managed to track down a bootleg *Love Boat* DVD (it hadn't been released officially), and he presented it to me during one of my last visits to the house. He left me alone for an hour while I watched an episode of *Love Boat* on the same TV, and in the same spot on the living room floor, as if it was 1984 all over again.

Kit's attention to detail, and his ability to really tune in to people, didn't just affect his relationships, it also influenced his art. It can be seen in his photography, his design work, his obsession with fonts. He saw the world—and people—in his own unique way. If you've ever browsed through his Instagram feed, you know what I mean. Many of the photos are of his grandmother, whom he'd call his muse, I think because she was like a living time capsule. As was her home. They both remained unchanged from his childhood. Even when life moved at a breakneck pace, he could always count on coming home to his grandmother and finding her exactly as he'd left her. And her house exactly as he'd left it. He would spend hours taking pictures there of the most mundane things—or the most *seemingly* mundane things—like the inside of her refrigerator, or the items on her end table, the way her toiletries were resting in her bathroom. His grandmother would often say, "What are you taking a picture of now?"

In spite of his massive talent, Kit never bragged about it. He was confident, don't get me wrong. He knew he had a gift. But he never wanted the attention that came with it.

And then this past year, all of the good parts of him just grew exponentially while he fought this battle. After he was diagnosed with neuroendocrine cancer, we interviewed four different oncologists to find the right fit, and the prognoses were all over the map—except for one thing: They all agreed it was bad. We knew it would take a miracle for Kit to beat this. The doctor at Sloan Kettering that we ended up going with basically said up front he had a year to live. So right from the outset, we knew that there was a decent chance his days were numbered. And what Kit did on the afternoon he received that grim prognosis at Sloan Kettering set the tone for the entire year to come. After crying his eyes out for a half hour or so, he hopped in a cab, went to city hall, and he got married.

It sounds corny, I know, but he spent the past year living like he was dying, and I feel so privileged to have had a ringside seat for what turned out to be his farewell tour. Which sounds depressing but was actually spectacularly inspiring. We should all be so lucky as to be brave enough to go out with such gusto.

And the Universe did not make any of it easy for Kit. He would often say, "My numbers just aren't coming up." And he was right. He was dealt one setback after another. Treatments that were supposed to work didn't. Pain remedies that should've made him comfortable made him feel worse. This man went through hell this past year, and that still didn't deter him from scheduling almost daily visits with friends and, on five different occasions, enduring the three-and-a-half-hour ride to his beloved hometown of Millersburg despite the fact that sitting down in a car triggered some of his most intense pain.

In late July, Kit took advantage of a period of relief from his symptoms brought on by radiation and escaped to his happy place, the Hamptons, for an extraordinary week of beach time, long naps, and meals with his friends and colleagues at Wyeth. He spent much of the rest of the summer camped out on our tiny deck in the West Village, soaking up the rays, listening to music, playing games on his iPad. He built a fence around the deck so that Mister Scooch could accompany him out there without fear of him falling over the ledge. I'll never forget what it was like to come home from the gym to the sight of Kit— who was in the middle of a rough pain phase—constructing this metal fence around our deck by himself. It took him a little longer than it normally would have, but dammit, he finished it. And it looked incredible. For the first time ever, our cat got a taste of the outdoors, and he loved it. They both did. One of my most precious lasting memories will be looking out the bedroom window and seeing those two out on that deck just chilling together, like best friends.

Along the way, Kit also made sure that his time with friends and family was meaningful. During one of his parents' many visits to the city, he blocked out some individual "private time" with each of them to make sure that nothing was left unsaid. Once again, the ultimate gift-giver.

Even on his worst days, when the pain was so bad he just wanted to die, Kit would say to me, "Someone, somewhere has it worse. Someone always has it worse." There was no self-pity. Sure, there was deep sadness, anger, maybe a little fear. But never pity. He wouldn't want our pity, either.

Before he was diagnosed, one of our favorite ongoing jokes involved untimely death. If we were out to dinner and one of our friends was in the bathroom a little too long, or was just running late, one of us, without missing a beat, would assume tragedy had struck and go, "Eh, he had a good life." Some people were taken aback by the dark humor, but mostly, everyone got it. *We* got it, which is all that really mattered.

So when you think of Kit, and the tragedy of his life cut short, and you're feeling pain, may I suggest that instead of letting it bring you down, you look up and say, "Eh, that Kit Cowan, he had a good life."

The original plan for the Millersburg ceremony on February 15 had us scattering Kit's ashes in the Susquehanna River right before the reception. But that was scuttled when the mercury dipped to two degrees (literally the coldest day of the year), rendering any kind of outdoor activity—particularly one set on a riverbank!—untenable. So Marilyn, Bob, and I resolved to delay the ash-scattering until summertime. We also decided to keep things simple and limit the guest list to just the three of us and Kit's maternal aunts Martha and Marie, the latter of whom he was extremely close to growing up. Marie's second husband, Ron, was also present.

When the Uber driver closed in on Millersburg, my heart broke in two as we passed Kit's beloved Sorrento's Pizzeria, home of his favorite Italian submarine. ("Just take a bite of the homemade bread," Kit would beg me, to which I would shake my vegetarian head and demur. "No. The meat touched it.") There was an awkward tension in the car as the male Uber driver clearly saw and heard me crying my eyes out in the backseat but said nothing. My breakdown only intensified as we rolled into Millersburg and drove down Main Street, past the gazebo and the old hardware store and the now-shuttered five-and-dime. I instructed the driver to ignore the address I'd entered into the app and directed him toward the river.

I stepped out of the car, and the view was just stunning. Weather-wise, it was a perfect day. Hot but not *too* hot. The riverbank was empty, save for the stray squirrel or bird. Kit would always say that the town's residents took for granted that the Susquehanna was right in their backyard. But Kit never did.

I walked over to one of the benches and took a seat, resting my backpack with Kit's ashes down beside me. And I just stared out at the sparkling, peaceful river. I felt close to him. I started to talk to him, mostly just to remind him how much I loved and missed him. And how lonely Millersburg felt without him.

As the warmth of the summer sun beat down on me, it was suddenly 2003 again, and Kit was excitedly taking me for my first ride on the nautical icon that was the Millersburg Ferry. I remembered him pointing out the mini rock islands that would jut out when the water level was low.

"I would spend hours walking along the mounds, collecting rocks, looking for frogs with my friend Jen," he shared, adding that on weekends he would cross the river on the ferry to get to neighboring Liverpool, where his aunt Marie and now-deceased uncle Cloyde would be waiting to whisk him off to their nearby house for a weekend of fun and games.

It was on that maiden voyage of mine that Kit confided the unthinkable to me.

"If I go first, I want my ashes scattered in this river," he told me. "Please promise me you will do that."

After pausing for a moment to wrap my head around what he'd just said, I replied, "I promise." And then as we stood there silently, I dwelled on two thoughts: How beyond moved I was that after only a year and change of dating, Kit was already entrusting me with such an enormous ask; and, *Please God—I beg you*—let me die before Kit.

And now that I was here, it felt like every bit of the nightmare I had imagined it to be on that fateful summer afternoon in 2003. But I also felt a ripple of peace encroaching on my pain. The peace that came with knowing with your whole heart that this moment was fated. I was meant to be on that ferry with Kit twelve years ago. And I was meant to be back here again today, with his ashes in my backpack.

After about ten more minutes of meditative silence, I made my way up the hill to Bob and Marilyn's house. Per tradition, I eschewed ringing the front doorbell and snuck around the side of the house toward the back porch, which I guessed was where they were hanging out. My suspicions were confirmed when I got halfway down the side path and began to hear voices, then saw the faces of Bob and Marilyn as well as Martha, Marie, and Ron. They were all sitting in a sorta circle, casually gabbing away.

"Well, look who finally showed up." Bob playfully ribbed me, to a chorus of chuckles.

I smiled and extended a round of "Good morning," which was followed by a round of hugs. When I got to Marilyn, I held her for a few more additional seconds than perhaps she was prepared for. And I started to cry. I missed her. And Bob, too. It hit me how dramatically our relationship had changed on February 5. Instead of clinging to me, as I'd feared might happen, they had done the opposite; they had pulled away. After either talking to or seeing them every single day during the eleven months Kit was sick, I could count on one hand the number of times we had spoken in the last five months. And, for the most part, I had been the one initiating the communication. It had never dawned on me that I would need them more than they would need me.

Instead of simply scattering the ashes from the shoreline, Bob and Marilyn had chartered Kit's beloved ferry for a full hour. As the six of us walked toward the docking station, Marilyn took us past the town's new swing sets that the two of them had donated in Kit's name. They asked me if I would sprinkle some of his ashes near the swings and along the riverbank. I took a deep breath. I'd been avoiding making eye contact with the ashes. Missi had handled the Tupperware transfer for me last night at my apartment. I cracked open the container and lightly dusted the ground with . . . pieces of Kit's heart. And his slightly crooked front tooth. And his lazy eyelid. He was really gone. Seven months ago we had walked along this riverbank together. Seven months ago Kit had stood in this exact spot. And now he was gone. A pile of ashes in a blue Tupperware container.

As we climbed onto the rickety-but-oh-so-perfect ferry, the captain and his copilot greeted the five of us solemnly, and before I knew it we were pulling away from the dock. The captain anchored the boat in the middle of the river, halfway between Millersburg and Liverpool, and we all gathered at the front. I said a few words about Kit's affection for this stretch of the river and for his hometown in general, and concluded by telling him how much we all loved him and that he would never be forgotten. I then knelt down, cracked open the Tupperware container, and then slowly released his ashes into the water below. His family immediately tossed flowers in so we could follow the path of the ashes down the river.

As I watched the ashes drift downstream, I felt outside my body for a moment. Like I was in a dream. Like I couldn't possibly be depositing pieces of the person I had loved more than any human being ever into the Susquehanna River. But I also felt something else. Closure. Complete, utter, transcendent closure. I hadn't realized it at the time, but Kit had given me an enormous gift the day he made that request of me. And I was suddenly overcome with gratitude.

I stood up and gave his parents a hug, as tissues were passed around. I then slowly made my way to the back of the boat, alone. I searched for the flower petals now off in the distance. I found them. And I kept my eyes fixed on them as I reached into my pocket and pulled out Kit's wedding ring. I then slipped my matching band off my finger and placed it on top of Kit's ring in the center of my palm. And for one last time, they clinked.

I stared out at the river, with Millersburg in the background, and I whispered, "Thank you, Kit."

And I tossed them in.

Flash-Forward

"Happy Holidays," I cheerily say to the young female patron as she makes off with her $11 in greeting card purchases. I lean on the counter and discreetly observe the only remaining customers in the store—a modish, mid-forties gay couple that have been dawdling for some time now. I'm *thisclose* to politely informing them that the shop closes in five minutes. But it's Christmas Eve and I don't want to be a Grinch. At the same time, it's Christmas Eve and I have cookies to bake (a lie) and presents to wrap (the truth). And because of the heavy foot traffic today from procrastinating elves, Mister Jibbs never got his mid-afternoon walk in. He's probably upstairs crossing his legs, going, "What the eff, yo? Dog's gotta pee!"

The well-coiffed pair—who I'm guessing are city folk visiting family in the greater Hudson Valley area—do not look anything like me and Kit when we were their age. But something about their easy, slightly antagonistic banter feels familiar. From what my eavesdropping ears can gather, the taller, blonder of the two is majorly coveting the Finn Juhl low table near the entrance. But the shorter, beefier one can't get past the $10K price tag. And the air of financial authority the latter is giving off tells me that the literal buck stops with him.

I'm tempted to alert them that there's a holiday promotion currently under way on insanely expensive furniture that will shave 20 percent off that price, but my gut tells me that it won't move the needle enough to resolve their stalemate. If anything, it'll just prolong the little couples dance they're engaged in. And as amusing as it is, the clock's ticking.

Just then, the tall one steps away from the table and approaches me at the register, dropping what appears to be $20 worth of cards on the counter. His frugal other half is right behind him.

"Is this everything?" I ask, pleasantly but rhetorically.

"Yep, I think that's it." He hedges, while perusing the nearby point-of-purchase items (miniature NYC-inspired water towers, fortune-cookie scrapbooks, cunt coloring books, ceramic middle-finger statues inspired by Atlantic City's once-iconic 99-cent outlet, etc.). "You have a very cool store."

"Thank you," I reply, genuinely, because I never tire of hearing that compliment. Hudson, New York, has no shortage of eclectic, charm-soaked boutiques. But this is the only hybrid greeting card/novelty item/midcentury furniture establishment in town.

"The furniture is gorgeous, but a little out of our price range," he says, taking a subtle dig at his partner.

"A *little*?" the BF/spouse retorts.

"OK, it's a *lot* out of our price range," the tall one begrudgingly clarifies.

"That Finn Juhl piece you were looking at is one of my favorites," I tell him. "You have very good taste."

"If Santa leaves us a suitcase full of cash under the tree, we'll be back for it," he jokes.

I ring up their selections—a pair of cat-themed holiday cards designed by an up-and-coming artist I met at the Brooklyn Flea, and a Pretty Bitter original: a twelve-pack of Dirty Doily greeting cards. I also never tire of seeing someone snap up one of Kit's heritage items. It makes me wistful for the good ol' days, while also filling me with pride for the small role I played in helping make Pretty Bitter a reality.

"Your total comes to twenty-four dollars," I inform him (I was only $4 off!), as he pulls up his iPhone and hovers it over the Apple Pay sensor. The transaction goes through. I place the items in a bag and hand it to him.

"Happy Holidays to both of you," I say with a smile.

As they head out, the taller one stops to admire the table one last time, but he's quickly shooed along by you-know-who.

I check my watch—it's 5:05 p.m. It's time to blow this popsicle stand. I walk over to the front door and lock it, before dimming the interior lights, sending a clear message to the public that this joint is closed.

"*Hey, ChuckleNutz—we have presents to wrap!*" I shout across the empty store while walking back to the counter to begin crunching today's sales numbers. As I hunt and peck away on the keyboard, I look toward the rear of the store, waiting for a certain human to appear. But it's crickets. "Hey," I bellow. "It's Christmas! Santa's coming! Let's *goooooo!*"

Still no response.

I glide over to the little office/stock room at the opposite end of the shop. My guess is he's on the phone with a customer explaining that the online order they placed *this morning* is not going to arrive in time for Christmas. I open the door and stick my head in—it's empty. And then suddenly I hear the faint sound of voices coming from . . . the *other* room.

I head toward an archway covered with long blue-and-white dangling beads. The closer I get, the more I can hear two distinct voices. One I recognize; one I do not.

I pull the beads back, step into the room and—*ahhhhhhh*—I take a moment to enjoy the still-thrilling sensory assault. Hundreds upon thousands of Smurfs, tastefully displayed within twenty gorgeous white museum-quality cabinets. There are also a half-dozen dioramas depicting holiday-themed Smurf village scenes, including one centered around an ice rink that if you look close enough is actually a pocket mirror hidden under fake snow. And right in the center of the room rests my pride and joy—a wall of eighty clear square compartments stacked one on top of the other, each block holding hundreds of identical Smurf figurines. Picture, if you will, the jellybean dispensers that anchor any candy store you've ever been in, only instead of bright-colored confectionaries the cases are filled with Smurfs.

I've walked into this room countless times since last year's low-

key ribbon cutting, but the sight of my fully realized, lifetime-in-the-
making Smurf shrine still takes my breath away. If I keel over while
transitioning the dioramas from St. Patrick's Day scenes to Easter mi-
lieus I will die a happy man.

I step further into the 750-square-foot room, past the main case
housing the plush Smurfs, and into my line of sight appears a middle-
aged woman. She's deep in conversation. I lean in and . . . there he is.
The guy I've been searching for: Kit.

Maybe it's his positioning under the subtle track lighting, but my
silver fox of a husband is looking particularly fetching at the moment. I
dare say he's even sexier than the fateful night three decades ago when
I first laid eyes on him chomping on that cocktail straw at Webster
Hall. Not only has he maintained his full head of (now *very* gray) hair
without the aid of a single Propecia pill (grrrr), he can still fill out a pair
of khakis like nobody's business. And his wardrobe game continues to
be on point. His red V-neck sweater is layered over a green-and-white
striped button-down shirt, the perfect mix of timeless style and holiday cheer.

And the best part—this hot piece of tail is all *mine*.

The cabinet with the pricey figurines is ajar, and Kit is giving the
patron a close-up look at the rarest of rare pieces, a Smurf holding a
red apple inscribed with "I Love NY." I check to make sure he's wearing
gloves. Lucky for him, he is. I loiter quietly and listen in.

"Only about a hundred of these were made," Kit explains to her,
adopting his best museum curator voice. "This one is actually not for
sale. It's part of my husband's *private* collection."

It's not often that I get to see the Smurf Expert side of Kit in action.
It feels like Santa is giving me an early Christmas present. It's hard to
imagine that this is the same person who, back in 2002, walked into
my Bloomfield, New Jersey, apartment and nearly suffered an aneu-
rysm upon seeing the Smurf-filled vomitorium that was my bedroom.
Watching him enthusiastically embrace this part of me fills me with a
certain full-circle joy.

It's worth noting that Kit still hasn't made *total* peace with my
nostalgic obsession. To wit, he originally tried to talk me into putting
my blue oasis upstairs in our third bedroom, a suggestion I vetoed

outright. But instead of being a total Gargamel, now he's more like Grouchy Smurf after a glass or two of chardonnay.

Uh-oh. I've been caught. Kit notices me lurking.

"Michael, meet Elizabeth—she's one of your oldest stalkers, er, *fans*," Kit jests, as the visitor rotates her head, sees me, and promptly turns a bright shade of red.

"I used to read 'Ask Ausiello' all the time," she gushes. "And I loved you on *Gilmore Girls*—both episodes!"

"Neither one recognized by the Emmys, it's worth noting," I sigh, as I shake her hand. Kit, meanwhile, carefully places the "I Love NY" figurine back in its airtight home.

"I saw the photos of your Smurfs online, but it's much more impressive in person."

"Thanks for coming to see it," I tell her with enthusiasm. "I'm pretty proud of it."

Kit glances at his Apple watch and exclaims, "It's already 5 p.m.?!"

"Yeah," I confirm. "We've got presents to wrap!"

"Oh, God, I'm sorry for keeping you," our guest exhales.

"No worries," I assure her.

"I'm going to bring my niece and nephew here next week," she says, as the three of us walk out into the main store, toward the exit.

"We're closed the day after Christmas but open the rest of the week," I inform her. "Please come back."

As Kit unlocks the door to let her out, my number one fan turns to me and sheepishly says, "I have a small favor to ask . . ."

Before she can even finish her sentence, Kit reaches for the smartphone she's purposefully clutching in her hand. "I'll take it," he playfully harrumphs.

"I'm sorry!" she exclaims, handing Kit her device.

"No need to apologize!" I assure her, as I place my arm around her shoulder and smile for the camera. "I love posing with my public, especially when there are witnesses."

Kit snaps a half-dozen photos and we exchange some final pleasantries with Elizabeth before sending her off into the merry night.

With just Kit and me left in the store, he turns to me and exclaims, "It's Christmas! Let's get going!"

"I'm ready!" I tell him giddily because *it's Christmas!!*

I walk briskly to the counter to grab my keys and to confirm that the computer is shut off. While there, I adjust the slightly crooked "Ask Me About My Smurfs" sign on the wall. Kit, meanwhile, flits about the store, tidying up the greeting card rack and lightly zhushing a few items on a nearby display case. We meet up at the exit, he shuts off the store lights, and we step out into the cold.

"It's my turn to walk him," Kit reminds me, as I lock up the store. "You can get started on the wrapping. And order us some dinner. I'm starving."

I pause for a moment.

"You know what," I begin, as Kit is now unlocking the adjacent door to our home. "Bring my jacket down. We'll walk him together. I feel like taking in some Christmas lights."

"OK, but just a few blocks," he demurs. "It's fucking cold."

As Kit heads upstairs, I step away from our quaint circa-1800s row house and take in the gorgeous store window and the unassuming sign above it advertising its name, "See You Next Tuesday." And then I look up at our beautiful six-over-six sash windows on the second and third floors and . . . I wait for it. And I keep waiting for it.

Come on, what's taking so long.

And then, just like that, all six windows on both floors simultaneously light up with multicolored C9 old-timey bulbs, all diligently measured out for peak symmetry. The collective brightness casts a glow over not only the sidewalk but part of the street itself. It's magical. It's also the best Christmas display along Hudson's storied commercial district—by a landslide (not that it's a competition or anything, it's just that, at the end of the day, *you better fucking believe it's a competition*).

Sixty seconds later, the front door opens and Mister Jibbs—our lovably rambunctious black Labrador retriever—bounds out and races toward me as Kit hands me my jacket.

"Jibber Jabs!" I exclaim, while grabbing the leash from Kit, Jibbs's tail wagging away. "We're sorry we neglected you, buddy, but we had a busy day. Oh, yes, we did. *Oh, yes, we did have a busy day.*"

Jibbs immediately takes a piss on the sidewalk as Kit steps away from the door toward the curb to admire his holiday handiwork for the umpteenth time this season.

Jibbs finishes tinkling, and just as we're about to step off for our nice Christmas Eve stroll, our four-legged little man transitions from a pee position right into a poop stance. Kit flashes me his signature "Eww, gross" face.

"Come on, Jibbs—not right in front of our store," Kit sneers. "We trained you to unload your brown business in front of the CVS around the corner."

I faux-cringe. "Oh, no. It's gonna be a juicy one. It's a double bagger."

"The neighbors are staring, Jibbs," Kit scolds him, while tearing off a doggie bag in preparation for the waste removal. "I hope you're proud of yourself."

As the two of us stand there playfully berating our beloved successor to Mister Scooch while he innocently relieves himself on the sidewalk in front of our dreamy home/store on Christmas Eve, I take a moment to bask in my immense good fortune and immeasurable gratitude.

"Stinky poops." Kit grimaces as he cleans up after Jibbs. "Big ol' stinky poops."

My adorably bundled-up, teeth-chattering husband turns back to me and catches me staring at him, smiling.

"What I do?" he asks, intentionally ratcheting up the cuteness quotient.

As I lean to give him a kiss, Mister Jibbs begins tugging on the leash, cutting our winsome PDA moment short. He wants to get going. I hold out my hand and Kit promptly grabs it. He catches me smiling at him again.

"Merry Christmas, Kit," I say, earnestly.

My favorite recovering Scrooge ekes out a sweet grin, before playfully replying, "Let's go, Santa."

And with that, we begin to make our way down the quiet, twinkling street.

Together.

ACKNOWLEDGMENTS

David Duhr, my book coach from WriteByNight, thank you for your game-changing notes, spirit-boosting pep talks, and keeping me (mostly) on schedule. To my editor, Rakesh Satyal, for believing in this project and, more importantly, me. My brothers, David and Pete, for not giving me TOO much grief for skipping out on two years of holiday get-togethers to stay home and write. To my therapist, Tony, for talking me off the PROVERBIAL ledge once a week for forty-five minutes. To Kit's BFF and artistic soul mate Jen Renninger, for helping me sift through Kit's intimidatingly vast photo archive in search of missing narrative puzzle pieces and chapter-opening art. And to my habitual NYC writing spots—Think Coffee, Fiddlesticks, and McNally Jackson—thank you for providing ample seating, a chill vibe, and tasty low-cal beverages.

ABOUT THE AUTHOR

Michael Ausiello is the founder and editor-in-chief of TVLine.com, a television entertainment website owned by Penske Media Company that launched in 2010. Ausiello began his publishing career in 1997 at *Soaps in Depth* magazine before moving on to TVGuide.com in 2000, where he debuted what would become his signature, spoiler-tinged "Ask Ausiello" column and established himself as a major player in the world of TV journalism. In 2008, he jumped to *Entertainment Weekly*, where he penned a column in the magazine as well as an award-winning blog on EW.com (both titled "The Ausiello Files"). He currently splits his time between New York City and Los Angeles.